# *Forgotten Foods*

## *Memories and Recipes from Muslim South Asia*



EDITED BY
SIOBHAN LAMBERT-HURLEY,
TARANA HUSAIN KHAN,
CLAIRE CHAMBERS

PICADOR INDIA

First published in India in 2023 by Picador India
an imprint of Pan Macmillan Publishing India Private Limited
707 Kailash Building
26 K. G. Marg, New Delhi 110001
www.panmacmillan.co.in

Pan Macmillan, 6 Briset Street, Farringdon London EC1M 5NR
Associated companies throughout the world
www.panmacmillan.com

ISBN 978-93-95624-35-0



Illustrations by Ranojoy Hazra



5 7 9 8 6 4



Typeset in Perpetua Regular by SÜRYA
Printed and bound in India by Replika Press Pvt. Ltd.

MIX
Paper | Supporting responsible forestry
FSC™ C016779

## Praise for *Forgotten Foods*

'There are all kinds of food books. Some are a collection of recipes, others are autobiographical and some claim to be rewriting the history of what we eat. Some enterprising authors trace the journey of a samosa or a jalebi, a kebab or a pulao to the subcontinent along the Silk Route or describe the export of Indian curries. Rarely does one come across a volume that blends all these ingredients beautifully to present a delicious dish, but this anthology is a rare exception. The book delivers amply on [its] premise and promise' – **Pushpesh Pant, *Tribune***

'Peppered with recipes, *Forgotten Foods* spans a vast spectrum of Muslim cuisines and customs from across South Asia' – **Rahul Verma, *Frontline***

'At a time when war, religious conflict and food bans are becoming common, a book about Muslim kitchens serves as a tangential tool to understand a community and how they shaped world history' – **Jahnabee Borah, *Mint Lounge***

'Representation finds its rightful seat at the table through 33 non-fiction essays in *Forgotten Foods*' – **Jehan Nizar, *Vogue India***

## Copyright Acknowledgements

For Josh,
For Qamar,
And for Rob

# Measurements

## Liquids

| Metric (ml) | Imperial (fl oz) | US cups |
|---|---|---|
| 250 | 8 | 1 |
| 180 | 6 | ¾ |
| 150 | 5 | ⅔ |
| 120 | 4 | ½ |
| 75 | 2 ½ | ⅓ |
| 60 | 2 | ¼ |
| 30 | 1 | ⅛ |
| 15 | ½ | 1 tbsp |

## Weight: Imperial to Metric

| Imperial (oz) | Metric (g) |
|---|---|
| ½ | 15 |
| 1 | 30 |
| 2 | 60 |
| 3 | 90 |
| 4 | 110 |
| 5 | 140 |
| 6 | 170 |
| 7 | 200 |
| 8 | 225 |
| 9 | 255 |
| 10 | 280 |
| 11 | 310 |
| 12 | 340 |
| 13 | 370 |
| 14 | 400 |
| 15 | 425 |
| 1 lb | 450 |

# CONTENTS

## PART TWO: IDENTITIES IN FLUX

## PART THREE: SURVIVAL AND REVIVAL

## PART FOUR: A DISH IN TIME

# Preface

*Siobhan Lambert-Hurley,*
*Tarana Husain Khan and Claire Chambers*

Food is an urgent necessity, but it may also be an enlivening topic issuing forth hope. Whenever we talk about food, we inevitably talk about culture. Food in various contexts means different things, and around itself cuisine can shape a culture. The subject provides us with a way of thinking about regions and their history through the lens of food rather than politics. That said, food, waste, servitude and the supply chain can also function as political allegories.

The cooking, serving and eating of food is a language, perhaps even a universal language. It offers a way of expressing feelings, which can even shade into abuse – often across the fault lines of gender, class and religion or race – but also has the potential to be a love language. Meals are a way of communicating across boundaries, including those that divide generations and time periods. Cooking and eating together brings people around the table. Particular dishes bespeak memories, others foretell futures.

This anthology of essays, anecdotes, recipes and reflections on food emerges from a research and public engagement project entitled 'Forgotten Food: Culinary Memories, Local Heritage and Lost Agricultural Varieties in India'. The project was funded by the Global Challenges Research Fund through the Arts & Humanities Research Council in the United Kingdom

(2019–2023). Specific to this funding was a requirement to use academic research to 'improve lives and opportunity' by addressing the United Nations' sustainable development goals. All three editors of *Forgotten Foods* had central roles in this project: Siobhan Lambert-Hurley as the overall project lead, Tarana Husain Khan as the main consultant in India and later research fellow and Claire Chambers as the lead on literature and creative writing.

We had our initial project meeting in Allahabad in November 2019. It was the first time our core team had met in person, and the coming together of such a diverse array of people was inspiring. Academic historians, literary scholars and plant scientists met writers, heritage practitioners, filmmakers and chefs. Over several days, we not only shared our experiences and visions for the project but also, at the generous invitation of Samina Naqvi, attended the Sanchari Sanskritik Parv (see chapter 25). We were treated to the most delicious regional delicacies, as well as lively festival sessions featuring writers, bloggers and foodies, including the inimitable food historian Pushpesh Pant.

On our final day, we set aside some time to discuss ways in which we might shape the project to our collaboration. A key focus was how to share the expertise and knowledge among our diverse group with the widest possible audience. Perhaps we could put together a series of articles, in English or Hindi, for a mainstream newspaper or magazine? In the months that followed, we took action by pitching the idea of a column to various mainstream outlets. A first draft of this collection's introduction was written at that time to place our endeavour in its wider context, and offer a justification for our intention 'to open the channels of communications between practitioners and scholars'. The series was picked up by the fearless online digital news publication, *Scroll*, and given ballast by its editor Naresh Fernandes' enthusiasm.

Then, in the midst of our plans for the first columns, the Covid-19 pandemic took hold. *Scroll*, like most news outlets, was overtaken by daily statistics, hospital updates and the extraordinary crisis of migrant labour. Our plans for the 'Forgotten Food' columns were themselves momentarily forgotten, as we, like everyone, grappled with lockdowns, food shortages, online working environments, home-schooling and caring for those most in need. By the summer of 2020, however, there was a general hunger – literally and metaphorically – for something to enliven the strange monotony of life in a global pandemic. Our first columns appeared in July 2020. Rana Safvi's evocative account of the 'bountiful' breakfasts of her Lakhnavi childhood – complete with a historic recipe for Roghini Roti Khassagi – unlocked an outpouring of content (chapter 3).

A global pandemic, it turned out, was a good time to write about the histories and cultures of food. People the world over were full of nostalgia, longing for an indeterminate moment in the past when life was more certain. Food seemed to provide the best way to get there: everyone will remember how banana bread became a transnational craze! Cooking and eating also offered a means for armchair travel when physical journeys weren't possible. Across the world, families and friends set up WhatsApp groups to share recipes, TikTok was inundated with cooking videos and Instagram turned into a veritable visual feast of home-cooking triumphs. Our columns mixing food and history struck a chord, attracting a wider audience than we had ever imagined. Though we initially only intended to curate the column for a year, its success meant that, like the pandemic itself, it carried on much longer.

In selecting articles and themes, we placed particular emphasis on food stories and histories from Muslim South Asia. This focus was neither exclusive nor explicit – and thus not all the excellent columns in the original *Scroll* series are included here. It was, however, intentional: a response to the devastating assault on food cultures connected to Muslim communities in contemporary India. Some may (and did) question this focus, highlighting shared culinary customs across region, caste or class, irrespective of religion. We may think here of the celebrated

Ganga–Jamuni tahzib – the distinctive and shared Hindu–Muslim culture of north India's central plains – evoked in chapters here too (11 and 25).

As scholars, though, we were attentive to how what had come to be labelled as 'Indian' food had been constructed in line with idealised patterns of 'Hindu' consumption throughout the twentieth century and beyond – often to the detriment of Indian Muslims. This was despite the fact that the arrival of Islam in India from the seventh century onwards had radically reshaped cooking and eating in India, making Indian food what it is today. A primary aim of our bigger project was thus to counter and complicate received ideas about history by aiming for the recovery, preservation and renewal of the rich food cultures in and from India's cities and locations with significant Muslim heritage. These places include Delhi and Lucknow, of course, but also Bhopal, Hyderabad, Manipur, Ladakh and elsewhere. Food history and literature, we argued back to our critics, offered a means to draw positive attention to a marginalised group within the Indian polity.

Inevitably, the pandemic also shaped what we would and could write and publish. Interviews, like that with Head Chef Naved Nasir featured in Claire Chambers' essay on the restaurant sensation Dishoom (chapter 21), had to happen over phone or the now ever-present Zoom. As food festivals became off limits, organisers wrote about them instead – cue Noor Khan's article about the Mahindra Sanatkada Lucknow Festival (chapter 24), which was originally published to coincide with the cancelled event in early 2021. Lockdown curbs on special occasions with loved ones meant Farah Yameen's article on her family's Eid gatherings in Bihar (chapter 8) gained a new poignancy. So did Sadaf Hussain's ode to India's street food vendors (chapter 20) as city streets were being emptied by government orders.

For the historians in our group, the pandemic was a particular conundrum. The archives that held our precious historical sources were closed overnight. Moreover, those academics based in Europe or North America could no longer travel to the peoples and sites of their research in South Asia. In this new world, the *Scroll* column became a way to create a new online archive of food memories. Restricted within our own national borders, yet strangely free of them in the virtual world, we invited authors from across the usually impermeable India–Pakistan border to reflect on their family's alimentary histories. The articles by Bina Shah (chapter 4) and Moneeza Hashmi (chapter 2) were the initial results. Muneeza Shamsie then produced a three-part series, which has been combined here into a longer piece to open this book (chapter 1). Over time our new realities informed the collection as a whole, with its focus on culinary memories and heritage recipes often preserved in families.

Simultaneously with building this archive, the 'Forgotten Food' project embarked on many other activities later documented in the *Scroll* column. At Benazir Farm near Rampur, we worked with plant scientist Duncan Cameron and a visionary farmer, Birendra Singh Sandhu, to resurrect heritage rice varieties previously vital to the textures, tastes and smells of local cuisine. Indeed, our first crop of Tilak Chandan came to maturation through the fraught summer and autumn of 2020 (chapter 23). Ideas were also crystallizing for a cookbook of historic recipes mined from nineteenth-century Urdu and Persian manuscripts in the Rampur Raza Library and translated by Tarana Husain Khan. Experimental cooking sessions took place when and however possible, with local chefs Suroor Khan and Aslam Khan in Rampur and Sadaf Hussain in Delhi (chapters 26 and 33). A documentary on Rampur's forgotten foods was also in the planning stages with filmmaker Yousuf Saeed – though, inevitably, new Covid waves and restrictions kept interrupting the production schedule.[1]

In fits and starts, depending on the risks and restrictions, we also undertook a comprehensive programme of oral history to capture memories around unique culinary practices, cultures and histories. As a researcher Farah Yameen was marvellously intrepid, finding ways in an era of quarantine and social distancing to undertake a vital set of interviews in Delhi with Muslim respondents from different social, regional and occupational backgrounds. Concerned with our reach under Covid constraints, academic partner Saumya Gupta at Janki Devi Memorial College also trained her students – confined to their own homes and engaging primarily by mobile phone – to gather oral histories from parents and grandparents on how their family's engagement with food had been transformed by migration to the capital.

In the spring of 2020, we still imagined a planned European Conference on South Asian Studies scheduled for the July of that year might go ahead in Vienna. It was to involve many of the project's academic contributors in a panel on 'Cooking, Eating, Remembering: Dynamic Histories of Food, Culture and Place'. The conference did not take place, predictably enough, but the essays came together in the end for a special issue of the academic journal *Global Food History*, co-edited by historians Jayeeta Sharma and Siobhan Lambert-Hurley. Some of the pieces were later rewritten – free of jargon and footnotes – for a broader audience, encouraging other academics to also convert their scholarly work of food histories into new forms (chapters 9–12, 14, 16–17, 22, 28).

In the autumn that same year, researcher Razak Khan persisted with his project plans to develop a contemporary performance piece based on rekhti poetry with scriptwriter Danish Iqbal and dastango Fouzia and Saneya. The original idea was for this production to be held live. However, amid pandemic realities, we took the opportunity to rethink, innovate and produce new digital content for the era of Zoom and online viewership. Across social media, YouTube and email, a transnational team created an experimental video featured in our July 2021 column.[2] Focused on the metaphors of food, flavours and taste, it draws on an Urdu rekhti text, *Musaddas tahniyat-i jashn-i Benazir* (Felicitation for the Incomparable Festival), written in 1867–1868 by Mir Yar Ali 'Jan Sahib' (1818–1886) about a public festival in Rampur.

Another landmark moment came in December 2020 with the publication of *Desi Delicacies: Food Writing from Muslim South Asia*, commissioned and edited by Claire Chambers. A planned output of our project from the start – if not in the global conditions we had imagined – it offered a mix of short stories and essays by some of South Asia's best-loved writers, historians and chefs. The idea was to capture South Asian and diasporic food cultures in prose by putting personal experience and expressiveness at the centre of gustatory writing. Authors were challenged to translate conversations about food cultures into imaginative and genre-bending prose pieces. We discovered the beauty of descriptions, and the pleasure that we take in describing and reading about food. There is a sensuality to food writing when it is well done. And, assuming that you are reading on a full stomach, this is a pleasure that is complete in itself.

The public response to *Desi Delicacies* was staggering to us. The book flew off real and virtual shelves, with reviews and features in the popular press, blogs and social media across India, Pakistan and Bangladesh. Online events in pandemic circumstances enabled energetic panels by contributors from India, Pakistan, Bangladesh, Britain and the United States at multiple literary festivals and universities. In due course, local editions came out in the UK (from Beacon Books, 2021, with the alternative title *Dastarkhwan*) and in Pakistan (from Liberty Books, 2022). Clearly, publications of this type can attract many hungry and appreciative readers. We could not have been more grateful.

We could also not help but heed a few caveats in otherwise glowing reviews. Many of the stories were those of the elite, with some time-intensive recipes often requiring expensive ingredients. Would there be a follow-up on more diverse households and the labour required to produce those feasts? In focusing on Muslim South Asia, the volume bridged populations in India, Pakistan, Bangladesh and their diasporas – but what about other regions, particularly in the south of South Asia? The project's oral history programme was already attentive to social and regional diversity – but, as the *Scroll* column flourished and took on its own life, we began to reflect consciously on how we could fill these gaps in another public output too. In addition, *Desi Delicacies*' essays proved more popular than its short stories. That is why we decided to concentrate on non-fiction for this volume, and to include a greater plethora of perspectives. We wanted to focus attention on a wider range of food and the contexts from which it emerges.

At promotional events for *Desi Delicacies*, certain themes also kept emerging in the public discussions around heritage foods – in particular, an often nostalgic desire to preserve 'authenticity' and 'tradition'. Plainly, the attention given to these qualities reflects their culinary value in today's societies. We can all observe how customers are lured to an upmarket restaurant or even a supermarket ready meal by the promise of a taste genuine in terms of origin and history. But these terms can also make historians bridle in suggesting that flavours or culinary practices can be fixed to a time or place. As a discipline, history demands close attention to how rhetoric shifts and contexts facilitate specificity and change. It seemed more reflection was needed here.

A new idea thus began to coalesce around bringing together the 'Forgotten Food' columns with a much larger set of commissioned articles for a second collection – a kind of *Desi Delicacies II*. Each chapter would take the reader on a journey through a different terrain – from the warm sweetness of childhood memories to the narratives of revival, from the intimacy of household kitchens to the gritty realities of the street-food stall. The texture of regional cuisines would be at the heart of this journey, enabling us to draw out how local dishes and tastes are rooted in specific foodways – crops and vegetables and animals – themselves the product of a place and its history. More often than not, that history is unstable, meaning that the borders of a region are made flexible by movement and migration, even as they are tied to a soil, a water, a climate.

We planned the four sections that now structure this book after the incomparable Teesta Guha Sarkar, our editor at Pan

Macmillan India, picked up our idea and ran with it. The first, simply titled 'Memories', captures some of the family histories from distant and more recent pasts to which we've alluded already as a function of archiving. The second, on 'Identities in Flux', is also historic in focus, though in a more scholarly vein, tracing the ways in which culinary cultures have evolved as a function of broader societal transformations. The third section, on 'Survival and Revival', acts as a tribute to food warriors – from individual families, street vendors and restaurateurs to farmers and festival organisers – who are preserving and bringing alive fading or lost culinary traditions today and into the future. For the final part, 'A Dish in Time', individual dishes act as an invitation to explore the jubilant particularities of regional cuisines.

Upon whetting the reader's appetite, each chapter concludes with the offering of an heirloom or historic recipe. The sheer diversity may come as a surprise as well as a delight. Food from Muslim kitchens is often identified in common parlance with meat dishes – and there is certainly a rich selection of those here. But the non-vegetarian recipes are far from just kabab and qorma, biryani and nihari. What's more, we include many different varieties of greens, grains and vegetables – from a Keralan kanhi and a Pangal eromba to Allahabad's nimona and a Kashmiri saag. And, of course, no meal would be complete without pickles in accompaniment and dessert to finish – though a Sri Lankan Malay achar and Rampur's adrak halwa may be new to many. Drawing on Unani traditions, we even include recipes for skin remedies.

From this chronicle-as-preface, we hope you will see that *Forgotten Foods* is a memorial to our initial intentions, the pandemic struggles and the bigger project. It also attests to our collaboration and friendship. As a team of three, we are intensely aware that we each bring unique qualities to the editors' table. Siobhan Lambert-Hurley and Claire Chambers are professional academics engaged with history and literature, respectively and in tandem; and Tarana Husain Khan's work as a food writer, novelist and heritage practitioner is indispensable. Together, we have sought to underpin more popular writing on heritage food with scholarly rigour, while translating nuanced academic approaches into accessible, elegant forms. Passion and compassion unite us in our endeavour.

We now invite you, dear reader, to join us for this feast of culinary writing from Muslim South Asia. From the present appetiser to final desserts are entire courses showcasing the diversity of these cuisines. We hope you savour our spread of slow-cooked enjoyment.

*Further material:*

1. Watch the documentary:

2. Read more about the transnational team's experimental video on *Scroll*:

   Or watch the performance video:

# INTRODUCTION

## Heritage Food and the Need for Collaboration

*Siobhan Lambert-Hurley*

Wherever you turn in India today, heritage food seems to abound.

From Amritsar to Chennai, food festivals are bringing delicacies from various regions, cities and neighbourhoods to a general public hungry for food with provenance. At local cultural events such as the Sanchaari Sanskritik Parv in Allahabad (see chapter 25) and the Mahindra Sanatkada Lucknow Festival (see chapter 24), audiences are treated to morsels of food history and traditional cuisine alongside literature, music, cinema and dance.

If you are on the five-star circuit, you may be drawn into luxury restaurants showcasing the finest dishes from historic royal courts. In September 2019, the Conrad Pune celebrated the 'royal flavours of Rampur' with a special dinner curated by Chef Suroor Khan. On the menu were 'lost recipes' from the glory days of the former princely state. Visit the ITC website and you'll read about the hotel group's 'relentless pursuits in presenting the gastronomic traditions of India's centuries-old heritage' through signature restaurants such as Dum Pukht and Dakshin.

More accessible eateries have turned history into franchise. The famous Karim's Hotel opened near the Jama Masjid in old Delhi in 1913, when the British Empire was still in its heyday.

But, since branching into Nizamuddin West in the 1990s, it has spread across Delhi–NCR, taking its famous kababs everywhere. History is also a part of newer restaurants such as Naimat Khana in Lucknow, which are bringing heirloom recipes passed down the generations to the table.

There are growing opportunities to carry historic flavours into your own home too. Browse the shelves of your local bookshop and you will be treated to lush cookbooks promising the best recipes from the 'last thousand years' of India's rich culinary heritage. Neha Prasada and Ashima Narain's *Dining with the Maharajas* (Roli Books, 2012) even provides a handy paperback 'kitchen copy' of recipes. This means you can recreate a royal banquet at home without messing up the lavish illustrations of the coffee-table book.

Increasingly, recipes come with memories attached. A delightful example of this is *Daastan-e-Dastarkhan* (Hachette India, 2019) by *MasterChef India* contender Sadaf Hussain. Combining 'stories and recipes from Muslim kitchens', the book embeds 'easy-to-follow' instructions for mouth-watering dishes within an autobiographical account of his culinary journey from Bihar to Delhi and beyond.

One difficulty in recreating historic recipes can be the availability of ingredients. India's Green Revolution in the mid-twentieth century increased rice productivity by around 50 per cent. But, as government programmes pushed high-yielding varieties, so the number of India's rice varieties dwindled from over a hundred thousand to just a few thousand. Now heirloom rice is making a comeback, buoyed by concerns over biodiversity, obesity, nutrition and, of course, taste. Handy online providers, like spiritoftheearth.in, bring it straight from the farmers to your door.

There is plenty in India's heritage food boom for armchair aficionados too. A major series, *Raja, Rasoi aur Anya Kahaniyaan*, originally shown on the Indian channel Epic TV, was bought by Netflix because of the runaway success of its first eleven-part season in 2014. Taking a regional approach to Indian cuisine, the show claims to offer an 'inside look' into the kitchens of India's former royals. If you prefer the written word to the moving image, you can read the writings of bloggers and journalists, who have also hit on food heritage as a means of exploring local cultures and mediating difference.

And yet, as one Delhi-based columnist and blogger Sourish Bhattacharya noted in the 'Fortune Cookie' column for *Mail Today* in 2015, much of the hype around 'lost recipes' and 'heritage cuisine' in India remains mere 'chatter'. Practitioners have been successful in transmitting heritage food into the public domain. However, to do more than 'scratch the surface', they need bona fide historians. In other words, trained scholars are required to gather oral testimony and mine the archives for original texts to provide historical meaning and texture.

That brings me from heritage food to the world of academic food history. Here there is a broad array of scholarship that addresses the preparation, consumption and distribution of food in historical context. As Concordia University professor Rachel Berger observed in her article 'Alimentary Affairs' in the academic journal *History Compass* in 2018, food history is only just beginning to coalesce as a defined area of study in South Asia. But the potentials for understanding the past's relationship to India's present are clear.

For heritage food to achieve its full potential, we need to open up channels of communication between practitioners and scholars. This exchange is at the heart of our project. Bringing food historians, sociologists, literary scholars and plant scientists into dialogue with heritage practitioners, authors, cooks and street vendors, it addresses challenges linked to local communities and food sustainability in India.

And in the process, you'll see we have recovered some great recipes and delicious food too!

*part one*

# Memories

# ACROSS INDIA, PAKISTAN AND BRITAIN

## A Family's Culinary History

*Muneeza Shamsie*

### For starters

I grew up in post-Partition Karachi, in a family where cooking was considered an art. My father, Isha'at Habibullah (1911–1991), a company executive at Pakistan Tobacco Company (PTC), was a gastronome. Cooking was his great hobby and he loved to prepare meals for friends. The range of his cooking is encapsulated by his famous brunches. The dishes at these brunches ranged from those considered desi nashta such as paya, nihari and aloo puri, to an eclectic mix of Euro-Anglo-American food including paté de foie gras, waffles, scrambled eggs and several salads. In the centre of the table, there would be a cake prepared by my mother, Jahanara Habibullah (1915–2003): for example, devil's food cake or Christmas cake in winter. Cake-making was my mother's contribution to household cooking. Sometimes she would make a pickle or chutney to supplement those created more frequently by my father.

My mother was very particular about every household detail. In our home, at every meal, the dining table of gleaming dark wood would be laid with placemats, matching table napkins, good cutlery and china. All our meals were served by a bearer or two in white livery. The food was almost always reviewed while it was being eaten; each dish was expected to be exactly right. This was invariably followed by a 'post-mortem' – a comment on this or that ingredient which my parents would elaborate on with their incomparable cook Maqbool. He was pivotal to our household and its culinary traditions.

Maqbool joined us as a young man two or three years after Partition. By then, my younger sister Naushaba had been born and we were living in Karachi in a block of company flats – a colonial building of yellow Gizri stone – on Clifton Road. In our breezy apartment, with its arches and verandahs and patterned floor tiles, the back verandah ran past the dining room and led off at a right angle towards the pantry and a traditional kitchen. The latter was equipped with a chula built into the far wall, with holes on top for cooking and another underneath where burning coals glistened; a dark, sooty chimney rose up overhead.

## Going away

In the mid-1950s, the company replaced this colonial building with a modern block of nine spacious flats. We lived on the top floor. There was an enclosed verandah with big windows, but the remaining area – hall, drawing room and dining room – were open plan, divided by the angle and structure of walls. The dining room, however, had a side door which opened into the pantry from which another door led into the kitchen with a modern gas cooker and possibly a metallic sink.

My memories of Maqbool preparing our meals, and indeed those of my parents' brunches, date back to this era. I associate Maqbool with the modern rather than the old-fashioned kitchen, always dressed in an apron while preparing food.

By this time, both Naushaba and I had been sent to boarding school in England, as my father and his brothers had been a generation earlier. This was the norm in our Anglicised milieu in Karachi (though mostly for sons) with due foreign exchange permissions. I was nine when I left and Naushaba joined me after she turned eight. We came home for good a full ten and nine years later, respectively.

My parents visited London every other year during the summer holidays. Naushaba and I came to Karachi in the alternative summers and would also visit our widowed grandmothers in Rampur and Lucknow. All this provided a huge contrast to our lives in England and, of course, the food we ate there. We had inherited our father's genes and were plump little girls devoted to food, to the despair of our slim, elegant and restrained mother.

## Eid, Christmas and events for 'ladies only'

In 1961, my father was appointed chairman and managing director of PTC and became the first Pakistani to head a major multinational corporation in the country. We moved into the chairman's house next door, a two-storey colonial building with a white exterior, sloping red-tiled roof and windows with green wooden louvres to filter the summer sunlight.

In this house we 'inherited' Rahim, an exacting, super-efficient majordomo. He was well acquainted with the social demands of a chairman's life as well as the British company directors who came from London on official visits. They stayed with us, as was the norm. On these occasions, daily meals were very formal, consisting of cut-glass tableware, the finest cutlery and china, and three courses of English or European food, followed by coffee.

This was the house where, as a child, I had attended Christmas parties, Santa Claus and all. Once my parents moved in, the rituals of Eid and Ramzan became the major house festivals. At the former we ate mince pies, Christmas cake and sandwiches; for Eid we were served traditional fare including samosas, seviyan and halwa.

Rahim also supervised the 'ladies only' events held by my mother: coffee mornings, bridge and mahjong parties as well as milads where two or three women with beautiful voices would sing or chant verses celebrating the life of the Prophet. At these milads, guests would sit against bolsters scattered on white cloths spread over the drawing room carpet before enjoying a sumptuous tea.

After my father's retirement as chairman of PTC, we moved into our own home: the modern house my parents built in the then comparatively new Defence Housing Society. Maqbool and his family came with us, as did Rahim.

This new house was divided by a central courtyard with patterned floor tiles and edged with potted plants and a small fountain in one corner. The kitchen was long and rectangular and had a small storeroom at the far end for crockery and glassware. There was no pantry. The gas cookers and sinks were located near the wide windows. Opposite, smaller windows were created higher up for cross-ventilation, but most of that wall was lined with cabinets at upper and lower levels.

A sliding serving hatch opened out onto the adjoining polished wooden cabinets in the dining room. My father's kitchen utensils bought on his trips to England – special kitchen knives, different thermometers and cutters, together with the various beaters, processors and cake tins that my mother used – were all stored in this section of the kitchen; the gas cooker my parents used stood nearby. My father now had more time to spare despite many distinguished appointments in the corporate sector, and would prepare food for his friends, children and grandchildren. I particularly remember the soup or stock he would leave to cook on the stove for hours on end. The gas cooker that Maqbool used daily was further down in the same row.

## Maqbool, a great cook

Throughout this time, Maqbool held his own, producing the finest food. He managed this whether he had to cater just for the family (and later Naushaba's little children and mine), or on a grander scale for the formal and informal dinners my parents hosted. At these, there were both Pakistani and visiting (mostly British) guests as well as diplomats and public figures – the latter were often old family friends.

My parents were aware of the traditional culinary world of both Lucknow and Rampur to which they belonged. Maqbool also came from Rampur. He had clearly revealed his talent early, because he had worked in the royal kitchens of Khasbagh Palace, albeit in a junior capacity when he was very young. He understood the careful melding of spices which my mother often declared to be the essence of good cooking. This was considered one of the great attributes of Rampuri food and included the restrained use of chillies. In Karachi, Maqbool was trained further by my father, who greatly valued Maqbool's culinary skills.

Maqbool's repertoire was vast and he paid great attention to detail. The koftas and shami kababs he made were stuffed with a very fine-chopped mixture of green coriander, green chillies and onions. The qiwami seviyan were cooked in such a way that each seviyan strand, plumped by the sugar syrup it had absorbed, glistened with the sheen. Then there was the crisp toffee he shaped into baskets with curving handles above – one basket per serving – filled with fruit salad in thick cream.

There was one specialty that I have never seen elsewhere: a pudding made of a large Swiss roll covered with thick white cream and dots of yellow-coloured cream, to resemble a corn cob and with green leaves made of marzipan on either side.

Once, in my early twenties, before I was married, I asked him if he would teach me to cook. He said, '*Arre, aap! Aap ko kya seekhaoonga? Aap to khansama rakheingi!*' (What, you! What can I teach you? You will keep a cook!)

In my parents' homes in Karachi, spicy desi food was usually a special treat two or three times a week. Most days we ate 'Angrezi' food, which included those everyday dishes so popular in the subcontinent and which I never encountered during my years at boarding school in England: potato mince cutlets, cock rolls and crumb chops. Then there were the usual soups, roasts, spaghetti, salads, baked fish and fried fish. Sometimes we had soufflé or lobster thermidor or crab au gratin. Maqbool also made the lightest pastry imaginable – flaky pastry for vol-au-vents and mille feuille and shortcrust pastry for quiches, jam tarts and other puddings.

Maqbool died of a massive heart attack in the late 1970s. Both my daughters, Saman and Kamila, were very young little at the time, but both remember him with great affection. Their grandparents loved to have them over and, each time, the two little girls would be asked beforehand, 'What would you like to eat?' They adored all Maqbool's food, but their absolute favourite was lemon meringue pie. Saman makes this dish to this day. She became an enthusiastic pastry maker, aged eight or nine – and lemon meringue pie was an early dish she learnt from her first cookery book.

Kamila's culinary skills developed much later – after she settled in London. She became a rather inventive cook, as was her grandfather. But in her second novel, *Salt and Saffron*, a description of iftar, of breaking the daylong fast during Ramzan, recreates for me the delicacies my parents would have served. She writes:

> We started with the requisite date, of course, to symbolise fidelity to the first Muslims in the deserts of Arabia, but then…on to gluttony! Curly shaped *jalaibees*, hot and gooey, that trickled thick sweet syrup down your chin when you bit into them; diced potatoes drowned in yogurt, sprinkled in spices; triangles of fried samosas, the smaller ones filled with

> mince-meat, the larger ones filled with potatoes and green chillies; *shami kababs* with sweet-sour *imli* sauce; spinach leaves fried in chick-pea batter…

Maqbool lives on in family memory. My parents did not find a cook equal to him again. By the time he died, it was rare indeed to find one with his repertoire, particularly when it came to European food, puddings, pastries and halwa.

## Maqbool's successors

My parents' subsequent cooks and other staff came from different regions of Pakistan, but there was another Rampuri cook vital to their household after Maqbool was no more. This was the elderly Amjad. He used to work for my mother's cousin, whose daughters were my childhood friends. I seem to have known him forever. He was certainly a household name in my maternal family. He was reserved and very polite – and I always associate him with the churidar pajama, sombre sherwani and dark cap he invariably wore. I have no memory of him in the kitchen per se. He gave up his full-time job eventually and started to cook freelance for us and a few of our relatives, preparing specific dishes such as that Rampur showstopper, adrak ka halwa, or his amazing dahi bara on important occasions.

There was also Sabir who, like Maqbool and Amjad, was of Rampuri origin. He had a rather chequered career and, from time to time, would just vanish from our lives. He worked for my parents a couple of times, decades apart, as a bearer; and once for me. In between he was a factory worker and trade unionist. Occasionally he cooked specific dishes for my parents in the post-Maqbool era. He had a shock of black hair, wore shalwar kameez and moved around with great agility; then at some point he disappeared entirely.

## My mother's love of food

In all these years I took my mother's knowledge of food for granted; it never occurred to me to question how or why she came by her information, since she didn't cook any of these dishes. After she passed away, I was surprised to find that she had left behind four whole exercise books scribbled with recipes, some in English, mostly in Urdu, plus little envelopes with recipes folded inside.

Among these papers, I found one recipe for sheer khurma, but three different recipes for qiwami seviyan in three different books. One is marked 'Qiwami seviyan tarkib Sultana Masood', namely, the method given to her by her friend and relative, Sultana Masood. There are three recipes for adrak ka halwa, including one attributed to Amjad and Sabir each (though I have no recollection of Sabir's version). There is no indication of any date.

As far as I can remember, adrak ka halwa was regarded by my family and select guests as a great treat, but it seems to be virtually unknown in Pakistan today. My Karachi friends have certainly never heard of it and, if I ever allude to it, the usual response is that the mere thought of such a thing – a halwa made out of ginger – is so off-putting. I have often wanted to rectify this and make the dish one day – the finest of halwas (just my opinion!). The taste of the ginger blends with all the other ingredients (cream, milk, sugar, almonds, kewra, asli ghee) to give a wonderfully nuanced flavour.

Other traditional desserts include loki ka halwa, shahi tukra, kheer, firni, plus two versions (including Amjad's) of gajar ka halwa and ande ka halwa. My mother has also written down three recipes for khichra, a main course usually associated with Ashura, the tenth day of Moharrum and distributed as niaz. Among other main courses, I discovered an unusual salan hara dhania, alongside Amjad's murgh musallam, Sabir's qorma and Sabir's aloo ki katliyan. The latter is so easy that I was surprised to find it there, until I came across several other straightforward recipes – even one for an omelette.

I soon realised that these recipes, along with those of the usual meat–vegetable combinations, such as saag gosht, provided that essential knowledge which ensured everyday fare for the family. Throughout this extensive and varied collection, there are recipes attributed to friends or relatives, including one each by Naushaba and me, as well as tamatar ka Hyderabadi cut az Sorayya Mazari, baingan ki sabzi az Gaiti, tarkib machli az Bajia, Tuba's biryani, and lime pickle by Begum Amjad Ali. There are two more lime pickle recipes (one typed in English, the other handwritten in Urdu) and a wide range of pickles and chutneys from achar shaljam khatta, achar aam and prawn achar to nauratan aur aam chatni, tamatar chatni and imli ki chatni.

There are no recipes by Maqbool. I can only assume that my mother wrote most of these methods down to instruct future cooks after he passed away. One exercise book has a solitary date, November 1975, very much within Maqbool's lifetime. However, it refers to my mother's culinary signature – Christmas cake – with an added note: 'The recipe is not quite right.' In an envelope, I found a letter dated 1976, written on the official letterhead of the British Deputy High Commission, Karachi and signed Nellie Eaden, with a recipe for plum pudding attached. There is another plum pudding recipe and one for crème Suisse, both seemingly written by British visitors to Pakistan.

The list of recipes is endless: scones, walnut bread, coffee cake, brownies, Swedish tea ring, two for cake icing and a detailed description of how to make mango ice cream in a special ice cream machine given by another friend, Yusuf Bhabha.

Then there are recipes for Chinese dishes so popular in Pakistan, and a slew of Angrezi dishes including mulligatawny, plucked partridges and parsley potatoes, roast duck and lots of patés including one made of kidneys by my father. Added to this are some basic essentials: white sauce, chicken stock and apple pectin.

For me, these recipes are an extraordinary walk down memory lane. Both the recipes and the people my mother mentions evoke so many images of a bygone past. I finally understood how my mother kept herself informed about different dishes and their ingredients, and the constant possibilities for improving every dish. I believe this work was common to many women of her generation.

## My own relationship with food

I learnt to cook gradually, and only after I married, from some recipes given to me by my father and some from cookery books recommended by him over a period of time. The only recipe I 'inherited' from my mother was her Christmas cake, which I make almost every year. The recipe was originally given to Saman. I ventured to try this a year or two later – and it worked perfectly! I had been intimidated by its intricacies at first. I was never told by either my parents or my husband Saleem Shamsie what I should or should not cook.

Somehow, I seem to have collected recipes, and made kheer, ande ka halwa, gajar ka halwa, sheer khurma and qiwami seviyan long before I made cakes: I can still see my father sitting there at the end of his dining table, sometimes flicking through a cookery book or two, at other times just giving me the details straight from memory/experience, pausing to ponder a little as he dictated these recipes to me.

One such recipe is the qiwami seviyan, a traditional dish that my parents always served at Eid, as I do too. In the old days, it used to be decorated with finely beaten silver foil (chandi ka varq) alongside the almonds and pistachios, but these days I don't risk it unless I can be sure it really is silver and not some unhealthy metal made to resemble varq.

## My parents' life writing through food

I discovered the long history of my parents' culinary fascination when they wrote their memoirs. Unfortunately, my father Isha'at Habibullah was very ill when he began his autobiography, which remains incomplete. However, he did condense the pre-Partition sections into a four-article series published in *Dawn Magazine* in 1991 under the title 'Memories of the British and Feudal India'.

Around this time, my mother Jahanara Habibullah, encouraged by her two sisters, began to jot down her own memories as therapy to help her cope with my father's failing health and, later, her widowhood. These writings became a book, *Remembrance of Days Past: Glimpses of a Princely State during the Raj* (2001), translated from the Urdu by Tahira Naqvi.

Later, the original Urdu was published as *Zindagi ki Yadein: Riyasat Rampur ka Nawabi Daur* (2003). The English version was brought out first, as the Pakistani branch of Oxford University Press had not yet started publishing in Urdu. Both of Jahanara Habibullah's books are soon to be reprinted in a second edition, with an introduction by Razak Khan.

Each of my parents incorporate references to food as an intrinsic aspect of life in pre-Partition Lucknow and Rampur.

## My father's colonial childhood

In my father's first *Dawn* article, he says that in his childhood he and his two older brothers were brought up by an English governess. This was because their Anglophile father, Sheikh Mohammed Habibullah, a taluqdar of Awadh (and later Vice Chancellor of Lucknow University), had decided that his three sons would later be sent away to England to receive 'the best of English education'.

My grandfather and others in his social circle entertained often, and used to serve European and Indian food as well as vegetarian dishes prepared by Brahmin cooks. My father's earliest memories include one such lavish dinner, which was thrown by his uncle, Sheikh Shahid Hosain Kidwai (father of the novelist Attia Hosain). There my father's English governess gave him some jelly to eat. He expected it to be sweet, but, to his horror, it was salty. This was his introduction to chicken aspic, and it made him feel quite ill. My father wouldn't touch this savoury jelly for years, but he must have come round, since I remember aspic concotions being served as some of his favourite dishes in our Karachi home.

My father and his brothers would accompany their father on shikars in the winter, which my father enjoyed very much. These hunts were very 'sumptuous affair[s]' with 'a whole enclave of tents' being pitched among mango trees and in other scenic spots. He has very little to say about hunting otherwise. Instead, he writes of the delicacy and beauty of his father's shikar elephant.

He particularly enjoyed the food: sagpaita dal, les ke chawal, kababs and qormas cooked in fresh ghee. Then there was the delicious rasawal, which he described as 'kheer made with sugar cane juice eaten with very cold milk and wads of fresh balai'. As he noted in his first *Dawn* article, he much preferred these foods to 'the elaborate cuisines of Lucknow'.

## Lucknow

A generation later, after Partition, Naushaba and I would accompany our parents across the border from Karachi to Lucknow to visit my widowed grandmother, Huzoor Ammi (the activist and writer Inam Fatima Habibullah) – if we got a visa to do so. During one such trip, I remember there was great excitement at the dining table because someone had sent us a gift: a beautiful earthenware pot filled with rasawal. Truly delicious it was too, though it is a dish I seldom encounter in Karachi. As for the balai, I have never seen any as thick as the one in Lucknow. I was fascinated by the round layers and layers of solid fresh cream, which were stacked one on top of the other into a pile, having been skimmed from the top of the milk.

As far as I can remember, these stacks were never homemade. Instead, a vendor would come through the back garden to the few steps leading up to the open-air landing near the kitchen door. I would watch with fascination as he removed the requisite number of layers and weighed them on the scales, or tarazu, he carried across his shoulders.

Another Lucknow treat were the special seekh kababs which were unique to Kakori, the village to which my grandmother belonged. Special cooks would come from the village to prepare them for us on a charcoal anghithi, or brazier. In my memory, Kakori kababs remain unique, with a lovely glossy and soft texture and subtle flavour, all of which made them more delicious than other kababs.

The kababs were served on long oval dishes on my grandmother's long dining table. She always sat at the head with two generations of her family gathered there during these reunions. Large colour photographs and paintings of her and my late grandfather and other forebears looked down at us from the walls.

Hidden from view, behind a carved wooden screen near the rear door, sat a huge copper bowl on a wooden stand; a flat filigree brass top stretched across the bowl. This was where we washed our hands, with water being poured from the spout of a silver lota by a servant, a bar of soap at hand on a small shelf.

My grandmother was extremely fond of paan. There was always a silver paandaan by her side in the drawing room with a silver spittoon nearby.

My other great memory is of the pickles my father made during one of my trips to Lucknow. I have no idea what the pickle was, but I do know that in Karachi my parents would leave pickles to mature in sealed jars for at least a year. Even then, imagine my amazement in Lucknow one winter when three or four huge ceramic pickle jars around two feet in height were brought out to the driveway and placed before my father. While my grandmother looked on proudly, my father proceeded to unscrew the lid of each jar and inspect its contents. The pickle had been made on his last trip to Lucknow and had been sitting there waiting for him ever since.

## European influences

During my father's childhood, his English governess always took his brothers and him to Nainital, the hill station now in Uttarakhand, to escape Lucknow's summer heat. By 1919, at the age of eight, my father 'was struck by the fact that aristocratic ladies who observed purdah in Lucknow did not do so in Nainital'. The hectic social life for which the hill stations were famous included wonderful picnic parties where 'the ladies used to be busy cooking' their specialties. This made a profound impression on him and influenced his 'gourmet propensities', he told his *Dawn* readers.

Many of these ladies were European – and so he became particularly interested in European food. This proclivity perhaps also stemmed from the fact that he knew he would be leaving to study in England soon.

In February 1920, my grandfather accompanied his sons to England. In his incomplete draft memoir, my father describes a delicious breakfast in Paris en route to England that year. He also mentions that, at school in England, his fellow pupils were amazed that as a Muslim he was not allowed to eat pig and was instead served kippers or haddock. To my surprise, Christmas festivities, which meant a lot to the Habibullah brothers in both their British and Indian lives, receive only passing mention, as does the rich Christmas pudding embedded with silver sixpence coins.

My grandfather left his eldest son, Ali Bahadur ('Sonny'), at a public school, Clifton College, in Bristol, and the two younger ones, Enaith ('Bubbles') and Isha'at at a prep school in Rottingdean, Sussex. After joining his school, my father only came to Lucknow once, during a short trip in 1931, before he returned to the subcontinent for good in 1935. However, the Habibullah brothers saw their father again in 1924 when he came on a visit to England with their five-year-old sister Tazeen. Their mother Inam Fatima was also present, and she described that trip in her Urdu travelogue *Tassurat-i safar-i Yurap*.

The journey to England was her first by ship, and she had just come out of purdah. She had never seen Bombay before, let alone the sea and, once on board, she felt very worried about the food. What was halal and what haram? She dared not eat anything but boiled vegetables.

Her fascination for the new worlds she discovered, including the workings of government, the women's movement in Britain and the Muslim world, and the work of modernising Muslim scholars, brings imperial, interwar Britain vividly to life. She was, however, rather unimpressed by that choice English meal served so often by the privileged – roast meat and boiled vegetables – which had a disparaging effect when translated into Urdu as bhuna gosht and ubli hui sabzi.

## Tears of happiness

Sections of *Tassurat* have been elegantly translated into English for a chapter in the book *Three Centuries of Travel Writing by Muslim Women* (2022), edited by Siobhan Lambert-Hurley, Daniel Majchrowicz and Sunil Sharma. One passage captures Inam Fatima's joy at being reunited with her sons during their Easter holidays. She, my grandfather and Tazeen arrived at Dorchester Station. The three Habibullah brothers, with their English guardian, were at the station to receive them and accompany them to the house my grandparents had rented in Dorchester.

She writes that the cooks 'had prepared food for us, but at that moment I was neither hungry nor thirsty. I was seeing my darlings after an eternity. Tears of happiness and joy flowed from my eyes.'

Her descriptions of England include a trip to the seaside resort town of Weymouth, where she became acutely aware of the culinary deprivation of her sons:

> There is a restaurant here called Trocadero. The boys told me that they serve a 'gravy,' or sauce, that is better than the ones you get in India. We went for lunch. The poor boys haven't had an Indian meal in such a long time that they were thrilled to eat there. I thought it was terrible.

During his sixteen years in Britain, clearly my father continued to long for desi food. In 1921, after my father and Bubbles joined Sonny at Clifton College, my father and Sikander 'Siku' Baig became particularly good friends. Siku's father, Sir Abbas Ali Baig, was posted at the Indian Council at Whitehall and had a house near the school. Every Sunday, Lady Baig would invite her sons and the Habibullah brothers to lunch and, according to his published memoirs, gave them 'sumptuous desi meals' of biryani, qorma and kababs.

## Oxford and after

In 1929, my father went on to study at Oxford University. There he came to know many more Indians. He made lifelong friends, joined their various clubs and societies and identified strongly with India. He recalls in the third article of his *Dawn* series: 'We were a most united lot and our friendships were not monopolised by feelings of religion or region.' There are references in his writings to the social life he enjoyed, including *thé dansants* (teatime dance parties), and reasonably priced three-course menus, but in neither case does he specify what the food was like.

In his draft memoirs, he adds that, in London while working for his bar exams, he and his friends frequented the famous Indian restaurant Shafi's in Gerrard Street. Apparently, they had been taken to it by Nawab Ali Khan of Akbarpur. Known as 'Nawab Chakkan', this man was described by my father as a 'a great gourmet' who had also introduced 'items of Lucknow cuisine' such as 'karelas and several daals' to the restaurant's menu.

In 1935, my father returned to India. He had been away so long that he experienced great difficulty in adjusting. He notes in his memoirs that he felt like 'a fish out of water' and thus tried to 'Indianise' himself by wearing sherwanis and churidars and chewing paan. Eventually he defied his father, giving up the legal profession to join what was then the Imperial Tobacco Company in Calcutta, and later in Lahore. He loved the Bengali metropolis, as he did Lahore. In both cities, he had many Oxford friends and a great social and gastronomic life.

His work, however, took him across many other regions. In his memoirs, he refers to the 'excellent food' he was served in the paddleboats he travelled on between Khulna and Narayanganj. He explains that, in Bengal, he discovered new vegetarian and non-vegetarian foods, claiming that the meat there 'was much more tasty…than elsewhere'. In Lahore, thanks to his friend Nawab Muzaffar Ali Qizilbash, 'whose table was well-known', he was introduced to 'Pathan food' such as khichri kuroot, shalgambatta (a form of shab degh) and chapli kababs, which he describes as 'not as spiced as in the UP or Calcutta'.

He also referred to the exquisite French cuisine of André Malik, the French wife of his friend, Tufail Malik. His friendship with Syed Babar Ali, another great gastronome, with whom he shared an insatiable love of food and cooking, as far as I can remember, dates back to this time too.

Living in Karachi later, my father continued to indulge his love for seafood and the only sport he excelled at: deep-sea fishing. In the early days after Independence, lobsters, prawns and crabs – products that now earn millions as exports – were readily available too.

A favourite Karachi outing when I was a child was to go 'crabbing'. We would hire 'bunder boats' manned by local fisherman who would sail us round the harbour, providing us with fishing line and baits to catch crabs. The fisherman would cook them there and then on the boat to serve fresh with our dinner. On our Sunday trips to the company's beach hut at Sandspit and later Buleji, fishermen would come by and sell us freshly caught shellfish, including lobsters for a rupee or two.

## An extensive culinary bookshelf

I remember that my father had a habit of sitting around reading cookery books and magazines in the way others sit and read fiction and non-fiction. These ranged from *Gourmet Magazine* to a recipe book dating back to the time of Wajid Ali Shah of Awadh. His bookshelf also included many other books, including those by the fiction writer and broadcaster Attia Hosain.

She was my father's first cousin and also married to his eldest brother Sonny. She had lived in London since 1946. Her novel *Sunlight on a Broken Column*, published in 1961 – and chosen recently as one of the seventy books on the Queen's Jubilee Book List – has a passage capturing the ambience of different festivals, ranging from Diwali to Eid, with a brief reference to food: 'Bowls of Sivain [seviyan], rich golden threads of honey sweetness decorated with silver beaten into paper light as whispers, flecking one's lips, and jugs of steaming milk, and thick many layered cream.'

In 1962, she published *Cooking the Indian Way*, co-authored with Sita Pasricha. This was one of the earliest post-war, diasporic cookery books. The co-authors drew on personal experience to make traditional South Asian cooking feasible to the busy housewife. Kamila, who now lives in London, still uses this book, as I do in Karachi; the various dishes I make include stuffed pepper curry, dhansak, vindaloo, khatti dal, mulligatawny and sukhe aloo chilke wale. I inherited the copy that Attia had signed for my father: 'Isha'at, thanks for the help.'

My father seldom followed a recipe exactly, but tended to throw in a 'dash of this or that'. If I consulted him over a recipe from a cookery book, he would pore over it and tell me how to adjust it to local ingredients. Though he dictated some of his recipes to me, I never knew him to write any of them down.

In the late 1970s, however, Zuhra Karim, a family friend and editor of the women's monthly *She*, invited him to contribute recipes to her series 'Man in the Kitchen'. He did so for several months and was given an entire page each time. Sometimes he would present an Angrezi and a desi dish alongside each other such as 'Chicken Fricassee or Blond Chicken' and murgh musallam. In another issue, he focused on two puddings, trifle and Crêpes Suzette, both of which are particular favourites of mine.

His 'Iftar Specials' consisted of his 'four favourite sherbets': imli (tamarind), kairi (mango), falsa (blackcurrant) and kaghzi nimbu (lemon). There were also recipes for two types of shami kababs and two types of seekh kababs, plus a mushroom pulao using black morel mushrooms (guchchi) found in Hunza and Pakistan's Northern Areas. Of course, he could not miss out on his favourite seafood and included a 'prawn curry' and 'Lobster à la Reine'. I rather think the recipe for the former is his own invention and I still use it frequently. It has one added advantage: if I have a guest allergic to prawns, I substitute the shellfish with skinned boneless mackerel (surmai) boti cut into cubes – and it still works very well.

## My mother's rootedness in Rampur

I realise now that my father's fascination for cooking, his adventurous approach to new and different foods, are closely linked to his tale of displacement, exile and a quest for self.

In marked contrast, my mother's awareness of good cuisine and the importance she attached to it is largely rooted in, and an assertion of, the culture in which she grew up. Both my parents shared an abiding interest in Rampur's cultural and culinary heritage.

My parents were married during my father's pre-Partition Lahore posting. They had met during my father's visit to the hill station Mussoorie, when he had gone to call on her father, Sahibzada Sir Abdus Samad Khan, who was an old friend of his family.

My mother, Jahanara Habibullah, was born and brought up in Rampur. Her father was the chief minister of the princely state. Her eldest sister Rafat Zamani Begum was married to the ruler Nawab Raza Ali Khan. Both their families were Rohilla Pathans but my mother's forebears, the rulers of Najibabad, had been executed for the mutiny of 1857. Both the Rampur and Najibabad families and that of the princely state of Loharu, to which my grandmother, Lady Abdus Samad Khan née Sahibzadi Aliya Sultan Begum belonged, had all intermarried across several generations.

*Remembrances of Days Past* has the 1911 Coronation Durbar on the cover and a photograph of my stunning sari-clad mother at the back. The book interweaves the history and cultural heritage of Rampur with anecdotes of family life. A detailed chapter, 'The Royal Tables at the Court of Rampur', explains that Rampur menus were famous throughout India and 'the chefs here were superb craftsmen and each had his designated skill'. There would be a qaliya master, a kababchi, a specialist in rice, another who concentrated on desserts, such as halwa and so on.

Her words remind me of our family's talented cook Maqbool. I wonder how many of these chefs he would have known, or heard of, or remembered – even though he had been very junior in those pre-Partition years. I wonder, too, what he would have thought of her reminiscences.

My mother describes the various dishes prepared in the royal kitchens. She points out that two main dishes prepared in Rampur kitchens were the qaliya and the qorma: 'the former contains turmeric; the latter is made with coriander'. She names a wide range of qaliyas and also refers to a special white chicken qaliya with milk, yoghurt and green chillies as its main ingredients. She describes the Mughal dish shab degh as a qaliya too. This dish involves hours of slow cooking and the addition of koftas, which are prepared separately, also whole turnips, as well as gur (raw sugar), 'lightly fried with turmeric', and saffron and kewra water. My mother clarifies that this is a different variety to the famous Kashmiri shab degh.

*Remembrance of Days Past* additionally contains much discussion of rice dishes. My mother describes dum pukht pulao made of whole partridges, quail or a leg of mutton. She refers to yakhni pulao, which consists of rice and mutton stock. Meanwhile, biryani entails meat first cooked as a qorma, then mixed with 'half-done rice and sprinkled with saffron and kewra'. She moves on from the savoury to an astonishing array of sweet rice dishes, beginning with mutanjan. This dessert 'has a sweet and sour flavour', with sugar four times the weight of the uncooked rice, tiny gulab jamuns studded across the dish as a garnish and tiny spicy mutton koftas for decoration!

Then there is muzaffar, which has less sugar than mutanjan, and fruit preserve (murabba) is added to it. Safaida, a sweet dish of white rice, is cooked in such a way that it completely absorbs the sugar and ghee and 'each grain stands out…and is so white that the sugary syrup coating has the sheen of diamonds'. She also writes of an anar pulao served in special silver bowls called qabs. Each one is laid out with 'four pomegranates crafted from sugar and red colouring', the pomegranate seeds created from almond slivers coated in petha – a transparent sweet made of pumpkin. She also refers to a sweet grape pulao and a pineapple pulao.

My mother continues to explore the extraordinarily creative and imaginative abundance of Rampur's fabled dishes – foods that most of us cannot even imagine today – in her section on kababs. Here are descriptions of kabab urus-i behri, which is made of sanwal, a freshwater fish, cooked, ground and reconstructed to resemble a fish two feet long – with scales, tongue and tail, each of which has a different flavour.

Rampur was also known for its legendary halwas and sweets. Several had very poetic names too. There is 'dar-i bahisht (gateway to paradise), a flaky sweet made of almonds or pistachios, ghee and sugar and cut into squares'; naan-i santara (naan of oranges) 'made of orange peel, orange juice, ghee and sugar and shapes into small flat rounds like a roti'. Hardly anything is within the realm of the ordinary by today's standards. The khase ke laddoo made of gram flour might resemble the laddoos of today, but were so large that they weighed 'about a quarter pound each' and the gram flour was mixed with 'ground pistachios, almonds and whole raisins'.

She writes of other delicacies, some of which I had the good fortune to taste during my visits to my widowed maternal grandmother, Ammajan, in Rampur with my parents in the 1950s and 1960s. My grandmother lived in Rosaville, the family home. My aunt, Fakhra, her husband, Sahibzada Masuduzzafar Khan, and their children, my playmates, were nearby, in Lalazar, their resplendent art nouveau house. There Fakhra, a talented artist, had painted beautiful murals across entire walls, created unusual furniture, drawn women with bangles and flowing skirts on the cupboards of a bedroom, sculpted a gargoyle in the lush garden as well as herons and frogs around a fountain, and much else. I was completely enchanted by the place.

Often we were invited to meals at Khasbagh Palace next door. Sometimes my eldest aunt, Rafat Zamani Begum – known to me as Khala Huzoor – and Nawab Raza Ali Khan would insist we stay there for a few days too.

The meals at Khasbagh were stunning. I still remember the crispy diamond-shaped loz-i Jahangiri named after the Mughal emperor. These sweets were made of 'almonds, ghee khoya, sugar…with layers of crushed pistachios'. Then there was halwa sohan, made of wheat, which is 'the king of halwas' and still available today. The difference is that the halwa sohan I ate at Khasbagh was far superior to any I have eaten elsewhere in Rampur, or indeed my hometown of Karachi. In the Khasbagh version, the grain was very fine, the colour darker and each piece sat on the serving dish cut into beautifully neat shiny squares.

I remember too, the puris made of clotted cream, 'collected layer upon layer to form a cake and served with sugar' – as my mother describes them in her memoir.

Above all, I was spellbound by the nimish, 'a great delicacy made by collecting layers and layers of froth from sweet milk'. I was fascinated to learn that it was made by pouring sweetened milk from a height from one dish to another, over and over again, to create a froth, which was then left on the rooftop in the cool of the night under the dew. It was eaten with a tunki, a very crisp, thin and large roti, which my mother rightly describes in her book as 'biscuit-like'.

I was very taken by a simply delicious main course, murgh musallam dumpukht pulao, and was equally spellbound by its appellation – such a wonderfully rhythmic and guttural pronunciation.

On the other hand, I seem to have had my first taste of paya in Rampur too, though I am not sure why. The Angrezi schoolgirl that I was, on a summer holiday from school in Sussex, was just horrified at the sight of all that jelly, the bones and marrow in such a dark liquid! The paya had been made especially for us, but I could hardly touch it. I felt quite ill to see the grown-ups, our friends and family tucking in and saying, 'Wah! Wah!' while commenting on the superlative quality of the dish. In later years, I realised my husband Saleem would have greatly enjoyed that meal. After I got married, I learnt to appreciate paya and nihari, thanks to him.

In Khasbagh Palace, we would be served these peerless meals in a beautiful wood-panelled dining room hung with oil paintings. The two or three round tables arranged for us would take up but a small portion of that huge space where banquets must have once been held. My memories date back to a time when the princely states were no more, of course – though I would imagine there were still separate kitchens in the palace for European and Brahmin food.

## Angrezi food

My only memory of Angrezi food there is from a stopover one year with Khala Huzoor in her modern Delhi home. There was some delay over lunch because one of the adults had been held up somewhere. After a while Khala Huzoor suggested that since it was getting late, my sister Naushaba and I should go ahead and eat first. We were led into the dining room which featured a long gleaming table laid with due formality. We did not find this unusual, nor the fact that the food was served formally by a bearer (because that was the norm in our Karachi home too). But we had never imagined a lunch with quite so many courses: soup, fish, roast meat, desi dishes, desserts and fruit. Being well brought-up little girls, we thought we had to partake of every single dish. By the end, we staggered out, our eyes glazed. My mother couldn't stop laughing. She told us that the staff must have thought, 'Mashallah, what healthy appetites!'

In her childhood before her first European trip, my mother was probably little acquainted with Angrezi food. This was despite the fact that her Anglicised father was well travelled and her three brothers Yusuf, Yunus and Yaqub were being educated at British India's well-known English schools. In 1931, however, my mother and her sister Fakhra discarded purdah, aged sixteen and seventeen respectively, because Fakhra was recommended a sanatorium in Switzerland to cure her tuberculosis.

After she regained her health, the two sisters and their mother travelled in Europe, spent some weeks in London and returned to a greatly changed, modernised and Westernised Rampur under the newly crowned Nawab Raza Ali Khan. In her memoir, my mother comments on the delicious Italian food they ate en route to Switzerland via Genoa on board a Lloyd Triestino ship. When it comes to her description of London, though, she merely says: 'English food is plain, but the puddings and tarts are delicious.'

My early memories of Rampur are very vivid. This is because in that (unimaginable) time, when visas between India and Pakistan were not an issue, Naushaba and I were entrusted to the care of Ammajan in India for several months. This was when my father was sent to Britain for a training course by his company and my mother accompanied him. I loved the family house with its fluted arches and verandahs, elegant interiors and spacious grounds, lily pond and rose garden, as well as its own private mosque. At some point I learnt that the front part of the house, including the bedroom where I was staying and the elegant dining room and drawing room had once been a part of the mardana, for men only.

The back door of the dining room opened out to a long, wide passage – part of which, in my time, served as the pantry where the fridges were kept – which divided the house between mardana and zenana areas. The entrance to the zenana opened onto a large courtyard at the back, and at one end was a staircase leading up to first floor where all the bedrooms (and more open-air verandahs) were. I am not sure where the kitchen was, though I have a notion that it was in the vicinity of this courtyard somewhere. Perhaps it was near the area in the far corner next to some low steps where, as a small child, I had been fascinated by a woman sitting behind a circular chakki, grinding wheat into atta.

## Ornate rituals

*Remembrance of Days Past* covers a different dimension of Rampur and its food traditions than I could ever have imagined. This includes descriptions of ornate rituals which were held in purdah. One such ritual was the sawani celebrations during the rainy season, which was welcomed by songs and music, new clothes, special foods and young girls sitting on swings. She explains that since the monsoon embodies romance and the quickening of life, sawani was a wedding ritual too, celebrated by the bridegroom's family to welcome a young bride. She includes Khala Huzoor's description of her own rich and sumptuous sawani ceremony held by her father-in-law, Nawab Hamid Ali Khan, culminating with her and her bridegroom, the future Nawab Raza Ali Khan, being positioned together on a swing. Here the references to food, the 'trays with a variety of snacks [which] had been provided for the guests' and 'arrays of delicious dishes elaborately laid out on tablecloths', are integral to the atmosphere: the music, the guests and their sumptuous attire.

My mother also refers to the symbolism of food in elaborate rituals. Her description of her sister Fakhra's wedding includes the ma'yun ceremony when round sugary sweets (peendiyan) are symbolically placed on the bride's upturned hands for good luck, while fruits are placed on her lap. My mother devotes an entire chapter to various wedding rituals, well known across the subcontinent, and how they were conducted in Rampur. Several of these, such as ma'yun, mehndi and arsi mushaf, continued to play a vital part in post-Independence Indian and Pakistani weddings. This includes my own nuptials and those of all my friends and relatives, although these rituals were greatly toned down compared to those in times of yore.

Similarly, foods served on religious occasions or festivals in my mother's time are not dissimilar to culinary traditions today. Her account of Eid ul-Fitr in Rampur is filled with wonderful descriptions of joy and celebration when the Eid moon is sighted, marking the end of the month of Ramzan. She recounts that her father always broke his fast after Eid prayers with sheer khurma, which is seviyan cooked in milk, though she says it can be prepared in different ways. She writes of qiwami seviyan, which is cooked in syrup with four times the amount of sugar, while muzaffar has less sugar but is cooked with saffron. She gives a detailed description of how the yellow vermicelli-like strands of seviyan are made at home from kneaded farina.

Of course, today seviyan are bought dry and packaged from supermarkets or grocery stores. They are synonymous with Eid ul-Fitr and served in every household, but usually as a sheer khurma version prepared in milk. Sheer khurma was always present at my parents' home on Eid and served to visitors who came to call and also for sit-down Eid lunch *en famille*. The same can be said of homemade qiwami seviyan, alongside other sweets bought from the shops, such as barfi, halwa sohan and rasgullas. I have only seen qiwami seviyan occasionally in Karachi.

## Qiwami Seviyan

**Ingredients**

2lb (around 1kg) sugar
1 pint (around ½ litre) water
½ tsp saffron threads
2 tbsp kewra
8 oz (around 225g) seviyan (vermicelli)
8 oz (around 225g) unsalted butter

2 tins evaporated milk (about 400ml each)
1 packet 200ml cream (or use 6 oz/170g fresh cream)
chopped pistachios or almonds (skinned)

**Method**

1. Heat oven to 150°C/300°F.
2. Butter an ovenproof dish. I use a Pyrex 12" x 8" x 2 ½".
3. Crush saffron strands and soak in kewra. Put aside.
4. Dissolve the sugar in water and bring to a boil. A clear syrup will be formed. Put aside.
5. In a separate pan, heat butter. Add the seviyan and brown them (but make sure they do not burn).
6. Add one tin of evaporated milk, ½ pint syrup, and 1–2 tbsp of cream. Bring to the boil, then lower the heat slightly and cook for about 5–10 minutes. The mixture will thicken. Stir regularly.
7. Add the second tin of evaporated milk, ½ pint syrup and 1–2 tbsp of cream. Bring to the boil, then lower heat slightly and cook for 10 minutes or until the mixture starts coming away from the edge of the pan while you are stirring.
8. Add the rest of the syrup and cream, kewra and saffron and stir well. Bring mixture to the boil, then lower the heat slightly and cook for another 20 minutes.
9. Pour mixture into the ovenproof dish. Cook in the oven at 150°C/300°F for 15 minutes.
10. Turn down the oven temperature to 135°C/275°F and cook for another 30 minutes.
11. Take the dish out of the oven and let it rest for 20 minutes or so. Scatter with chopped pistachios or almonds.
12. Serve warm with cream.

# Memories of My Father
# Faiz Ahmed Faiz

*Moneeza Hashmi*

I do not have clear memories of all of us, the whole Faiz family, sitting down at the dining table to eat together every day. Neither do I recall any particular occasion when we would all get together for a family meal. This was probably because my father, the poet Faiz Ahmed Faiz, was rarely home at mealtimes. Moreover, my mother, Alys Faiz, being a working mom, had to keep to the schedules of her office, as well as making sure we young girls, my elder sister Salima and myself, were never late for school.

What I can remember from my schooldays, back in the 1950s, is that each day during the winter term we would receive from home a tiffin, as we called it, or lunchbox. All of us school friends would sit together in the grounds and share our lunch while we laughed and talked non-stop during the long lunch break. The food in that lunch carrier was always simple. One roti and one curry, sometimes a dal and sometimes veggies.

Our dinner at home would mostly be snack food. Perhaps omelettes and toast or cured meat sandwiches. Maybe dal and plain rice. When we had a treat, it would be a sort of pancake made with mashed potatoes and cabbage with a fried egg on top. I used to look forward to that as it was a hot meal.

Our dining table seated four. My father always sat at the head, and my mother next to him on his left-hand side, with me on his right and my sister Salima opposite him. The table itself was not too big, made of rather cheap wood and rickety, with a plywood top, and the chairs were straight-backed and simple. The tablecloth was cotton. The pattern, I remember, was a handblock print from the famous Jhandoo Khan who had a shop in the Mozang area of Lahore. The colours were turquoise and bright blue with matching napkins. We always had placemats too, but I don't recall their pattern. The plates were white and made from simple china. Our cutlery was the most basic forks and spoons. The glasses were again straight and plain.

The dining room was next to the pantry, so our bearer would be in and out carrying the food. The kitchen was a few steps down, but the food was never cold when it reached us. These were not the times of microwaves or ovens, but we did have a toaster in the pantry, as well as a kettle to warm the water for my parents' tea.

## Kitchen cabinet

There was never much talk at mealtimes. I cannot remember us eating together often, as lunch was always between my sister and myself or in school during winter. Dinner was usually a threesome as my father was almost always in the office at that time. Now and again, we had breakfast together on Sundays, but, on reflection, that too was not as frequent as I would have liked.

We had two servants in my childhood whom I can remember clearly, even to this day. Mohammad Ali, our cook, was a Punjabi and spoke only that language. I am surprised even today thinking how well my British mother Alys Faiz conversed with him. He stayed only in the kitchen and was never found in the main house.

The second servant was something of a Jeeves figure who was known as 'bearer' throughout his life. I remember him as an oldish man who spoke only fluent Urdu. Again, how he and the cook got on is beyond me, but I never heard of any arguments or disagreements happening in the pantry or the kitchen. Our bearer used to double up as a kind of nanny for us two sisters as well. Since my mother worked for a newspaper, her hours were long and we would be left in the care of this male nanny. He looked after our food and our laundry, making sure we did our homework and at times even putting us to bed. He would cycle home late every evening after the dishes had been washed and dried. He was there too in the early morning to give my parents their 'bed tea' and see us off to school after serving breakfast. He was with us for so long that I cannot recall how many years it was exactly. I do know my father depended on him for everything and my mother would admonish him at times for spoiling my dad.

## Modest resources

What I can remember of my father's eating habits was that he was always completely dressed before he sat down to breakfast, which consisted of a fried egg, toast and tea. He would always eat his egg on his toast with a fork and knife and sip at his tea. His lunch, if at home, was again simple: a roti and possibly dal and some vegetables. We were not a meat-eating family, probably because we could not afford it. Both my sister and I were brought up with simple tastes in clothes and food. Now, I reflect this must have been the case because of the strains on our parents' finances.

My father was fond of eating spinach in all forms, so I am told. He liked the desi palak and also sarson ka saag (mustard greens) with missi roti. My paternal grandmother would sometimes send us exotic sweetmeats, which she must have learnt from the other Afghan wives of my paternal grandfather who lived in the same house. I loved to eat them and can recall their aroma even today. Unfortunately, nobody from our family learnt the recipe from Bebe ji, as we called our grandmother.

I recall my father as quite a modest eater. Perhaps his smoking killed his desire to eat. By the time he sat down to food, he was either too tired or too stimulated for getting on with the next engagement. However, when he did sit down at the table, he ate slowly and carefully, chewing his food quietly and cleaning his plate completely.

I am told he liked koftas with gravy. He preferred roti to rice. I can still see him breaking his roti into small pieces and picking up the meatballs one by one. He liked chutney made of coriander and green chillies, but was not a fan of hot spices. Pickles were something he was partial to, and his favourite was a mango variety. He also sometimes liked to have a paratha, a roti which preferably had butter mixed into it and was then fried. This bread is rich, but so filling and satisfying. Parathas are still usually enjoyed in the winter as they keep you full and warm.

## Simple tastes

His morning and afternoon tea habit continued throughout his life, almost like a ritual. In the morning, his newspaper accompanied his cuppa. The afternoon tea was just a simple cup without any snacks. He would sip the tea slowly and gently with a cigarette in one hand, usually remaining silent.

When we shifted to London in 1962 for two years, and lived in Cornwall Avenue in Finchley, I remember he started liking steak and kidney pies, as did I. During those days in Britain, our evening meals were again simple. Usually, we had fried eggs on toast and baked beans, sometimes chicken sausages. My mom probably did not want too many dishes piled up to be washed, and so she kept it straightforward. Also, in Britain there were no servants, so it was only my mother doing all the housework. I was still going to school and my elder sister Salima was at university.

Yes. We were a simple family with simple tastes and simple needs. I think we still are.

## Sarson ka Saag and Spinach

**Ingredients**

1½ kg sarson ka saag (mustard greens)
½ kg spinach
½ cup fresh fenugreek leaves (methi)
15–20 cloves garlic
2 tbsp yoghurt
10–12 green chillies
2 tbsp maize flour
5–6 whole red chillies
½ cup ghee
1½ tbsp ginger–garlic, finely chopped
ginger, finely chopped into batons or strips, to garnish
2 tbsp butter
salt to taste

**Method**

1. Boil water in a large pot. To the boiling water, add mustard greens, spinach and fenugreek. Also add garlic and green chillies. Cook until the greens are tender and then remove the excess water.
2. When the boiled ingredients have cooled a bit, chop them up. I use an electric chopper or food processor.
3. In a handi (or pot if necessary), heat ghee. Fry the whole red chillies and ginger–garlic paste, then add the chopped saag mixture.

4. Add yoghurt and maize flour to the pot and mix thoroughly. Leave to simmer for 30 minutes. The water should completely evaporate and the saag should have a thick consistency.
5. When ready, spoon into a serving dish and garnish with ginger and butter. Serve with maize flour roti (makki ki roti).

# Impoverished by Modernity

*Rana Safvi*

*Go meve hazaron hain aur hain ne'maten lakhon*
*par sab se saris ham ne maza naan mein dekha.*
Although there are millions of bounties
I have found the most satisfaction in a naan.

– Nayan Sukh

For anyone who grew up in north India, particularly Punjab and western Uttar Pradesh, this verse will strike a chord of resonance. For us, no meal is complete without some bread, be it paratha, roti, puri or naan. Rice, to most of us, is secondary.

In our region, rice was cooked rarely and never just boiled – it had to be made into a khichri or biryani, pulao and tahiri. If someone had an upset tummy, they were fed rice because it was considered easier to digest.

As a child, I was an outlier. I loved rice but would only be allowed to eat it after finishing my share of the chapati, which for some reason was deemed healthier than starchy rice. We looked forward to the winters because they meant hot puris or parathas for breakfast and lunch. I can still feel the sun on our freshly washed hair on Sundays as we sat in the aangan (courtyard) for lunch. In summers, the service arrangement would be reversed and we would have dinners in the aangan. There were no air conditioners in those days, of course, and we lived in sync with nature. Summers meant earthen surahis (pitchers) and ghadas (pots) kept out on the grass to cool in the dew-laden night. Winters were made for heating bathwater in huge iron pots on wood or coal fire. But I'm digressing: let me return to the subject of wheat delicacies.

Wheat has been grown as a staple grain in India since ancient times. The food historian K. T. Achaya writes that what we know today as wheat was evolved in the Fertile Crescent area of West Asia between 8000 and 3000 BCE. A variety of it from around 6000 BCE was found in Mehrangarh in present-day Rajasthan. Excavations in Indus Valley sites too revealed wheat and barley as staple grains.

Over the course of centuries, India became home to a multitude of flatbreads and bread dishes, but modernity corralled many of them into restaurants. We no longer have the luxury of time to plan meals, so toast is an easy breakfast option. I still remember the days of my childhood when everyone wasn't pressed for time, when the breakfast table was bountiful.

A favourite breakfast was roghini roti and aloo ki qatli, a unique Awadhi dish. My mother would knead the dough for the roti (roghini means oily) in balai, or cream, skimmed from the surface of the milk used at home. In fact, balai ('bala' means above) would be saved for this meal.

I haven't come across this breakfast in other states. It is something I still cook at home, but today, in keeping with modern sensibilities, I only use milk instead of balai in the dough. The khastapan (crispness) of the roti depends on the dough, so it's crucial to use milk that contains cream at least.

A small digression: I have always used the word khastapan for savouries, such as samosa, namak para and kachori, but never really wondered about it. To me, it meant crisp. As I looked for the meaning, I realised that the Persian-origin word 'khasta' is used for something ruined, crumbling or in tatters. We use khasta for crisp food because the crispness makes it crumbly.

I found a cookbook published at the beginning of the twentieth century, *Khwan-i Ne'mat-i Kalan*, that lists forty-four varieties of roghini rotis. I am sharing one called khassagi – from khasa (food for royalty) – which has all the ingredients of a bygone era.

## Roghini Roti Khassagi

### Ingredients

1 ser (around 900g) maida or atta (white or wholemeal flour)
½ ser (around 450g) ghee
2 cups milk
3 masha (around 3g) saffron
3 masha (around 3g) cardamom
3 tola (around 22g) salt

### Method

1. Boil and reduce the milk until it becomes thick and creamy.
2. Add the balai (from the boiled milk) and ghee to the maida/atta.
3. Dry grind the saffron and cardamom finely, then knead them into the dough.
4. Divide the dough into balls (each weighing approximately 35g) and roll out.
5. Cook the rotis on a tawa (on medium–high heat) or in a tandoor.

This book presumes we know the recipe of making the tikias (what we called rotis because of their small size) but I will spell it out here.

1. Make small pedas (balls) of the dough (each weighing approximately 35g) and roll.
2. Leave them slightly thick.
3. Prick the surface so that they cook inside.
4. Cook on very low heat and turn when done on each side.

These rotis may be accompanied by aloo ki qatli and lahsan–mirch ki chatni. I am offering here my family recipes.

## Aloo ki Qatli

### Ingredients

½ kg potatoes
2 tbsp oil
¼ tsp cumin seeds
¼ tsp peppercorns
2–3 cloves
1 whole red chilli
1 onion, finely sliced
salt to taste

### Method

1. Peel and cut the potatoes into wafer thin round slices and place in cold water.
2. Heat oil. Add cumin seeds, cloves, peppercorns and red chillies. Sauté till the spices start crackling. The cumin seeds should not turn black.
3. Add finely sliced onions and fry until golden brown.
4. Add potatoes, and a little bit of water and salt.
5. Cook covered until potatoes are tender. The water should have evaporated and oil should be visible. The potatoes should take on a beautiful caramel hue from the fried onions.

## Lahsan-Mirch ki Chatni

### Ingredients

1 pod (bulb) garlic
2 whole red chillies
1 tsp desi ghee

### Method

1. Grind the peeled garlic and chillies together into a fine paste.
2. Heat the desi ghee in a small pan and sauté the other ingredients.

# In Praise of Nabi Bux

*Bina Shah*

In the old days of the grand houses of South Asia, both before and after Partition, it was common practice to employ more than one cook to prepare the food for the household. So many people – servants and family members – populated these establishments that they were like small countries of their own, with many tastes and preferences which needed to be catered to and indulged, and a constant demand for meals at all hours of the day.

So, the big houses would hire multiple cooks: one solely for the servants, another for the masters' standard Pakistani food, and where there was an appetite for European fare, a third expert in Western dishes alone. The regular cook was called a borchi, but the expert was called khansama, or chef. The Nawabs of Awadh, seated in the capital Lucknow, had started this tradition in the post-Mughal era, which found its way to different parts of India. This included Sindh, where my paternal grandfather lived as a prosperous landowner in the mid-twentieth century.

According to Anoothi Vishal, writing in *No Ordinary Cooks: The Rise and Decline of the Tradition of Khansamas*, the khansama was a product of the Mughal courts, of feudal India and the British Raj, one born in 'dak bunglows, bureaucratic homes, Railways catering, army messes and elite clubs'. And while the khansama tradition faded away when feudalism was abolished in India, it found traction in Pakistan, in both feudal establishments and the well-to-do families of the city-dwelling upper classes.

## A rare talent

One such khansama, a slight, unassuming man called Nabi Bux, prepared the Western dishes in my grandfather's bungalow at 17 Civil Lines in the cantonment area of the Pakistani city of Hyderabad over a period lasting about thirty years. Anyone who tasted his exquisite food fell under his spell; he was known as a man of rare and unusual culinary talent. No other khansama in Sindh could compare.

Nabi Bux, who did not have a last name that anyone knew of, was from Lucknow. He came with his family to Hyderabad, Sindh, from Delhi in 1947, on one of the trains that brought Muslim refugees to Pakistan. As a young boy he worked for a British family in Delhi as a member of the general household staff. Peeking in the kitchen, he soaked up all manner of English and continental dishes which he saw the khansamas prepare. Somehow he learnt all their recipes and brought his knowledge with him to the new country, looking for an opportunity to reinvent himself as a khansama.

We know very little about his life in India, and nobody knows where he worked in Hyderabad when he first came to Pakistan. However, he arrived at 17 Civil Lines in 1954, and stayed with our family long after my grandfather died in 1961.

My grandfather, Muhammed Ali Shah Jamote, was the sardar, the head of his Syed clan, a powerful position of influence and honour in those post-Partition days. At that time the political establishment was still shifting, and influential figures of the area provided a certain amount of stability in a time of transition. A steady stream of visitors, family members, political figures, military officers and ambassadors poured through the Hyderabad bungalow and my grandfather's ancestral home in Matiari, a village twenty-nine kilometres north of Hyderabad. Zulfikar Ali Bhutto, who would one day become Pakistan's prime minister, was a frequent visitor.

At 17 Civil Lines, guests attended formal sit-down dinners with ten or twelve courses served on Royal Albert crockery and

Sheffield-made silverware with bone handles. For dinners like these, Nabi Bux prepared almond or tomato soup, fruit or shrimp cocktail, then roast meat; his specialties were saddle of lamb, mutton chops with mint sauce, and steak and kidney pie. He made baked fish with tartar sauce, followed by a heavenly almond soufflé or a steamed pudding for dessert. His showstopper was a basket made of delicate orange peel, filled with carved oranges and Chantilly cream.

Afternoon guests were served tea in a Shelley tea set, for which Nabi Bux prepared an English-style cream tea, complete with tiny fairy cakes, scones and cucumber sandwiches.

The dining room at 17 Civil Lines was not a luxurious grand hall; it was round and of average size. But it did boast one luxury item from the 1950s: a refrigerator that hummed impressively in a corner. In the style of the old cantonment bungalows, the dining room had one window covered in patterned drapes, plain whitewashed walls, and colourful floral floor tiles. Even with only a punkah whirring overhead and no air conditioning, the room always remained a little cooler than the rest of the house. Guests crowded around a small table covered with a white tablecloth, the important ones sitting at the table, others standing behind with plates in their hands. Large glass-fronted cabinets held wine and shot glasses for the drinks served at these meals.

## A garden buffet

If more than ten or twelve guests came to lunch or dinner, then a buffet was laid out in the garden of the bungalow. This was a beautiful green space with sweeping champa and tall palm trees, manicured hedges, a multitude of prize-winning flowers, and comfortable stone benches. A shamiana, or canopy, was set up on winter evenings; guests helped themselves liberally to a table heaving with fresh fruit, Viennese-style cakes from Hyderabad's famed Bombay Bakery, and other appetisers while waiting for the main meal. The Jamote household was known for its hospitality; no expenses were spared to keep guests well fed. That expense included Nabi Bux's salary, which at Rs 75 per month in the early 1960s was more than what any other servant in the household received.

When the masters of the grand houses travelled, the cooks would accompany them, taking up residence wherever needed. The cook helped bear the strain of additional people at the host's table, impressed the guests with his expertise, and provided the master with favourite dishes he simply couldn't bear to be away from for too long. My grandfather's guests would journey to the family farm outside Matiari for shooting parties in the vicinity; they all needed feeding in a style which complemented the reputation of the Jamote household.

Away from the kitchen and proper ovens and utensils, Nabi Bux was a master of improvisation. He made vegetable soup over an open fire; he would prepare the day's catch, grilled partridges or a wild rabbit, on a spit over hot coals. When King Hussein of Jordan came to Pakistan in 1955, he visited Tando Mohammed Khan, a nearby village, to shoot partridge; Nabi Bux was sent to the home of the King's host to cook for him.

Nabi Bux lived in Hyderabad with his wife and children, and every day he would arrive for work at 17 Civil Lines on a bicycle. A literate person, he made a habit of reading the newspaper in the morning before starting the day's work. On Sundays, he cycled to Kotri and went fishing in the Indus River. Although he was a reserved man, almost aloof in his demeanour, he made a firm friendship trio with my grandfather's driver and valet, the three of them forming the upper echelons of the servants at the bungalow.

Nabi Bux stayed on at 17 Civil Lines after my grandfather's death, continuing to cook for my father and his older brother, the latter of whom inherited the title of sardar and carried on the lifestyle that came with it. In the 1960s, my uncle hosted Presidents Ayub Khan and Yahya Khan when they both came for shoots to Matiari, and Nabi Bux cooked for them too.

In the 1970s, my father, mother and I settled in Karachi after spending five years in the United States. Nabi Bux travelled often from Hyderabad to stay at our house for a few weeks, cooking the Western dishes that we craved after those five years in America. I liked nothing better than to come home from school and find a plate of sliced jelly rolls waiting for me, a tureen of hot custard standing beside the plate.

By this time, Nabi Bux was an old man; our small family's demands were much easier to fulfil. My grandfather's driver, Abdul Ghani, also came to work for us in his old age, and the two of them were the best of friends, always reminiscing about the old days at 17 Civil Lines. I spent many hours in their company, playing chess with Nabi Bux, while Abdul Ghani showed me pretend magic tricks with cards and Nabi Bux's reading glasses, which would disappear and then reappear in a flower pot or behind a stack of plates.

I'd known neither of my grandfathers, who had died before I was born. Both of them had had affectionate but austere, somewhat formal relationships with their children, my parents. They might have been less reserved with me, a small granddaughter, but I never had the chance to find out. Although gentle Nabi Bux and Abdul Ghani would not have thought of themselves as anything other than beloved family retainers, I saw them as substitute grandfathers, showering me with the love and attention that elders in our culture bestow upon the young.

One day in 1981, Nabi Bux was called to Rechal, the farm of my great-uncle, an hour away from Hyderabad in Tando Allah Yar. He was meant to cook Western dishes for the Lebanese ambassador. It was a job that required endurance and strength, as conditions on the farms in rural Sindh were still primitive. Nabi Bux had grown old; my parents and uncle made his workload lighter and easier in their more modern kitchens, equipped with ovens that ran on Sui gas. A lifelong smoker, he had become asthmatic in his old age. Beside his regular medication, my mother fed him a concoction that came from her mother: burnt peacock feathers crushed and mixed with honey, which he said made him feel better.

At Rechal, the makeshift kitchen was small and poorly ventilated; there was no oven and Nabi Bux was cooking on coals, improvising as he had in his prime. Racing to get the food ready on time, Nabi Bux inhaled the smoke that gathered in the close, stuffy kitchen, unaware of the danger he was in. He suffocated, then collapsed. He was taken to a hospital but could not survive the asthma attack that had overcome him, and he died on that hot summer day.

My parents and my uncle were inconsolable when they heard this terrible news: so was Abdul Ghani. My mother and father sat me down and told me gently that Nabi Bux had died. When I asked how, they said he'd been asphyxiated, but I was nine years old and I did not understand what that word meant. Later, I overheard my parents lamenting that Nabi Bux, old and frail, should not have gone to Rechal; he should have been spared the unsafe working conditions and been treated more gently, more carefully in light of his age and health.

We knew we had lost a gem, someone who linked our family to the days of the past, to the generations that were no longer there. A dignified, gifted man who had, I thought, overcome the difficulties of his life to become both friend and family to us all. How easily such illusions are shattered though, in the chasm between Nabi Bux's meticulous, disciplined life and his accidental, untimely death. My grandfather's *noblesse oblige*, my father and uncle's ideas of fairness and generosity were overshadowed by a vast, bottomless class inequality that Pakistan may never overcome.

My mother preserved many of Nabi Bux's simpler recipes, writing them down as he dictated them to her while he cooked in our house. But the secrets of Nabi Bux's most intricate dishes died with him. Only the memories remain.

## Nabi Bux's Jelly Roll

**Ingredients**

6 egg whites/4 egg yolks (separated)
½ cup flour
1 tsp baking powder
2 drops vinegar
½ cup sugar

**Method**

1. Beat the egg whites, then add the sugar and continue to beat until stiff peaks form.
2. Add the yolks and mix gently. Gradually add flour and baking powder.
3. Pour into a prepared square baking tin. Bake at 350°F (180°C) for 15 minutes until both sides become golden brown.
4. When cool, cover with raspberry jelly and roll up using wax paper.
5. Remove the paper, then slice the roll. Cover slices in powdered sugar.
6. Add cream or custard to serve.

# Life as a Picnic

*Taran Khan*

One Friday in Kabul I find myself thinking of monsoons in Aligarh. It is spring where I am, and friends are taking me for a picnic outside the Afghan capital. We are packed into a car, wedged into a traffic jam heading towards a river, a hill, any place with trees and a view.

In the trunk of the car is a huge degh full of mutton do pyaza – a meat curry with onions added in two stages. Melons are also rolling around between the large toshaks or mattresses. We flop on those mattresses in the shade of a tree by a swift-flowing river, rounding off our meal with fish scooped out of the icy currents and fried in front of our eyes. We return with the dusk, jammed between cars loaded with dozing children, their cheeks still aglow with the chill air.

I am thinking of the afternoons of my childhood when the rains came, darkness and coolness arriving together. Voices rose in the kitchen, dispelling the languor of the long summer. I entered the many-limbed tangle of cousins in the car, filling the back seat, joining the adults in singing old Hindi songs. We would find a spot to spread out our food, on a grassy patch by a canal, or on the dusty verandah of an old inspection quarter marooned in the semi-urban sprawl just outside Aligarh. On the chatais (mats) was fare that rarely appeared on our tables, which we ate off paper plates that buckled under the weight of the quantities we piled on: aloo qataliyan (sautéed potato slices), achar (pickle), roghani tikiyas (flatbread) and kababs or qeema (spicy sautéed mincemeat). The potato qataliyan were cooked with cumin seeds and dried chillies. The roghani tikiyas retained their softness with the addition of milk and cream to the flour batter. Sometimes there was khageena – scrambled eggs with tiny pieces of golden fried onions, green chillies and tomatoes. Generally, we had shami kababs which were prepared from boiled mincemeat and could withstand the heat of travel. This was before air-conditioned cars entered our lives and encased us in their controlled temperature bubbles. Our windows would be open wide while we blithely sang all the way there and back.

Growing up in northern India in the 1990s, 'outside food' was a concept that was hazy at the best of times. In a culture where hygiene and purity were given importance, and where resources were scarce, it came tinged with a hint of disrepute. Eating out carried a sense of living dangerously. The rules could be broken under certain circumstances, as when we enjoyed lassi and parathas at roadside dhabas. But for the most part, venturing outside the home meant carrying a part of our kitchens with us.

At the house of Nanna, my maternal grandmother, journeys were signalled by the appearance of her red kandiya, a capacious plastic basket with sturdy handles. It was unthinkable to leave home without the kandiya. On trains, buses and cars, it sat gleaming by our side, heavy with the picnic food Nanna had packed and with our anticipation. Years later, I can still recall the taste of each item perfectly. Hard-boiled eggs, tikiya, dry potatoes with a tempering of zeera. Mango pickle carefully drained of oil. A thermos of tea. Food that was easy to carry and eat on the move. Nanna woke up early in the morning to cook all this, and sometimes it wasn't even for us. She would prepare parcels of food for relatives whose trains were passing through Aligarh, to see them through the tedium of travel. To her, not offering such gifts of care was akin to abandonment, a mark of shame for both the traveller and the relatives living en route.

My phuppo, or father's sister, favoured a sturdy steel nashtedan or tiffin carrier for her escapades. It travelled with us on multiple visits to the Taj Mahal and other tourist sites across north India. Most memorably, she used it to pack our picnic dinners to the cinema, where she liked to watch the late-night show. Since she was not one to skimp on portions, this meant carrying substantial amounts of food into the darkened hall. As Bollywood dramas played out on the large screen, we passed down rotis, kababs, sweets and cold coffee through the long row of family members. The last touch was a toothpick packed specially for my aunt. No overpriced popcorn in glitzy cinemas can measure up to such luxury.

Adolescence meant rolling my eyes at these rituals, insisting on eating nothing but 'outside food' when I travelled. Over the years I experienced the riotous flavours that came with travel in India, even as India grew sophisticated about eating out and eating in.

I think of Nanna's unconscious frown of concentration as she peeled off the shell from hard-boiled eggs and seasoned them with the perfect mix of salt and pepper, the shadow of the window grill appearing and vanishing on her face as the train rushed past the flat countryside towards Kanpur. I think of the labour of all the women that accompanied us on all the picnics under the rain-laden skies of north India and the azure blue of the Shumali plains. Of the knowledge and expertise that made just what we needed to leave the house, and to take it with us. The secret ingredient in all these picnics, perhaps, was scarcity. The idea that we could not have everything that we wanted made these rare breaks from routine all the more exciting.

For the younger generations of Indians who came of age on aspirational images and easy access to fast food, our remembered picnic baskets seem bare, our high spirits at such simple outings unfathomable. Going out now, I am struck by the commercialisation of our leisure, of the linking of fun to global franchises offering poor-quality snacks. Even Nanna's train parcels would be irrelevant now, as travellers can order pizza on their mobiles and get it delivered at the next station. It is a landscape of uniformity, and overpriced, ever-present abundance.

When I was around nine years old, my family lived in the UK for a few years. Impecunious on my father's student budget and also finicky about bland London fare, my mother prepared sandwiches for us to carry on coach trips to heritage sites. I craved nothing more than the crisps and plastic-encased sandwiches other tourists bought and ate, and that were too expensive for us to purchase. For me, the store-bought food was a way of fitting in, of shedding the dreadful oddness we carried on our persons, in our bags of food. When I returned years later for my own studies, I bought the snacks. The pasty tuna on brown bread was as dreadful as my parents had promised it would be. Even today, the sight of British stately homes triggers the Proustian memory of my mother in her tiny London kitchen, mimicking Nanna in faraway India, packing her version of our kandiya, creating the perfect sandwich by layering spicy qeema between slices of thick white bread.

## Qeema Fry

### Ingredients

½ kg lean mincemeat
½ to ¾ cup mustard oil
1 large onion, diced
1 tbsp garlic paste
1 tbsp ginger paste
1–2 tsp red chilli powder (or as per taste)

1 tsp coriander powder
1 tsp turmeric powder
7–8 whole green chillies (deseeded if you don't want it too hot)
salt to taste

**Method**

1. Heat the oil in a pressure cooker or a pan. Add the diced onions and fry until they become golden.
2. Add the mincemeat and sauté until it changes colour. Add the rest of the spices and ginger–garlic paste and keep frying. Add salt.
3. Add half a cup of water and put on pressure for about 15 minutes. Alternately, let it slow-cook on low heat.
4. When the mince is tender, add green chillies and sauté until the excess water evaporates and the qeema is dry. The oil should be visible.
5. Garnish the dish with chopped coriander and serve.

# Gastronomic Adventures in Peshawar and Hyderabad

*Claire Chambers*

Two South Asian sojourns proved foundational for my gastronomic worldview. One was in Pakistan when I stayed there for ten months in the mid-1990s. The other took place in Hyderabad, India, where I was a student for four months around the turn of the millennium. These culinary exploits were not only formative for my tastes but also my general outlook on life. In those days, like many teenagers and twentysomethings, I possessed a prodigious appetite but conservative taste buds. The trips took me to a realm far from the loathed mushy peas and loved Yorkshire pudding of my northern English childhood.

My first-ever trip to South Asia was in my year off before university in 1993–1994. I spent this so-called gap year teaching English in Mardan and Peshawar, in the northwestern Pakistani region of Khyber Pakhtunkhwa (formerly known as the North-West Frontier Province or NWFP).

First I briefly taught at Fazlehaq College in Mardan. About ten years before my arrival, the college had been established by General Fazle Haq, President Zia-ul-Haq's right-hand man in Khyber Pakhtunkhwa. Not long afterwards, like President Zia before him, Fazle Haq would be murdered in mysterious circumstances. The school he left behind was modelled on a British public school and many of its (all-male) pupils came from army families. Aged just seventeen when I arrived and something of a hippie, I felt out of place at this august institution, with its bore cannon on display and Rudyard Kipling's bombastic poem 'If' proudly inscribed on a playground wall. Believing in the colonial ideology that linked spicy food with stagnation and self-indulgence, this boarding school's authorities served up dreadful, unspiced and oily meals. The boys and those of us teachers who lived on site were gifted lumps of gristly meat swimming in an orange ghee, with only a pinch of haldi to redeem the blandness.

Partly due to a sense of malnourishment, I shifted – or, what is closer to the truth, fled – to Islamia Public High School in Peshawar's University Town after just a short time in Mardan. Islamia was a day school with much lower fees and a more diverse student body than Fazlehaq College. About a third of the pupils were Afghan. As refugees, some of the Afghans were substantially older than their Pakistani classmates. They knew only Pashto, Dari or Farsi, and so had to catch up with their Urdu. One young man was just shy of six feet tall, with a ratty moustache and acne. The poor thing had to almost fold himself in two to get under the desk in the nine- and ten-year-olds' class to which he was allocated. Some pupils were so poor that three siblings would share a single pencil – or at least that's what they told this young and naive English teacher. It may just have been an excuse to get out of class. 'Miss, brother; Miss, pencil' became a common refrain even among kids I suspected didn't have a sibling in the school.

Despite having lost their homes, the Afghans brought with them a love of food. When I was occasionally invited to the homes of female pupils and their families, we would sit on bolsters on the takht or raised platform, eating the savouriest, crustiest yet fluffiest naans. The breads were used to soak up delicately spiced dishes of aubergine with yoghurt and various aromatic meats. I also have hazy memories of comforting plates of qeema with potatoes and peas.

To my relief, our school in Peshawar also taught girls and had no military regalia. I stayed on for the best part of a year, living with the headmaster – a dry, twinkling Punjabi – and his family. His brother, a youth not much older than me, vacated his bedroom for me and, without complaint, spent the whole year sleeping on a charpoi on the roof. I joined him and two servants up there for a few nights during the summer, when the heat seemed to radiate up through my bedframe, but the choking air did little to help me sleep.

The only thing to cheer me up in the furnace-like environment of a Peshawari summer was the richly sybaritic Chaunsa mangoes we would sometimes have for a treat, juice dripping down our forearms as we ate. Guavas were a slower burn for me. I was underwhelmed the first time I ate one, as it wasn't yet ripe and I didn't know what to make of the chewy pip-like seeds inside. Over time, though, I came to prize this strange fruit, and these days I regularly seek them out in my city's British Asian grocery shops.

The family food in Peshawar was exquisite and cooked with much love; a door was opened to my own passion for South Asian Muslim cuisine. My favourite dish was dal makhani, a Punjabi delicacy that made its way to our dining table at least once a fortnight, studded with occasional gems of fried garlic cloves. The headteacher's wife made this with a perfect blend of spices and heat, raising the luxury level through generous quantities of butter and cream. Less instant gratification came from karela, bitter gourd, which is notorious for being an acquired taste. With its gnarly appearance, bitterness and unusual crunch, I described karela in letters home as 'like eating a crocodile'. In those days I ate meat, so as well as karela stuffed with mince, I was also an aficionado of biryani. The dish was more of a treat than a staple in this household, but the layers of rice, tender chicken and occasional bursts of cardamom were like nothing I had ever tasted before.

There were two culinary misadventures. Both happened during Ramzan when I decided to fast along with my host family. I revelled in the sense of community after our feat of endurance as we would take iftar in the twilit garden, starting with dates just like the Prophet was said to have done. From there we would enjoy a wide range of curries, rice dishes and breads, plus a few fried dishes like pakoras or french fries. A few hours later, at around half past nine, we would squeeze in a light meal before bedtime and then an early rise for sehri, the pre-dawn meal before another long day of fasting.

One night I was in the kitchen heating up some leftovers for us to pick at before retiring. I did this by candlelight, due to one of Pakistan's many load-shedding power outages. Turning to get a spoon for testing if the food was hot enough, my dupatta dipped in the naked flame of one of the candles. It was winter and over my shalwar kameez I was wearing a thick sweater from Saddar Bazaar. Being young, I had opted for the cheapest jumper to be found in the market. It was flammable and instantly combusted, burning some of my curly hair with it. Shocked and not knowing what I was doing, I flung the jumper off and stamped out the flames. I was unhurt. What seemed more important at the time was that my hair was long and I could afford to lose a few inches when it came to trimming the singed ends. Reflecting on this accident many years later, I think of the many 'bride burnings' or 'dowry deaths' that scar the subcontinent every year. These are attributed to young wives catching their dupattas alight while cooking when in fact they are perpetrated by their families in anger over dowry shortfalls.

The other mishap was no accident. After class one day, two fifteen-year-old Afghan girls offered up a small fruit that resembled a crab apple for me to try. This was nothing unusual, for the strong hospitality ethos in this northwest region meant that both Afghan and Pakistani students liked to bring in nuts and fruits for their teachers. I did wonder why they were exchanging looks and struggling to suppress giggles, but took a bite anyway and politely praised the tart produce. They then burst into open laughter, having tricked this Ramzan novice into breaking my fast. I am still irritated that this cruel ruse meant I didn't quite complete the thirty days without food or drink from dusk till dawn.

## Hyderabad

Five years later, as an informal postgraduate in Hyderabad, Telangana, I once again became a nutritional migrant. In the early days of this trip, I lived in the undergraduate hostel. The food in its canteen was teekha in the extreme, too much so even for most students from other parts of India. Hyderabadi food is famous for its chilli heat and ubiquitous long black strands of zeera. But just as at Fazlehaq College, here too the institutional food at Central Institute for English and Foreign Languages (CIEFL, now the English and Foreign Languages University or EFLU) bore little resemblance to the wonders outside the ivory tower. My mouth on fire yet my taste buds left cold, I could hardly eat the hostel food. Instead I subsisted for a few weeks on mithai for my evening meal, my favourite sweet being buttery badam ki jali. Occasionally I felt so sorry for myself that I would splash out on Indo-Chinese or perhaps Hyderabadi food at Hotel Shadab, not far from the landmark Charminar in the old city.

I ran away again, to stay at the nearby Osmania University guesthouse. Its mosquitoes were so vicious that I hardly left my room after 6 p.m. and was fully dependent on Good Knight plug-in insect zappers. I would sortie into the dining room with DEET insect repellent sprayed on my few exposed bits of flesh, wearing suit-of-armour-like clothes so the winged beasts couldn't bite me through thin shalwar kameezes. I only ventured outside my fortified chamber for gastronomic adventures.

If the guesthouse's downside was the wildlife, its repasts were so wonderful that I put on twelve kilos. Even though I'd skip lunch each day, breakfasts and dinners were an irresistible summons to gluttony. I had to go on a strict diet once I reached Sydney, Australia, my next travel destination.

In truth, though, the morning meals were largely *kuch khas nahin*, nothing special. A revolving cast of academics, students and alumni would breakfast at the guesthouse each morning, starting with chai served from chipped floral cups and saucers. For me, a life-long drinker of 'separate tea' – very weak with a splash of milk and no sugar in the Angrez style – this was an entirely different beverage. Recoiling from the sweetness at first, over time I became addicted to the drink's rich copper colour, notes of ginger and cloves, with a subtle black pepper providing warmth in the finish.

As for the food, boiled eggs were accompanied by double roti, which I couldn't help compare to the lighter and infinitely more savoury breads of home. One quirk this nashta did give me for breakfasting over the rest of my life was the pairing of cornflakes with hot milk, as the French also do. Though I usually stick to cold milk on cereals, if I am very tired or run down then warm milk reminds me of this time and makes me feel looked after, even cared for. Yet so far, so bland. The only morning excitement was the piquant omelette studded with green chilli and scooped up with flaky, moist parathas.

Culinary energies were saved up for bravura evening meals. The guesthouse's chef was the late Sabith Ali, who was renowned for his hybrid take on Mughlai food. He used to rustle up some outlandish desserts like custard apple kheer, alongside his famed biryani and the puris like delicious puffballs. A plethora of eclectic fare was laid out each evening, making dinner worth saving my appetite for and braving the mosquitoes.

During this Indian sojourn and in the aftermath of a few stomach upsets, I developed a nostalgia for Heinz baked beans. For those blithely unfamiliar, these are orange in colour: mushy legumes made of haricots soaked in a sugary tomato sauce. Despite the sheer imagination and chutzpah of the dishes I sampled in Hyderabad, I sometimes longed for the foods of my childhood. When I got home and opened my first post-India tin, though, it was a sad disappointment. Before long I found myself in England frying onions, garlic, ginger, haldi and garam masala to create a tarka for my beans!

How could I be content with orange processed food after swashbuckling my way through biting insects in order to eat crocodile-like vegetables, chillies to make me cry, or puffball-puris? It was then that I knew the subcontinent had forever changed my taste buds for the better.

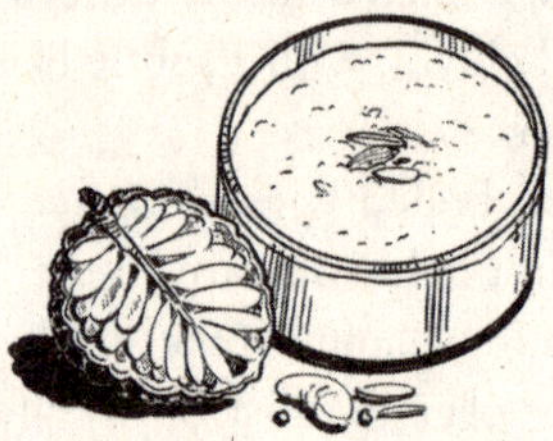

## Custard Apple Kheer

### Ingredients

3 large sitaphal (custard apple)
5 tbsp washed and soaked rice (preferably short-grain)
750 ml full-cream milk
5 tbsp sugar
1 tsp green cardamom powder
1 tbsp cashew nuts (toasted and chopped)
1 tbsp almonds (toasted and chopped)
1 tbsp pistachios (toasted and chopped)

### Method

1. Place a strainer over a bowl, cut the sitaphal into halves, scoop out all the pulp and mash them well; the seeds will separate from the pulp. Set it aside for now.
2. In a heavy-bottomed pan, bring the milk to a boil.
3. Boil on low for 5–10 minutes, or until the milk has reduced slightly.
4. Stir in the washed and soaked rice for 12–15 minutes, or until

the rice is cooked and the mixture thickens. Keep the heat on low–medium.

5. After 10–12 minutes, add sugar, mix well and cook for another 3–5 minutes.
6. When the mixture reaches the desired thickness and pouring consistency, turn off the heat, remove the pan from the stove and stir continuously until the mixture cools.
7. Mix in the cardamom powder thoroughly.
8. Stir in half of the roasted cashew nuts, almonds and pistachios.
9. Stir in the custard apple pulp.
10. Pour into a small earth bowl (sakore) or bowl of your choice; top with cashew nuts, almonds and pistachios, or silver leaf (chandi varq), and serve cold.

# Sri Lankan Malay Cuisine Walks the Tightrope

*Rizvina Morseth de Alwis*

One of my earliest memories is of my grandmother sitting on her haunches, hands dipped in a large earthenware pot, churning something vibrantly red and shiny, small red onions and slim long green chillies swirling like jewels as she tossed and turned them around until they were generously coated with the fragrant pickling sauce.

Years later, I would sit on the kitchen bench with my sisters and peel the niggling onions with tears pricking my eyes as Mum made the same gooey sauce in her blender, throwing in a handful of mustard seeds, a few pods of dried chillies, a whole cup of soaked dates and a generous splash of vinegar.

Malay achar is a dish I grew up with, one I carried with me everywhere, when I left home for college and subsequently overseas. No Sri Lankan meal is complete without Malay achar – and the same is true of watalappan, a creamy steamed custard that combines eggs, jaggery and coconut milk which my grandmother called sirkaya – its original name. These two Sri Lankan Malay dishes have earned a permanent place in Sri Lankan cuisine, an ode to its multicultural character and colonial legacy.

Sri Lanka is home to a multi-ethnic, multi-religious population of twenty million, comprising Sinhalese (75 per cent), Tamils (11 per cent) and Muslims (9 per cent), the latter including

Moors, Malays, Borahs and Memons. This makes Malays a minority within a minority, at a mere 0.2 per cent of the country's population.

With a complex history of migration dating back to the eleventh-century Chola kingdom, the ancestors of present-day Sri Lankan Malays arrived in the seventeenth century to serve in the Dutch army, among them exiled aristocratic families from Java. When the British took over in 1796, they 'martialised' the Malays (as with the Gurkhas of Nepal) and strengthened their forces by inviting more from Peninsular Malaya. With these successive waves of arrivals, Malays brought with them their women, children, food and culture. The community quickly deepened its roots in the country with a distinct culture and language of its own. This was not done without assimilating local influences, especially of the Moors, descendants of Arab and Indian traders with whom Malays share the Islamic faith.

Sharing common roots with present-day Malaysian/ Indonesian cuisine, Sri Lankan Malay food has evolved into a unique repertoire all of its own as it adapted dishes out of necessity (substituting traditional with local ingredients) and to accommodate the taste buds of local cultures. The ubiquitous Malay achar and watalappan exemplify how original dishes evolve and create new flavours whilst retaining their cultural significance.

Yet Sri Lankan Malay food is more than just achar and watalappan. Lesser known are daging–chukka, sukkun–goreng, kolak curry, kueh, pasthol and a range of other dishes with robust flavours of chilli, vanilla grass and lemongrass, rich in spices and usually simmered in coconut milk. Even the popular sweetmeat dodhol has Malay roots and so does bibikkan, a coconut cake influenced by the Dutch and made by the Sinhalese for their New Year. Yet these are facts barely known to the public.

Within this broad spectrum of Sri Lankan Malay cuisine is the less appreciated and much shunned babath–puruth, a tripe curry that usually accompanies pittu, a concoction of flour and coconut shavings steamed in a bamboo utensil to give pittu its cylindrical shape. While pittu traces its origins to Kerala, the babath/tripe curry is associated with Sri Lankan Malays, often with derogation. As a child I was called 'babath', a slur directed at Malays. This epithet reflects a history of racialised stereotyping of communities based on what they eat, particularly food perceived to be undesirable. The strong emotional reaction, if not revulsion, that babath or any offal dish evokes is a reflection of the fear of 'strange' unfamiliar foods, prejudice against other cultures, and sheer ignorance. Offal is a big part of Malay cuisine that encourages the prevention of waste in line with Islamic teachings. I grew up eating babath several days a week, but fought shy of acknowledging it publicly. In the face of my non-Muslim friends' exclamations, 'Yuck' and 'Gross', I did not want to be seen as one of the primary ingestors of this much-disparaged dish, reducing my enjoyment of it to a source of shame until I met my Sinhalese husband. His mother not only cooked it as deliciously as my own but served it with aplomb. As it turned out, Malays were not the only community that was consuming offal.

Today, with hoof-to-tail food trends gaining traction, popularised by television shows like *MasterChef*, it appears that attitudes towards offal may be changing again. At the same time, a new wave of veganism is countering that trend. As food bloggers battle out their differences, singing hosanna or decrying it, offal remains caught in a binary world of love and hate that misses nuances of culture, power and politics tied up with the colonial history surrounding food. Babath is thus still far from making an appearance in the menu of five-star hotels and posh restaurants. Yet efforts to reclaim and recuperate the 'offensive' dish are seen in several home-based Malay caterers who are boldly offering a range of offal curries with other Malay dishes, suggesting a demand that goes beyond the Malay and Muslim community. That said, I still have friends who return from holidays in Scotland with brave tales of trying out haggis and black pudding, but who continue to turn up their noses at babath.

These efforts to preserve an authenticity of Malay food in an ever-evolving hybrid culinary scene mirrors the community's efforts to maintain its distinct culture that is deemed to be at risk of extinction. The Malay community is known to be more liberal than other Sri Lankan Muslims. Ironically, this quickness to adapt and assimilate has also had an impact on the community's identity, traditions and language. As a result, the Sri Lankan Malays find themselves caught between modernism and a rising Wahhabism which seems intent on turning Islam into a monocultural global faith.

Growing up in a more culturally than religiously immersed household, I learnt from my grandmother, mother and a coterie of aunts the significance of food at social events and how what we eat distinguishes and defines us to ourselves and to other communities. Food served at weddings, funerals, festivals and religious events functioned as a primary cultural marker of our community. Our neighbours, full of curiosity, were eager to attend weddings and festivities in our home, I presume because these events presented an opportunity to experience difference.

I remember preparations at home for an aunt's wedding. These began weeks in advance with relatives arriving early to help with the chores, stirring up excitement and curiosity in the neighbourhood. A goat and a brood of chicken were slaughtered in the backyard to ensure the meat was halal. As children, we sneaked into the kitchen, looking for nibbles as potatoes bubbled in a pot of saffron waves, rendang simmered in large copper cauldrons and the smoky smell of satay roasting on open fires spread across the neighbourhood like an invitation. My childhood friend who lived next door was in awe, finding everything in our kitchen strange and different, and therefore enticing: the sights, the smells, the taste, just like the rituals of the wedding ceremony that evening, the singing of pantuns and the sumptuous dinner that followed, nasi–kuning expertly flipped from soup bowls to plates, placed before each guest like a personal yellow sun. Nowadays, serving rice shaped by a bowl is as predictable as sunrise.

For Eid, the house would smell divine with the spicy aromas of an elaborate meal being prepared. My sisters and I, dressed in new clothes, would carry bowls of watalappan to our neighbours mirrored by the kaveli and rich cake they would send us for Sinhala avurudu, or new year, and Christmas. My non-Muslim friends would come home to partake in the Eid feast: oxtail soup followed by a buffet of nasi–kebuli, ayam, satay, daging–goreng, qaliya, ubi, achar and sirkaya. A variation of this distinctly Malay menu would be offered at celebratory events, the birth of a child, coming-of-age and circumcision ceremonies, maulud recitals and almsgiving, where we would sit on the floor and eat from a large communal platter called the sawan.

Over the last few decades, these traditions have suffered a significant battering. Now Eid is celebrated by Malays with biryani in the tradition of other Sri Lankan Muslims, giving way to a variation of our own, Malay dum biryani, which has the distinct flavour of lemongrass and is also served at maulud, almsgivings and weddings.

Biryani is not the only 'foreign' dish to enter Malay cuisine. Samosa, a snack popularised in Sri Lanka by Moors, has usurped the pasthol, a traditional Malay pastry shaped like an empanada filled with minced babath/tripe. These days, for iftar we have samosa with congee instead of pasthol. More recently, Middle Eastern dishes like maqluba/majboos, shawarma, falafel, hummus and kunafa, which are particularly popular during Ramzan, have joined the Sri Lankan–Muslim culinary lexicon.

Of course, Arab influence is not confined to food. It is also reflected in the language, as Sri Lankan Muslims have taken to liberally peppering their conversations with Arab phrases. But it is most visible in the dramatic change in women's clothing. With the spread of Wahhabism, Sri Lankan Muslim women, especially the Moors, have been quick to adopt the hijab and abaya, abandoning the sari and shalwar kameez. The Malay community, who were once considered to be blasé about religion, are not entirely immune to the creep of conservatism. Growing up, I rarely bumped into a Sri Lankan Malay in hijab or abaya. My grandmother was always in baju–kurung. My mother alternates this outfit with a sari while I reserve it for special occasions, opting for Western clothes and sari, covering my head with a shawl when attending religious functions. Now I see more and more Sri Lankan Malays donning the abaya, making our community less distinguishable from other Sri Lankan Muslims.

As Moors and, increasingly, Malays started discarding their distinct cultural identities for an Arab makeover, anti-Muslim sentiments simmering beneath the surface kept rising. This cultural shift reinforced existing prejudices against Muslims who were seen as averse to assimilation, raising questions about Arabisation and cultural compatibility. These fears combined with political manipulation and global Islamophobia unleashed a series of anti-Muslim riots and campaigns against Muslim-owned businesses. It is no coincidence that these attacks were largely food-related – halal certification, beef stalls, boycotts of Muslim restaurants and a selection of insults with 'swine' or 'pig' taking the lead. These tensions eventually culminated in the 2019 Easter attack when nine suicide bombers, relatively young, educated men, hailing from middle-class and affluent Muslim families, blew up three churches and three five-star hotels in the country. These men killed over three hundred people and injured scores more, in an instant destroying a relationship built over a thousand years.

As the Muslim community reflected on the terror unleashed from within its own and began the long process of rebuilding trust and healing, stories of friendship between the communities surfaced on mainstream and social media, offering an alternative narrative to the dominant one of Muslims' presumed tendency to self-alienate. What struck me most was the role food played in these recollections: a celebrated cricketer eagerly awaiting the annual mosque feast to enjoy a kidu meal of ghee rice and curries; a bowl of watalappan sent to a new neighbour starting off a lasting friendship; a pot of congee and recipes shared over a fence triggering conversations about fasting and halal meat. These stories reminded me that food is far more than a material substance to fulfil a biological need. While food can be used to ridicule and attack a community and voice 'othering', it also has the power to demystify myths about the 'other', bring communities together and strengthen cross-cultural relationships.

The Malay community's resolve to integrate yet remain distinct whilst navigating the forces of modernism on the one hand and Wahhabism on the other in a context where Islamophobia is allowed to thrive is far more challenging than balancing the complex flavours of achar or reclaiming the much-maligned babath from its lowly place of ignominy. Yet a peek into my pantry, where Malay spices and condiments sit side by side with relishes and sauces from other cultures I've encountered, symbolises the potential food has to walk that tightrope.

## Sri Lankan Malay Achar

**Ingredients**

500g shallots
250g dates
100g green chillies
1 tbsp mustard seeds, finely ground
1½ tbsp chilli powder
2 tbsp ginger, minced
3 tbsp sugar
1¼ cup natural coconut vinegar
salt to taste

**Method**

1. Wash peeled shallots and green chillies and drain. Remove extra moisture with a kitchen towel and let dry for one hour or until free of moisture.
2. Pit dates and soak in ¼ cup of vinegar until they soften to a pulp.
3. In a dry clay pot (or ceramic or glass bowl), place the dates, minced ginger, ground mustard, chilli powder, sugar, salt and the remaining vinegar. Mix until combined into a thick sweet and spicy pickling sauce.
4. Add the shallots and green chillies and combine all the ingredients using a wooden spoon. Cover and leave it in a cool and dry place in your kitchen pantry until the achar achieves its perfect consistency (24–36 hours).
5. Store the achar in a dry, airtight container in or outside the refrigerator and use as needed.

# On Bakr Eid

*Farah Yameen*

The most striking Bakr Eid in our neighbourhood in undivided Bihar involved a camel. An elderly gentleman, known for fixing sprains and selling LPG cylinders on the black market, had attained the status of a Haji – one who has returned from a successful pilgrimage at Mecca. In an exaggerated show of piety, a camel was brought to the mohalla, stirring morbid curiosity, especially among the children. No one had sacrificed a camel in our neighbourhood of tiny streets and open drains before (or since).

Those who could not afford a sacrifice and had received the camel meat that year recall it as having been delicious and salty. It is another matter that the camel was slaughtered by a method not advised for camels under Islamic practices, as I learnt almost two decades later.

The qurbani, or sacrifice, is mandatory for any adult who is *nasb-i mal*, or a possessor of wealth. There are different schools of thought on what constitutes wealth. The Hanafi school in Islam, which my family and large sections of Sunni north India follow, considers any person in possession of the value of seven and a half tolas of gold or fifty-two tolas of silver as nasb-i mal. The amount has not changed for centuries.

A nasb-i mal must pay both the obligatory zakat during Ramzan and offer sacrifice from the tenth day of the Muslim month of Zil Hijj, the day we know as Bakr Eid, to the twelfth day. In more fortunate Muslim families, such as ours, there is often more than one nasb-i mal. Consequently, there is more than one animal that is offered as sacrifice on Bakr Eid. My grandmother went so far as to sacrifice one on my behalf well before I was an adult or in possession of anything other than an appetite.

In our neighbourhood, 70 per cent of the residents could not afford a sacrifice. Their Eid depended on the other 30 per cent upholding their end of the religiously mandated social contract of sharing their festive bounty. The percentages may vary, but this is still the case everywhere.

## Haves and have-nots

On the day of Eid, those who can afford the sacrifice are in their homes, directing the kasai, or butcher, to make specific cuts of meat for the kabab, the raan (whole leg), the qorma, the grail (slow cooked ribs and chops). Many of those who cannot are also in these homes, employed in their service, or tied to them by relationships of power informed by landed wealth and caste that have carried over several generations.

These include people who had once lived in the same villages as my grandparents and those who have worked for our family over the decades. Some run errands, some wash clothes, while others sweep the house or tend to the garden. There have been cooks who have stayed with us, and children of erstwhile cooks who have stayed in the house.

They will have claim to a third of the meat as advised by Hanafi jurisprudence – one-third for the family, one-third for the neighbours and one-third for those who are socially and economically vulnerable. As a child, when I was instructed in the benefits of Bakr Eid, this emphasis on religiously mandated philanthropy was foremost. Hence, one-third of the meat (and often more), one-tenth of whatever fruit our trees bore, and 2.5 per cent of our savings as zakat are still duly disbursed annually.

The higher purpose, my grandmother used to say, is to please Allah, who would send these animals to bear us across the thinner-than-a-hair, sharper-than-a-sword bridge that crosses over the fires of hell to the doors of heaven.

This Bakr Eid, as always, those whose families have not possessed seven and a half tolas of gold or its equivalent value in living memory will arrive at ours to remind us of our obligations. Shahnaz, who is our neighbour and our cook, will probably take the brain of the goat we slaughter to fry with a seasoning of pepper and cumin. 'Just like eggs,' she says.

Although it is a delicacy in many homes, my family does not care for the brain (maghaz): it seems slimy, and we prefer it stayed outside our threshold until Shahnaz can remove it from our presence when she is done with work. We will pretend that this is because Shahnaz enjoys eating the maghaz, and that it has nothing to do with our own deep-set notions of purity and pollution.

Bakr Eid is not Shahnaz's day off, even though it is a festival she observes. Every year, she busies herself with making the first meal of the day, the customary fry of liver and lungs (and, in some homes, the heart) that makes a late breakfast for the family. She puts the ribs and the chops on the stove to slow-cook for the grail. She eats some of this after everyone else is done. She will share the same cutlery as ours, but this is a practice that we have adopted only recently, with several rounds of self-congratulations on our enlightenment.

## Feudal relations

Disgust for the unfamiliar is not unique to our home. The stomach of the goat and its intestines on the earth are a recurring annual spectacle. The visual familiarity, however, does not temper our revulsion. The sira (head) and the maghaz (brains) we may be too queasy to eat, but the offal never crosses our threshold, or that of many upper-caste families. There are religious opinions that deem the offal makruh, a word of many interpretations, but in this case loosely meaning undesirable (as distinct from haram which is absolutely forbidden). Explanations range from 'there is filth in the gut' to 'it is unhealthy' and 'has germs from the excreta'.

Mehmooda, who is also a neighbour, and whose daughters were teenagers like us when they worked in our home several years ago, tells me that offal is delicious. She will wash the intestines at the tap in the garden and tear open the stomach. She will turn the gut inside out with a twig, like we pull the drawstring of our new Eid shalwars, and will then scrub the blackened inner lining with salt or lime until it is white. We will vehemently deny that Mehmooda's choice to eat the offal and our refusal to touch it has anything to do with caste. Islam, we remind ourselves smugly, has no caste.

Mehmooda will cook the meat in her own house in a vigorously fried masala of ground onions, ginger and an abundance of garlic to suppress the smell of the flesh. Our dishes are constructed on an edifice of spices, alliums and aggressive searing, so that we never have to smell the meat we eat. We call it bisaindh – a bad smell that must be exorcised out of all cooked meat and our homes.

Mehmooda also takes home choice cuts of meat from the hind legs for kababs and the ribs for grail. But she rarely returns to her own kitchen until she has run an errand. This could be as small as grinding the garlic for the qorma. It is not a favour asked of her. It is a residue of the anachronistic relationships that have carried from a rural zamindari past into our urban homes.

## Loyalty programme

Shaheen, who is employed as our cleaner, washes off the gore that has carried with the flesh into our home, our own delicate heads nauseous from the smell. The market price of nine kilos of the goat meat could pay Shaheen's rent. But we will rarely, if ever, ask Shaheen if she is making ends meet, or if she risks eviction. Instead we'll assuage our caste and class guilt with spurts of charity that will allow us to keep up the facade of moral superiority and religious piety.

For Bakr Eid, Shaheen will carry a kilo or even three of meat, that we will consider extremely generous. Perhaps she'll take cuts from the tongue and cheek, which she will cook into a curry, or the tail that she'll mix with the meat from the leg for a qaliya (meat with vegetables) or ishtew (stew) or a biryani.

She will salt the meat and heat it until the water evaporates, and preserve what she doesn't cook that day in large vessels covered with cloth. She will heat this meat every day, twice in warm weather, to prevent it from spoiling. We, on the other hand, have stuffed away the small amount of meat that our cramped freezers can hold, having lost all appetite for it, at least for the next few days.

Zinat, whose mother worked for us when I was a toddler, will take home the fat that Mehmooda does not want, melt it down to a crisp churri and use the rendered fat to fry onion pua and kachri (a close cousin of the pakora). Like Shaheen and Mehmooda, she will stretch the meat out for as long as it can last. If there are no more takers of meat, we will send the rest to the madrasa, where the children will be asked to remember those who fed them in their prayers. Our left hand may not know what our right hand gives, but the stomachs that received what we gave should not be allowed to forget it.

By late evening, the nasb-i mal will crumple in their rooms, still in their new clothes, exhausted from the day's altruism.

## Kaleji Fry

The morning of Bakr Eid in many Muslim homes often begins with a late breakfast of liver, lungs and kidneys from the sacrificed animal. Opinions are divided on this annual feast in our family. Men who rarely grace the kitchen with their presence actively get about setting up a makeshift wood stove to get the kaleji ready. It is a fairly elaborate process, and gender plays out predictably in the flex of outdoor meat cooking for men while women get the bread ready in the kitchen indoors. Many of the women, my mother and sister among them, will not touch the kaleji. It is one thing to buy meat from a butcher for whatever you are cooking that day, but quite another to be surrounded by the flesh of an animal you fed, one that perhaps even came to be loved and then sacrificed. That is a hard morsel for many to down. This recipe is from my uncle Naheedur Rahman, an excellent cook on all days of the year.

**Ingredients**

50g goat liver, chopped into inch-large pieces
100 ml vegetable oil
200g yoghurt
250g onion, chopped
4 tbsp garlic paste
2 tbsp ginger paste
¼ tsp deggi mirch (red chilli powder)
20 whole peppercorns, lightly toasted and ground
4 large cardamoms, lightly toasted and ground
coriander leaves for garnishing
salt to taste

**Method**

1. Heat the oil in a wide pan or wok. To the hot oil add onion and liver pieces. Fry on medium–high until almost dry.
2. Add the garlic and ginger paste, salt and red chilli powder. Cook with the lid open until the masala clings to the meat.
3. Add yoghurt, ground peppercorns and cardamoms, and cook until the gravy thickens.
4. Garnish with green coriander and serve.

*part two*

# Identities in Flux

# Islam on the Table in Bengal

*Jayanta Sengupta*

The most influential 'Muslim' food in India is arguably the biryani, with its near-ubiquitous presence on the subcontinent's culinary map. Bengal's version of this meat-and-rice dish, called the 'Calcutta biryani', holds a prominent place on this map. However, the dish also represents a chequered history of conflict, assimilation and adaptation.

Historically, the Islamisation of Bengal was gradual. Muslim immigrants in the region inherited the sum total of the material culture of pre-Islamic Bengal, which, in culinary matters, meant assuming the local dietary traditions based on the widespread consumption of rice and fish. The historian Ghulam Murshid has recorded that as late as the seventeenth century, Mughal officials in Bengal were contemptuous of the fish and rice eaten by the Bengalis, dietary practices they considered to be the markers of the community's inferiority. At the opposite end of the spectrum, the Muslim preference for meat – including beef and chicken – was mentioned in uncharitable terms by authors of the fifteenth- and sixteenth-century *Mangal Kavyas*.

For more than a century after the Muslim conquest and absorption in the Delhi Sultanate in the thirteenth century, Bengal continued to retain its distinctive regional culture largely isolated from outside influence. Islam's influence on the region's life, including its culinary practices, remained somewhat limited. The increasing use of meat, however – especially among the upcountry Muslim elites – brought about a significant variation in the foodscapes of Bengal. It also spawned some contempt among Hindus, as indicated by the Bengali poet Kavikankan Mukundaram Chakravarti's statement in his paean to the goddess Chandi, *Chandimangal*, written in the second half of the sixteenth century, that butchers selling cow meat did not merit a place even in hell. In another significant development, rice – introduced to Central Asia and Europe from the granaries of India – also came back to India in the form of new dishes like pilaf or pulao, enhanced by the use of aromatic spices.

The Mughal conquest of Bengal in the seventeenth century permitted an influx into the new provincial capital of Dhaka of an elite class of ashraf Muslims originally said to be from the Persianate world of Central Asia. This opened the way to Indo-Persianate food traditions. The Turko-Afghans had brought various ingredients, recipes and cooking styles to Bengal from places like Turkmenistan, Kyrgyzstan, Tajikistan, Uzbekistan, Azerbaijan, Kazakhstan, Armenia, Georgia and Afghanistan. To these the Mughals added recipes and styles from Iran. This combination shaped what would go on to become known as 'Mughlai' food.

In *Riyaz-us-salatin*, Ghulam Husain Salim wrote that natives of Bengal did not originally eat breads of wheat and barley, and also that the 'meat of goats and fowls and clarified butter' did not agree with Bengalis' digestive systems. This, however, changed over time. Mughal Dhaka was introduced to dishes like qorma, pulao, kofta, biryani and zarda, among many other delicacies. Dishes with a distinctively Persian touch included shahi morag (or murgh) pulao and tehari – a spicier but simpler variant of biryani made with rice and meat and eaten on ceremonial occasions. Also noteworthy was the use of yakhni – meat stock or broth, sometimes complemented with saffron – to flavour thick soups (shorba) or cook the rice in pulaos and biryanis. Such dishes became symbolic of the city's culinary practices. When the capital of Bengal moved from Dhaka to Murshidabad in the early eighteenth century, it became the new centre of an Indo-Persian culinary tradition. In general, the cuisine of eighteenth-century Murshidabad under the Nawabs evolved into a Bengali version of Mughal food that was slightly lighter than its north Indian version. However, like any Mughal dish, it involved the trademark slow preparation.

The rise of Calcutta (now Kolkata) as the new seat of British colonial power in the eighteenth and nineteenth centuries signalled a decline in the fortunes of Bengali Muslims. But the cultural tastes and social habits of the Hindu landed gentry and educated elite continued to display traces of the influence of Muslim culinary culture. The mid-eighteenth-century epic in narrative verse, *Annadamangal* ('In Praise of the Goddess Annada'), mentioned the cooking of qaliya, dolma, kababs and suchlike in Hindu households. Similarly, the Bengali poet Ishwarchandra Gupta (1812–1859) wrote poems that extolled the exquisite taste of kababs. His poetry also weighed up the merit of cooking mutton or lamb not with ginger and asafoetida – as had been typical in non-vegetarian Hindu households before the arrival of the Mughals – but with onions, which the Muslims added to Bengal's culinary landscape. The fondness for dishes like pulao, kababs, kofta and qorma among aristocrats like Raja Rammohan Roy and Dwarakanath Tagore is also well known from their memoirs and letters.

Manuscripts on culinary matters were of course not uncommon in India's regional literary cultures, but the first two cookbooks to be printed in colonial India were both in the Bengali language – *Pakrajeshwar* ('Royal Repasts', 1831) and *Byanjan-Ratnakar* ('A Goldmine of Recipes', 1858). They included a profusion of qaliyas, pulaos and kababs. These included several dishes referring to specifically Persian names, like Rumi pulao, Khorasani pulao and Shirazi pulao. The popular cookbook in Bengali by Bipradas Mukhopadhyay, *Pak-pranali* (1884), included recipes for lentils cooked in 'Shah Jahani' style, and khichris named Afghani, Kabuli, Jahangiri and Daud Khani (presumably after the eighteenth-century Rohilla Afghan chief Sardar Daud Khan). It also included pulaos with a distinctively Persian influence, kababs and qaliyas, and an entire section of dishes cooked with the dum pukht technique of Persian slow cooking. Prajnasundari Devi, a pioneering woman author of cookbooks in Bengali, included detailed recipes of kababs, koftas and pulaos over more than a hundred pages in her culinary magnum opus, *Amish o Niramish Ahar* (1902).

A landmark event in the evolving landscape of Indo-Persian foodways in Calcutta is often traced to 1856, when the Nawab of Awadh, Wajid Ali Shah, was deposed by the English East India Company and exiled to Calcutta. The gourmand Nawab was followed by chefs from the erstwhile royal kitchen who introduced the Awadhi biryani to the city, with further embellishment perhaps coming in the form of the addition of potatoes. Apocryphally, the cooks introduced this then less familiar vegetable either as a novelty element, or as partial replacement for the meat that the pensioner-Nawab was supposedly unable to afford for his large entourage. While there is no textual evidence that the Nawab himself ate this version, the fact remains that the so-called Calcutta biryani – with its aloo driving a distinctive interpretation of the Awadhi biryani – subsequently went on to become one of most iconic and ubiquitous symbols of Calcutta's culinary history.

Other waves of Muslim migration from Awadh and adjoining regions in northern India followed later in the nineteenth century. Many of these migrants – some of them claiming their ancestry from the royal chefs of the erstwhile princely state of Awadh – settled around the Chitpur region. As a result, eateries serving variants of Mughlai food came up in the area. Several of the most popular ones were located on Zakaria Street, around the Nakhoda Masjid, which was built in 1926. Even today, this mosque area is known as the 'Mecca' of quintessentially 'Muslim' foods like kababs and biryani. In December 2019, the Indian National Trust for Art and Cultural Heritage (INTACH) – the leading non-profit in India dedicated to the conservation of heritage – announced their decision to confer a 'heritage' tag on two Muslim eateries in central Kolkata. Shiraz Golden Restaurant (founded 1941) was honoured in this way for its biryani and Sabir Hotel (founded 1948) for its rezala.

One of the most interesting aspects of the legacy of Indo-Persian foodways in Bengal's culinary landscape is the remarkable extent to which these dishes have been adapted to local tastes and traditions. Such reworking has taken place through a range of different ways, most commonly by adapting new ingredients to Mughal-style culinary techniques. Vegetables like the potato and cauliflower and dairy products such as paneer (cottage cheese) have been subjected to the techniques of marinating and grilling to make their tandoori versions. Also – especially in Bangladesh – various kinds of fish, including the country's 'national' fish, the hilsa, have been used as a substitute for meat in pulaos. The diverse and pluralistic cultural traditions of Bengal, both in its eastern and western parts, have thus produced an encounter with Indo-Persian foodways that testifies to the permeable and hybrid character of the concepts of 'heritage' or 'traditional' food.

## Calcutta Mutton Biryani

### Ingredients

1 kg mutton (cut into large pieces)
5 whole potatoes
500g basmati rice (aged, long-grained)
150g onions (sliced)
150g vegetable oil (for deep frying)

*For the biryani masala:*

6 green cardamoms
1 black cardamom
¾ tsp cloves
3 cm stick cinnamon
½ of a whole nutmeg
2 pieces mace
2g shahi zeera
2g kabab chini
½ tsp fennel seeds
3g white pepper, whole
½ tsp black pepper, whole

*For the mutton marinade:*

100g yoghurt
10g fresh ginger
10g garlic
20g birista (thinly sliced onions fried in ghee or oil till golden brown and crisp)
8g biryani masala (see above)
5g kewra water (optional)
½ tsp red chilli powder
20g salt
½ tsp ground pepper
a little bit of water

*For the rice:*

6 green cardamoms
2 black cardamoms
7g cloves
6 cm cinnamon stick
7g fennel seeds
3g bay leaves
3 litres water
45g salt

*For assembly of the dum:*

6 to 10 bay leaves (to line the pan with)
40g dried plums (alubukhara)
1 tsp rose petals (optional)
15g birista (fried onions; see above for method)
5g biryani masala (see above)
50g grated khoya
200g yakhni (see method point 8)
5 ml lime juice
1 pinch saffron (steeped in warm milk)
1 pinch yellow food colouring (optional)
180 ml milk
5 ml kewra water
5 ml rosewater
4 drops meetha attar
30g ghee
20g butter

**Method**

1. Prepare the biryani masala by dry-roasting all of the spices and then grinding into a fine powder.
2. Prepare the mutton marinade by blending all of the ingredients into a fine paste. Marinate mutton pieces for a minimum of 1 hour.
3. Peel potatoes and keep whole. Smear them with yellow food colouring, if using.
4. Heat oil in a pan and fry potatoes until lightly browned on all sides. Remove with a slotted spoon to drain the oil and set aside.
5. Wash rice and soak in water for 30 minutes. Strain rice to drain water. Set aside.
6. Place fried potatoes at the bottom of a pressure cooker with the marinated mutton on top.
7. Add half a cup of water and pressure-cook on medium–low heat for 30 minutes. Allow the steam to release naturally for another 15 minutes before opening the lid.

8. Remove the potatoes and mutton pieces from the pressure-cook and place each in a separate dish. Set aside. Strain the liquid remaining in the pressure cooker (yakhni) and reserve.
9. Place the spices listed as 'for the rice' on a small square of cheesecloth and tie with a piece of twine.
10. Add 3 litres of water to a large pot. Add a pinch of salt and the spice bag. Bring to the boil.
11. Set the biryani pan you are using for dum on low heat and grease with ghee.
12. Cover the bottom of the pan with the bay leaves to impart aroma and buffer against burning.
13. Place the mutton pieces in a single layer, then the potatoes on top of the mutton.
14. Scatter alubukhara, birista and rose petals evenly.
15. Measure half of the biryani masala and khoya kheer for the assembly of the dum and spread evenly across the top of the assembled ingredients.
16. Add the yakhni and the lime juice.
17. Remove the spice bag from the boiling water and discard. Add the rice and cook until nearly done. The centre should no longer be hard, but the grain should still be firm.
18. Strain the rice and create a first layer in the biryani pan from half of the rice.
19. On top of this first layer of rice, spread evenly the remaining biryani masala and khoya kheer. Also spread evenly the saffron and food colour (if using).
20. Create a second layer of rice in the biryani pan from the remaining half, flattening gently.
21. Mix milk with kewra water, rosewater and meetha attar and drizzle over the second layer of rice. Add melted butter and ghee, drizzling it near the sides of the pan as well.
22. Cover the pan with aluminium foil, sealing the sides to prevent the steam from escaping. Place a tight-fitting lid on top. Alternatively, you can avoid the foil by sealing the lid with a wet flour dough.

23. Set pan on medium–low heat (dum) for 30 minutes. Turn off the heat and allow to rest for another 15 minutes before serving, with mint chutney on the side.

*Recipe adapted from one published by* Bong Eats *with their kind permission. There is an instructional video for this complex recipe on their website: https://www.bongeats.com/recipe/kolkata-mutton-biryani.*

# Ladakhi Muslims at the Culinary Crossroads

*Fida Hussain*

'*Saks sang kharji che sjim? Che sjim, stoks sjim!*' ('What is the most delicious food? The food that you eat, when you are the most hungry!') So says Aney Sakina, my sixty-five year-old aunt-by-marriage from the Shakar region of Kargil, with a smile on her face. Her words are an old proverb from Kargil itself. The proverb, with its suggestion of food scarcity, indicates the harsh agrarian and nomadic life of Ladakh in the past. People had to struggle through everyday life even for the most meagre of meals. Because of the need to work hard and earn it, the most basic food was satisfying and tasty.

In a remote society like Ladakh, which receives little precipitation and experiences harsh and extended winters, the crops produced are crucial in defining the region's food heritage. Unlike the plains of mainland India, Ladakh has a limited agricultural season and its variety of crops is minimal. This means we see a lot in common in the staple diets and cuisines consumed by families belonging to diverse ethnic groups, religions and geographical regions within Ladakh.

Aney Sakina was married to a distant cousin when she was roughly seventeen years old. At the age of thirty, she moved to Leh with her husband, who is now a retired employee of the local transport department. Aney Sakina had come to our house for lunch. We were chatting about how recent times have seen a whole new set of dishes which are gradually becoming part of our food heritage. Over the years, wheat flour and rice have become an integral part of Ladakhi cuisine, replacing barley which was the region's staple food for ages. Kashmiri dishes like rista (minced meatballs), kababs and yakhni (mutton cooked with curd) have come to replace the traditional dishes from Ladakh, as is apparent on occasions like weddings, iftar and Eid. This infiltration of food and cuisines imported from outside has in some ways eroded the local culinary traditions of the region.

Aney Sakina spent most of her childhood in her native village in Shakar. Her childhood experiences reflect the unforgiving agrarian and rural life of Ladakh. Her mother passed away when she was young, which exposed her to the vulnerability of being raised as an orphan under the shadow of her stepmother. Sakina recalled her childhood: 'We were a family of about eight siblings, and each one of us was fed with two cups of chanthug (a local variety of thukpa, where minced meat, dried green pea, barley and wheat are boiled and cooked in a mildly spiced broth), and a bit of paba (a kind of pudding prepared from barley mixed with butter tea). For lunch again, thukpa with mulak (a local word for turnip). Again for dinner paba and thukpa were the staples.'

Among the Muslim families of Ladakh the culture of food is mainly congregational. Everyone from the village would gather for any sort of religious or social event. They would cook food at a community level, gather together and eat it, distributing leftovers among themselves. The most visible of such events are weddings, Muharram majlis, Mamani and the 'Safar Thukpa'. Safar is a Turkish word for the second month of the Islamic calendar. Traditionally, during the month of Safar, Muslim families in the rural areas of Ladakh would cook chanthug. Another important festival which is usually celebrated in the Shakar–Chiktan belt of Kargil is the Mamani festival. The significance of Mamani is righteousness for the She-mi (deceased members of the family). Some people believe that the original meaning of Mamani was for offerings to be made to the local deities known as Lha. On the day of Mamani every household in the village is supposed to cook the best dishes they can afford for communal sharing. Among these are customary dishes like thukpa, rtsapkhur (ground sprouted white bread), khura (sweet deep-fried noodle-shaped biscuits) and puli (a pancake of buckwheat or wheat). Mamani usually falls towards the end of the harsh winter called Chile-kalan. The timing of the Mamani festival is significant. By the end of Chile-kalan, most families have run out of food stored for the winter. Whatever is left is redistributed at the time of Mamani, so even the poor have enough food to last the rest of the winter.

For centuries Ladakh's capital city Leh stood at the crossroads of the ancient Silk Route, connecting the caravan trails from Central Asia, Tibet and mainland India, through which all kinds of produce and other commodities passed. The staple diet of the people in this region has long been roasted barley (ngamphe) and noodles of various different shapes in a thick soup called skyu, timsthug or chu-tagi. With the advent of modernisation and globalisation, the Ladakhi diet is rapidly changing, particularly around the Leh urban sphere. The Food Corporation of India's flooding of Leh's market with subsidised rations and cheap food towards the last quarter of the twentieth century further replaced traditional foodstuffs with rice, refined flour, vegetable oil and other unfamiliar agricultural products. What is more, a sudden boom in tourism required modern kitchens. These new kitchens were designed to cater to the demands of the huge numbers of domestic and international tourists who started to flow into Ladakh in the early 1990s. Traditional Ladakhi kitchens and the type of foods cooked in them were pushed out.

Among the early Western travellers to have described the food of Ladakh was William Moorcroft. In his *Travels in the Himalayan Provinces of Hindustan and the Panjab (1819–1825)*, Moorcroft gives a detailed account of the various crops grown in Ladakh, the imports of fruits and other foods from Central Asia and Kashmir and the local cuisine. The writing of G. T. Vigne and David Fraser gives similar information about imports of tea to Ladakh from Yarkand and Tibet, as well as the introduction of vegetables like potatoes, spinach, tomatoes, radish and cauliflowers by the Moravian missionaries towards the end of the nineteenth century.

It is hard to draw a clear demarcation between Muslim and Buddhist food heritage in Ladakh. Food in Ladakh was primarily based on the regional topography of the region, and had less to do with religious identity. However, the cross-cultural connections with the Muslim-majority regions of Central Asia, Baltistan and Kashmir contributed to a rich food heritage in the kitchens of Ladakh. Such traditional kitchens were primarily used by the Muslim families living in Leh and its environs. Indeed, these Muslim families witnessed a strong influence of Kashmiri, Balti, Yarkandi and other Central Asian cuisines. By comparison, the families in more rural spaces of Ladakh were less dynamic in terms of cuisine and food heritage.

The Muslims of Ladakh do not belong to a single ethnic group. The Muslim population is spread all across Ladakh, and includes the Balti people of Turtuk and the western part of Ladakh, the Purigs of Kargil and the Argons of Leh. Although there has never been uniformity in the staple diet of the people belonging to different geographical regions of Ladakh, we see a lot shared in common. The main crops like barley and wheat are familiar to all. Balti people from western Ladakh, for instance, settled in the more fertile part of the region, so they have a vast and rich variety of dishes in their cuisine. Similarly, the Argons of Ladakh, because of their Kashmiri roots, have quite an influence from the Kashmiri diet in their dishes. Also, because the Argons were mainly trading families, it was easier for them to procure additional food ingredients like spices, sugar and several dried fruits, which were unknown to most people in Ladakh. The Changpas belonging to the eastern part of Ladakh were traditionally nomads. The consumption of dairy products and meat is more prominent among these nomadic peoples.

Our family name for Haji Zahra Bano is Ama Haji. She is my aunt and the eldest of my mother's six siblings. My maternal grandfather, the late Haji Hussain, was a trader from Skardu (in Pakistan), who accompanied his uncle on a trip to Ladakh and later got married and settled in Thiksey. Haji Zahra Bano spent her early childhood in Thiksey in eastern Ladakh. She later moved to Leh to live with Apo Jamadar, a widower and a close friend of my grandfather. Since Apo Jamadar had no children to look after him, he requested my grandfather to let him adopt his eldest daughter as his own. In those days it was difficult for a farmer to nourish six children, so my grandfather couldn't turn Apo Jamadar down.

Ama Haji moved to the Balkhang area of Leh when she was almost ten years old. Balkhang, meaning the place of the Baltis, has always been a hub for Balti traders. On their trade missions to Leh, these men would stay in the small inns around Balkhang, which is on the outskirts of Leh's old town. Although by the time of her childhood the trading caravans from Baltistan had stopped, Haji Zahra Bano still met Balti traders coming from parts of Kargil and other parts of Ladakh, who would stay in the inns of Balkhang. This was not only because of the influx of traders and merchants from various parts of Ladakh, who were still walking all the way to Leh to barter their goods. It was also because of the welcome from various families (by the names of Hor, Radhu, Kalon and Khwaja) living around Leh town, who are the living heritage of Ladakh as an ancient crossroads. Since Zahra Bano would often visit her friends from these families, in her early years she witnessed reminiscences about cross-border trade and cultural contacts in Leh.

Ama Haji recollects her favourite eatery from her childhood, run by a man of Yarkandi ethnic origin named Sadir Akhon, who later married and settled in Ladakh. She says that Sadir Akhon's small food stall was the only place in Leh which used to serve mokmok (a local name for momos or dumpling) and the famous Yarkandi pulao. It is not clear how Ladakh got acquainted with mokmok. Some believe it was Yarkandi traders from eastern Turkistan who first introduced the dish to the people of Leh. Others believe it was the local Buddhist monks who brought the dish's recipe from Tibet after finishing their religious studies. In those days only a handful of wealthy trading families around Leh had amokto—the traditional steamer needed to make mokmok—so it was not possible for ordinary people to cook the dish. Ama Haji recalls her failed attempt to cook mokmok at home once. Her sisters had come from their ancestral village to visit her. Since they didn't have the steamer back then, she decided to boil the mokmok instead of steaming it. All her sisters were curiously waiting for the new dish they had never tasted. After half an hour, when Zahra Bano finally removed the cooking bowl from the traditional clay stove, shredded chunks of the mutton were floating all around. Although the dish wasn't cooked the way it was supposed to be, her sisters still enjoyed the novel delicacy.

The alleys of Leh's old town echo Ladakh's longstanding cultural heritage. The bakers' street, also known as Chutey Rantag (rantag means 'mill'), even today contains the small bakery shops run by Kashmiri and Balti bakers. Bazari Tagi, which translates literally as 'bread from the bazaar', is popular among Muslim families to this day, especially during Ramzan.

A lot of Central Asian traders travelled across the Karakoram mountains. Many of them brought with them their local dishes, which stayed back and were passed from one generation to another. The Ladakhi tradition of baking, which is unknown to the rest of the Indian subcontinent, was inherited, probably from the neighbouring regions of Central Asia. There we see a variety of baked dishes which closely resemble what we have here in Ladakh.

Samso, known in Uzbekistan as samsa, is a baked bun stuffed with meat found in Chutey Rantag's bakeries. The Indian snack samosa is closely related to samso. The main difference between the two is that the samosa is usually stuffed with potatoes instead of meat, plus it is deep-fried instead of baked.

Another important local dish which is still quite unknown to the non-locals of Ladakh is the Yarkandi pulao (Yarkandi polla in the local tongue). Pulao is a Central Asian dish, which journeyed all the way to Ladakh from Yarkand in Eastern Turkistan (presently part of China's Xinjiang region). The Yarkandi polla reflects the cultural heritage of Ladakh as a confluence of cultures. The dish is a remnant of close ties between Ladakh and Central Asia.

The polla is considered haute cuisine. Its main ingredient is rice, which was unknown to the arid region of Ladakh until about seven decades ago. The Yarkandi polla's rice is cooked with huge chunks of mutton or goat meat, further enhanced by carrots, black raisins, nuts and animal fats. The meat and fat (clarified butter) are the other 'rich' ingredients apart from rice. The meat was always on the bone and came from the animal's leg and rib joints (raan and cham). The use of nuts as garnish is similar to Central Asian pulaos. The Yarkandi traders in Ladakh mainly used almonds, sweet apricot kernels and small black raisins, with the latter being picked on the way from Afghanistan before finally reaching Ladakh.

This is the only dish in Ladakhi cuisine that employs a few whole spices, distantly resembling the garam masala or ground whole spices that are popular in the subcontinent's pulaos or biryanis. It lends a subtle yet refined flavour and aroma to the rice without the feel of the spices in every bite. Otherwise, traditional Ladakhi cuisine doesn't use any masalas like turmeric or red chilli powder, which are synonymous with 'Indian' food.

Yarkandi pollo is most akin to the Afghani or Kabuli pulao, but it is not as sweet for Afghans sometimes garnish their pulao with caramel. Fellow Indians might find a striking resemblance to the Parsi pollo (as it is Persian in origin). Although we now call it 'pulao' or an anglicised 'pilaf', across Central Asia the word is pronounced 'pollo' or 'polla', which is also how elderly Parsis would pronounce it.

In the present day, this pulao is only sometimes cooked in the kitchens of a handful of Muslim families around Leh. Since my aunt Ama Haji was brought up in Leh seeing the prominent Muslim families cooking the dish, she was quite familiar with it. On the day of Eid, all of us siblings would fondly go to her place to eat Yarkandi pulao for lunch with great enjoyment.

## Yarkandi Pollo

Traditionally the Yarkandi pulao was slow-cooked in a heavy stone pot called a doltok in Ladakhi. The substantial weight of the stone lids of these pots did not necessitate the use of wet dough for sealing when cooking the pulao. The Yarkandi polla made the traditional way was said to be symbolic of the big hearts (read: deep pockets) of the hosts for their guests. This bounty was proven by the amount of fat/ghee dripping down one's elbows while eating. The recipe here uses just enough ghee and does not overdo it as did my ancestors.

### Ingredients

*For the meat:*

750g mutton (from the leg and rib joints) cut into 6 pieces (this is a medium size, but in earlier times the size of each piece would be almost double)
2 black cardamoms (bari elaichi)
1 tsp whole fennel seeds (saunf sabut)
¼ onion, chopped
1 tsp salt

*For the rice:*

630g carrots, finely julienned to about 1.5 inch long (not grated)
2–3 tbsp ghee
1 tsp cumin (shahi zeera)
2.5 level cups long-grain basmati rice

*For the garnish:*

2 whole onions, sliced and deep-fried
a handful of small black raisins
a handful of almonds and sweet apricot kernel mix
1 tsp ghee for frying the nuts
refined oil for deep-frying the onions

**Method**

1. Cook the meat with the chopped onion, black cardamom, fennel seeds and salt with enough water in a pressure cooker until the meat is tender. At lower altitudes than Ladakh, where cooking time is faster, the meat can be slow-cooked by boiling in a pan with the whole spices.
2. In another bigger pressure cooker, heat the ghee and add all the julienned carrots. Sauté this on a medium to low flame until the carrots are relatively reduced in quantity and look well cooked.
3. While the meat and the carrots are cooking, prepare the garnish by heating 1 tsp ghee in a kadhai (deep pan or wok) and gently toast the almonds and sweet apricot kernels.
4. When the nuts are toasted, remove them and add refined oil to the pan. Deep-fry the onion slivers until they are just browned and remove with a slotted spoon.
5. Once the meat is cooked, put the pieces on a plate and sieve the broth to get a clear stock without any whole spices or onion pieces. Measure the required amount of this broth (I use the same cup with which I measure the rice).
6. Shallow-fry the mutton pieces in ghee on a low flame (covered as the oil pops) until the pieces are browned on all sides.

7. To the cooked carrot slivers add 2.5 levelled cups of rice that has been washed well, the fried meat, 1 tsp of shahi zeera and the mutton broth. I also add the ghee the meat was fried in, but this is optional if you don't want your rice oily.
8. Once done, fluff the pulao (I usually use a pair of chopsticks) and layer it with dried fruits and fried onions, and serve.

# Qasbati Cuisine and an Urdu Cookbook

*Saumya Gupta*

Documenting domestic cookery is an elusive exercise. The culture of the kitchen is material, physical and pleasurable – and usually unwritten. Few women cooking three times a day would write cookbooks to formally codify their mundane activities. This is as correct today as it would have been in the early twentieth century. Thus, most cookbooks that document culinary traditions are either compilations of elite or royal cuisines, or a labour of love recording family traditions. However, from around the middle of the twentieth century, when print culture took root, we come across Urdu cookbooks written by and for middle-class Muslim households of Awadh, or central Uttar Pradesh.

The emerging print world of the early twentieth century gave rise to a host of journals and periodicals that aimed to define and refine India's sense of community and nation, tradition and modernity. A large part of this material centred on the figure of the modern woman. The burden of worldly progress and traditional ethics was squarely placed upon women, with enlightened domesticity their desired vocation. The balancing act between tradition and modernity was not always stable or smooth. Urdu journals and magazines reflect this cultural and literary encounter between the East and the West. Women's magazines, in particular, emerged as vehicles of social reform. They debated how women could become good wives while also becoming modern women. By the twentieth century, quite a few of these magazines had women as editors and authors. The publications emerged as a platform for women to express their own views about the home and the world.

Recipe columns in these magazines introduce us to the culinary concerns of the ashraf domesticity and middle-class rectitude. From these columns were curated cookbooks by discerning editors. The most well-known example is the journal *Ismat*, founded in 1908 in Delhi by the celebrated novelist Allama Rashidul Khairi, and edited by his son Raziqul Khairi from the 1920s. Raziqul's wife Amina Nazli wrote short stories and plays in Urdu as she co-edited the journal after her husband's demise. Nazli also produced at least seven cookbooks, of which the *Ismati Dastarkhwan* became most successful, going into multiple editions. After the Partition of India, the family and the journal *Ismat* relocated to Karachi, Pakistan, and further editions of *Ismati Dastarkhwan* continued to be published from there. *Ismati Dastarkhwan* earned a cross-border fan following. Rana Safvi from Delhi recounts how her first foray into cooking was through the recipes of this well-thumbed cookbook. Meanwhile Aamer Hussein, the celebrated Pakistani writer, remembered his mother regularly consulting the *Ismati Dastarkhwan*. This treasure trove of recipes and the memories of a shared culinary past transcended boundaries of orality and print, and Hindustan and Pakistan.

Much less is known about a comparable story of another recipe collection called the *Harimi Dastarkhwan*. This cookbook was published by the Idara-i Harim, an institution established by S. M. Naseem Inhonvi (also spelt Anhonvi) in Lucknow around 1928. The Idara brought out a monthly periodical for women, titled *Harim*, edited by Salim Inhonvi, and later by his son, the novelist Naseem Inhonvi. *Harim* continued to be published consistently from 1931 until the 1980s, when a fire gutted the press. Like *Ismat* and other popular women-centric Urdu journals of the time, *Harim* advocated reform and social work. However, it sternly declared that it was a magazine aimed at respected families, and refrained from publishing romance, ghazals, pictures and 'loose' advertisements.

A recipe column entitled *Dastarkhwan* appeared intermittently in *Harim*. Begum Saleem Inhonvi, the wife of the editor, and several readers contributed many of the recipes. Saleem Inhonvi put together a cookbook sourced from these contributions. This curation was titled *Harimi Dastarkhwan*, and was first published as a special number of the journal in 1949. It was made available to the annual subscribers of the periodical free of charge.

In the Preface, Begum Saleem Inhonvi listed the reasons for publishing the recipe collection. Expressing dissatisfaction with the existing Urdu cookbooks, she said she found them full of errors. For her, this was primarily because they were compiled and edited by male publishers. Even when the recipes were contributed by women, the inaccuracies persisted. Women knew how to cook but, ironically, not how to write the recipes; nor did the predominantly male editors and publishers apply the necessary rigour to correct the mistakes. These men, she wrote in the Preface, had little regard for the subtle intricacy of cooking or accuracy of measurements. Either the technique was wrongly noted, or the spices mentioned were missing, and the beginning and the end of the process was very often left unclear. So, Inhonvi spent two months perfecting recipes in the kitchen and then editing what her women readers had sent before *Harimi Dastarkhwan* could go into publication.

The book contains about four hundred recipes, of which almost half were contributed by the women of the Inhonvi family: Begum Saleem Inhonvi, Gazala and Mrs Naseem Inhonvi. Shahina Murad Ali, a reader from Lucknow, contributed sixteen recipes, and Begum Uzma Shamsi from Pilibhit gave eleven. After the Inhonvi family, the most prolific contributor was Srimati Kusum Kumari of Lucknow, who supplied a majority – thirty-three – of the vegetarian recipes. More contributions came from readers in far-off cities like Calcutta, Bombay, Karachi, Peshawar, Indore and Nagpur, and one from Delhi.

However, most of the contributions were from older UP towns like Sitapur, Itawa, Unnao, Rai Bareilly, Kanpur and Aligarh. Smaller qasbas, hardly larger than villages, like Suthan, Rudauli, Isauli, Sulaimanpur, Ballia and Kakori, were also represented. The listing of names and places of the contributions make *Harimi Dastarkhwan* a sociologically valuable collection. Indeed, it is a book that can justifiably claim to be representative of domestic cooking among Awadhi Muslim families of UP around the middle of the twentieth century.

The collection is quite comprehensive and provides the simplest of recipes alongside more difficult preparations. The recipe repertoire is divided into Breads (chapatis, puris, parathas), Meat Curries and Kababs (qorma, musallam, machli and kabab), Dals, Vegetables and Mashes (dals, tarkari and bharte), Pulaos, Mutanjan, Muzaffar (rice dishes, both savoury and sweet), and recipes for iftar. Included is an extensive section on desserts and sweets, categorised into three different chapters – one on halwa; the second on mithai and murabba (candied fruits); and the third on sheer, kheer and phirni. There is also a chapter on accompaniments followed by one on cakes, pastries and ice cream. Food is cooked according to the trademark techniques of Awadhi cuisine, namely dum (slow) cooking, cooking zamindoz (buried in the ground), producing galawat (tenderising), adding baghar (tempering) or dhungar (smoking).

Small familial stamping or fine-tuning of well-known dishes is reflected in the many contributions carrying the same name. So there are three murgh musallam recipes, each contributed by a different author, each suggesting a different technique. Interestingly, *Harimi Dastarkhwan* corroborates the much-publicised opinion that the Awadhi palate is partial to the lightly spiced pulao than the heavily spiced biryani: the biryani finds just three mentions in the book as against close to twenty recipes for pulao – from the mamooli (ordinary) pulao to the badam do pyaza ka laziz pulao, which can be loosely translated as a pulao laced with almonds and onions. There is no doubt that the pulao, combining rice and meat in myriad flavours, was the signature dish of Awadhi Muslim cooking. The many sweet preparations of rice – meethe chawal, zardas, muzaffars and mutanjans indicate the Awadhi sweet tooth. The culinary novelties that had become a part of the everyday desires of the middle-class urban families are represented through recipes like the Akhrot ki Coffee Icecream (walnut–coffee ice cream) or that of French toast sent in by Zehra Sultana Azhar Farooqui Faizabadi, who cooked it exactly as is done now.

There is a conversational quality to many of the recipes showcased in *Harimi Dastarkhwan*. These recipes are written in an everyday Hindustani idiom rather than chaste Urdu. The style is down-to-earth and simple, accessible to both newly literate and well-educated women. Measurements of main ingredients are usually given in reasonably exact units, though even the diligence of the Inhonvi editors could not keep the estimated 'andaz' out of the recipes. However, Mrs Kamal Kumari from Lucknow helpfully sent in the correct measure of spices for the garam masala, advising readers to make their own authentic mixture rather than depend upon the cunning grocers. Some contributions were quite outlandish, like that of Mrs Shamsi from Itawa, who offered suggestions for melting fish bones. One of these tips involved marinating the fish with a paste made of crushed heron bones, and then keeping it on the boil for twelve hours! She was, however, candid enough to accept that she had not tested any of the techniques offered, having only read them in another magazine.

The Awadhi spread is famous for its richness, abundance and variety. How could that be recreated in the middle-class household towards which these recipes were directed? Throughout the book, Begum Saleem Inhonvi dispensed advice on managing thrift and economy in the kitchen. She recommended that even if only half a kilo of meat was available, the good housewife should aim to cook three different recipes rather than just one dish of qorma or qaliya. It might well mean more work, but the reward would be greater praise from the assembled party!

For recipes requiring expensive ingredients like rose essence, cheaper alternatives like rosewater are suggested; for novel ingredients like baking powder, easily available substitutes like edible soda or sea salt are provided. Although she states that saffron and ghee are essential for enhancing taste, Inhonvi anticipates her readers' concerns about using such expensive ingredients. Many recipes end with the suggestion, '*Agar zaffran mil sake to dal dein, laziz ho jayega*' (Add saffron if possible, to make it tastier), implicitly recording the constraints of a middle-class kitchen. Unlike women's magazines in the West, which opened up the way to a 'consumption' kitchen, mid-twentieth century women's magazines like *Harim* stressed traditional cooking and advocated easily available substitutes. Cooking was not yet fully consumerised.

*Harimi Dastarkhwan* is a veritable repository of recipes from the Awadh hinterland. As in other parts of the world, the spread of a reading culture aided in the recording, writing, compiling, exchanging, testing, revising and dissemination of domestic recipes. By sending recipes to a journal like *Harimi Dastarkhwan*, qasbati women were breaking away from the restrictions placed by the small towns. Cookbooks like *Harimi* and *Ismati Dastarkhwan* created a community of readers who could transcend the limitations of their location, region or indeed religion. The recipes point towards a shared syncretic world of cooking and eating, of the Ganga–Jamuni tahzib. One can only speculate about the delight offered by the recipe columns in this familial, intimate print space. Like the many editions of the *Ismati Dastarkhwan*, fondly remembered by culinary enthusiasts in India and Pakistan, the *Harimi Dastarkhwan* also conveyed a sense of region and culture to its readers, as well as to the outside world.

Women's magazines have been mined for the reformist advice given to women, and for their venture into literary pursuits, associational activities and political advocacy. Educational initiatives and the rights of women have understandably been at the forefront of academic interest in this field. Recently, historians have looked in detail at Muslim women writing their world, illuminating how South Asian women came into their own through autobiographical and travel literature. A more affective domain of the woman's world – dealing with household management, home remedies, embroidery and cooking – has of late come under scrutiny. This helps to make visible the social world in which these women existed, and which they created. The spread of a print culture aided the process of recording, compilation, revision and dissemination of domestic recipes. Cookbooks with contributory recipes are valuable traces of a relayed past. Simple everyday dishes, the family tweaks and fine-tunings given to a well-known recipe; the concern with ingredients and expense, and the various alternatives that are suggested by the editors make this elusive world come alive. We find the women concerned not so much with princely recipes but with those more regularly cooked in their homes. Reproduced here is one such recipe from *Harimi Dastarkhwan*, which Ghazala Inhonvi listed as a particular favourite of the women of Awadh.

## Kadhi – by Ghazala Inhonvi for *Harimi Dastarkhwan* (1949)

**Ingredients**

125g besan (chickpea flour)
1 kg dahi (curd)
1 girah (bulb) garlic
1 girah (bulb) onion
1 onion, sliced finely
25g (approx) roasted coriander seeds
a bit (no measure given) of roasted black cumin

125g ghee
25g (approx) turmeric
a few cloves
a few green cardamoms
red chillies, as required
salt to taste

**Method**

1. Sieve the chickpea flour into the curd. Blend it well, so that there are no lumps. (You may pass the mixture through a sieve.)
2. Grind together an onion, garlic, roasted coriander seeds, roasted cumin, red chillies and salt. Take 125g ghee and add turmeric, cloves and cardamom and smoke it (dhungar). When the turmeric mixture is ready, add in the ground onion mixture containing the rest of the ground spices. Sauté for a while.
3. Put the curd and chickpea mixture into the pan and cook well until it thickens.
4. For the phulkiyan (small fluffy balls), combine the rest of the 125g chickpea flour with roasted cumin powder, black pepper powder and salt to taste. Whip it well, so that the balls come out light and fluffy. Then fry them in ghee or oil until browned. Add to the curd and chickpea mixture prepared earlier. Prepare a tempering of onions, red chillies and cumin and add to the kadhi.

# You Are What You Eat

*Siobhan Lambert-Hurley*

Fifteen-year-old Junaid Khan was travelling home by train from New Delhi to Haryana with his brother and two friends when he was stabbed to death in June 2017. Around two hundred people on the railway platform claimed not to have seen the Muslim teenager die. But reports from eyewitnesses describe how an altercation over seats deteriorated into a 'mob' attack on the four boys. This was vindicated on the basis that 'Muslims eat beef'. The murdered boy was a student at a madrasa in Mewar. Eid holidays meant that he had returned to his village, Khandawali, to celebrate with his family. That day, he and his friends had travelled to old Delhi, the largely Muslim enclave in India's capital, to buy new clothes, shoes and ittar, or perfume, in preparation. Remembering Junaid after the attack, his friends recalled some of his favourite things: cricket, kite-flying, bikes. His best friend, Yasin, also described his favourite food: 'While the rest of us ate mutton or chicken, he always wanted soyabean biryani. So every time he came home for Ramzan, his mother would cook him that. And those people taunted him and called him a beef eater.'

I open with this controversial incident because it points to how what one eats – beef or not – has come to be constructed as a fundamental marker of difference between religious communities in contemporary India. To communalists, the protagonists are undifferentiated and immutable. In order to challenge this politicised narrative, I offer here a longer narrative of how food has been used to indicate identity and difference among South Asian Muslims in the modern period. This focus will, perhaps surprisingly, move this discussion largely away from the communal politics of cows and beef-eating. Instead, I'll centre different Muslim histories to show how the symbolic meanings attached to food can vary within a nation, community or cultural grouping over time. The aphorism 'you are what you eat' is apt here. It captures how what we eat or drink – and, perhaps even more so, what we do not – plays a key role in constructing and signifying who we are.

Because I want to flag up more everyday experiences of food, I will favour a set of travel writings from Muslim South Asia that I gathered with two other scholars, Sunil Sharma and Daniel Majchrowicz, for our book, *Three Centuries of Travel Writing by Muslim Women*. I choose to focus on writings by women given that they were, historically if not also today, more occupied than their menfolk with the preparation and serving of food. It may surprise readers that, in the late colonial period and early Independence, a significant number of Muslim women wrote about their travels abroad in Urdu, English, Persian, Punjabi and Bengali. Most left Muslim-led princely states (Hyderabad, Bhopal) or major conurbations (Delhi, Bombay, Lahore, Karachi) for the Middle East, Britain and continental Europe, or, later, the United States. Low literacy in this period, especially among women, means most of these authors fall into the category of 'the elite'. However, the cast of characters that they depict is far more varied. My observation is especially true of culinary reminiscences being that food is most often grown, sold, cooked, served and cleaned away by those projected as 'subaltern'.

Reading these travel writings, we see how food was not solely, or even commonly, a means to divide Muslim from Hindu if we move back in time. Rather, depending on the historical moment and location, it acted as a marker of identity and difference between various social groupings: coloniser and colonised, men and women and those of differing social status. As this collection brings into focus for the present day, cuisine also distinguished Muslims coming from different regions and locales. Let me offer just few examples as a taster of how these themes play out in the often beguiling travel accounts by Muslim women in the colonial period and just after.

## Sharing papadums in Ohio

Though the emphasis in India now may be on internal differentiation, in the colonial period and soon after, food was most often used to draw a distinction between South Asians as a group – sometimes described as Hindustanis, desis or just Indians – and those in 'the West'. Any Muslim woman travelling to Britain in the early to mid-twentieth century found herself longing to share '*laziz Hindi khana*', delicious Indian food, with family and friends. 'Imagine,' wrote educationalist and author Atiya Fyzee in 1906 to her family and community of readers back home in India, 'how dal, chutney, etc, tastes after eating bland (*pheeka*) food for so many days. We Indians have such a craving for this kind of food.' A now tacit (if not always accurate) distinction between the 'bland' British palate and 'spicy' Indian fare fuelled subcontinental identities lived out from meal to meal.

Interestingly, these identities were expressed not just in terms of *what* food was eaten but also *how* food was eaten. Dining out in a restaurant – a form of bourgeois performance in Britain by the late nineteenth century – was one custom openly critiqued if not despised by many Muslim women travelling to the imperial capital. As Atiya Fyzee's sister, Nazli, noted wearily in her *Sair-i Yurop* (1909) of a day out in London: 'After strolling about, it was lunchtime, and we ate somewhere. At teatime we had tea somewhere. Sometimes I like this practice but at other times it irks me. How can one enjoy eating and drinking and doing everything in public?' For many women, eating under the curious gaze of others was only aggravated by the food on offer. Meat 'only nominally put before a flame' inspired Begum Inam Habibullah – notably, the grandmother to author Muneeza

Shamsie, whose food reminiscences are collected in this present volume – to make a brutal assessment of English cuisine in 1924: 'And the food, I think, can't but taste bad to a Hindustani.'

Even after the Partition of India in 1947, gastronomy still drew together South Asian travellers of different denominations and social groupings. A revealing example comes from an American travelogue, *Hamara safar o sarguzasht* (1956), written by a young woman from Hyderabad, Mehr un-Nisa. She arrived in Canton, Ohio, in 1953, to take a nursing course while her husband gained experience as a urologist in a nearby hospital. Throughout her narrative, she wrote on repeat about taking papadum and mango chutney whenever there might be a gathering of 'Indians', whether Muslim or Hindu, Indian or evidently Pakistani. As she recounted after one such enjoyable evening shared with fellow medical practitioners:

> Everyone liked the papadums we had brought, and the Indian doctors smacked their lips when I fed them my tasty mango pickle. As if we could eat home cooking from our native land and not be left licking our fingers!...Here in America, Indians had found a taste that warmed their souls, and memories of home had started filling their hearts until they were beside themselves. Otherwise, what was so special about papadums and mango pickle?

Food's deep-seated physicality and entrenched association with home inspired a shared desi identity when faced with postcolonial otherness in the United States.

## No ham in hamburgers

Muslim travel writers sometimes expressed their dietary differences from the colonial overlord, as well as from other non-Muslims in religious terms. In the interwar period especially, a real concern seemed to be that food provided abroad might not be halal, or permissible according to Islamic law. This worry was especially pressing if travelling to Europe on a British, continental European or American ship. There are many examples in surviving travel writing of how these fears of contravening food prohibitions accentuated divisions between Muslims and Europeans, whether passengers or crew. Begum Habibullah, introduced already for her dislike of English cuisine, wrote in the 1920s of being so unsure of what food was halal or haram that she only dared eat boiled vegetables all the way from Bombay to Marseilles!

The availability of meat products appears as more general theme too, though not always in the way one may expect today. Aboard the P&O ship *Moldavia* that took her from Bombay to Marseille en route to London in 1906, Atiya Fyzee was much less damning or fearful of English ingredients than Begum Habibullah nearly two decades later. She was still put off the local cuisine, curiously by the dearth of vegetables. As she explained: 'Since I am not fond of meat and there are no vegetables cooked there, it is truly difficult for me. If only I had brought some achar with me!' Her reaction points to meat-eating's historic association with ideals of masculinity in many parts of India. Women, including Muslims, were simply less likely – in the early twentieth century as now – to consume meat as regularly. Thus meat-heavy European cuisine could prompt a gendered response.

For these Muslim women travellers, the historical location most often linked to meat as a cheap and plentiful foodstuff was not an Islamic context, but the post-war United States. We may turn here to pioneering Pakistani journalist Zaib-un-nissa Hamidullah, on a coast-to-coast tour with her husband in the early 1950s. Her quotidian account, *Sixty Days in America* (1956), was saturated with food memories. One favourite reminiscence is the quintessential 1950s experience of visiting a drive-in restaurant. Having explained the unique arrangement of ordering, eating and paying 'without even once getting out of the car', she turned enthusiastically to the food: 'I had a *hamburger* and how delicious it was!' Attentive to the food injunctions of her Pakistani audience, she quickly followed up with an explanation: 'Now a *hamburger*, in case you're feeling suspicious, is a piece of beef between two pieces of bun with a lot of tomato sauce and pickle sprinkled on it.' Without any actual reference to forbidden pork, she pronounced her Muslim identity.

## That stinking Meccan ghee

Food preparation and consumption may be regulated by religious edicts, but in these travelogues, it could still be used to set *Indian* Muslims apart from *other* Muslims. Accounts about hajj or other Middle Eastern travel prove especially useful here in framing the historical contexts in which an alimentary line was drawn to divide one Muslim from another. They show that the forging of a Muslim other through food happened primarily when Indian Muslims went on religious pilgrimage, whether to Mecca or elsewhere. In other words, othering happened at the very moment when one might expect a heightened sense of Muslim unity, of belonging to the umma, or universal Muslim community. At high points for pan-Islamism – like the Khilafat Movement in the 1910s and 1920s – differences in eating practices could even disrupt the strategic aim of Muslim solidarity.

A culinary divergence between Indian and Arab Muslims emerges most sharply in Rahil Begum Shervaniya's pilgrimage narrative, *Zad us-sabil*, composed in the early 1920s at the height of the Khilafat Movement, though only published in 1929. The most revealing passages are those in which food was used to distinguish between the Indian Muslims aboard a hajj ship and the Meccan Muslims they were going to visit. The latter may have occupied the holiest site of Islam and yet, in a reversal of historic notions of 'centre' and 'periphery' within the Islamic world, many travellers did not consider them superior or even equal to their South Asian co-religionists. The following exchange between Rahil Begum and a fellow first-class female passenger is worth quoting at length for the intensity of sentiment:

> I asked her what sort of disaster she was expecting that she would bring so many supplies with her. She replied, 'Sister! We wouldn't be able to bear eating Mecca sharif's stinking ghee for a single day...We'd rather eat boiled food than their ghee. Even if we have to go without food for four days, we won't put that ghee into our mouths.'
>
> To which I replied: 'Well, then you yourself should take my canister of ghee. I will eat that sticky, rotten ghee instead.'
>
> She said, 'The wheat there is so bad that it clogs up your intestines,' and proceeded to trash every single grain in Mecca sharif. There were about twelve women there, each of whom took a turn to sing the highest praises of the items that they had brought with them, and to try and scare me by impressing upon me my impending suffering.

Clearly, Rahil Begum, from a prominent and accomplished family associated with the Islamic modernism of Sayyid Ahmad Khan and his Muhammad Anglo-Oriental College at Aligarh, did not place herself above eating the 'rotten' victuals of the Arab other. However, in holding this open-minded position she was clearly in the minority. Still, she recognised the mutuality of sentiment. Of one Bahraini family aboard ship, she commented: 'They seem to have some type of disgust for Indians ... I pass in front of their cabins often enough, but aside from finding that they are avid eaters, I haven't been able to learn much else about them.' As the final line here indicates, Indian Muslims could be set apart from Arab Muslims, not only by the quality of food consumed, but also the amount.

## Spitting paan into the wind

For these travel writers, food did not just segment Muslims across national or international borders. It was also used to differentiate Muslims from various status groups and regions *within* India. We've seen already how Rahil Begum Shervaniya, belonging to a family lauded for its associations with Aligarh reformism, sought to distinguish her modernist ways from the practices of other elite women. Hence, her passage on Mecca's 'stinking ghee' concluded with an oblique reference to the disparities between her (the narrator) and the women she was writing about (the narrated).

Her satirical style is evident from the way she wrote about the two groups in conversation: 'You are elegant and refined women from the city of Delhi, so how can a village-person like me, who is accustomed to eating whatever comes to hand, possibly be the equal of you?' She went on to explain that others aboard ship 'surpassed even this group' in terms of the volume and variety of their food stores, with many bringing live sheep, goats and 'baskets full of chickens' to be slaughtered on the deck each morning. 'Worst of all,' claimed Rahil Begum, were the large baskets of paan, some containing as many as 'five or six thousand [betel] leaves each', 'their size according to the status of their owner'. Her spirited account highlights how food's abundance – the ability to travel with half a farmyard and a crop of paan – operated as a status symbol or indicator of rank for these South Asian Muslim travellers.

At the same time, it is evident that Rahil Begum sought to distinguish herself, as a 'new' sharif, or noble woman, from the other elites with whom she travelled in first-class accommodation. That there was a false modesty in portraying herself as a 'village-person' in comparison with these 'elegant and refined' Delhi-types is clear when she is writing *about* them, rather than narrating what she said *to* them. Then, they do not appear 'refined and elegant' at all, but quite the opposite. This distinction is perhaps most clear in another passage on paan in which she records how 'our respected sisters' would spit the juices out against the wind – such that thousands of tiny drops blew back onto people's faces and clothes. 'Alas,' she concluded, 'I am compelled to write that these ignorant pilgrims are more suited to rickety cargo ships where horses and goats are given the same treatment.'

## 'Human or not, everyone has their own habits and tastes'

An ellipsis in the above block quote about 'Mecca sharif's stinking ghee' hides how Rahil Begum Shervaniya used dialogue with other female hajjis to point to a key observation about food, identity and difference. Faced with the other women's intransigence, Rahil Begum asked: 'Why? Aren't the residents of Mecca human too?' Their answer was definitive: 'Human or not, everyone has their own habits and tastes.' Her observation points to food's most basic quality: we all need food to live and so it should underscore our shared humanity. And yet, despite this – or more precisely because of it – food becomes a main mode by which we articulate our identity, as individuals and as social groups. Culinary others are differentiated and ranked by class, kinship, nation, ethnicity and religion.

My brief look here at women's travel narratives may be historical in approach, but it has important implications for how communal differences linked to food are constructed in India today, with all their bloody consequences. Far from fixed or fundamental, the Hindu–Muslim divide over the sacred cow has been one of many culinary markers of identity and difference for

South Asian Muslims in the modern period. These markers are not inconsequential, but also not exclusive. Just as past binaries reflected and illuminated a historical moment, so this one does our own: as a time when a politicised narrative around cow protection can authorise and embolden violence. Yet, even in this age of Hindutva, resistance can find its culinary expression. Here food mediates (rather than fosters) difference between religious groups. Food's significance to politics and the structuring of everyday life, then, is not just a story of historical continuities or rigid boundaries, but also fluidity, rupture and change.

*Note of acknowledgement:* This chapter employs sources from chapters by myself, Sunil Sharma, Daniel Majchrowicz and David Boyk in *Three Centuries of Travel Writing by Muslim Women* (Indiana University Press, 2022).

## Soyabean Biryani – in memory of Junaid Khan

I am grateful to Rana Safvi for sharing this recipe, which she prepares especially for her daughter, who is vegetarian.

### Ingredients

50g soya nuggets (Rana apa recommends the Andaz brand in India. The amount can be adjusted to preference.)
2 cups basmati rice, soaked in water for an hour
salt for cooking rice
bay leaf
1 whole onion
2 tbsp oil

1–2 green chillies
a few sprigs of mint leaves
orange food colouring or a few saffron strands
2 tbsp warm milk
flour dough for sealing the pot

*For the marinade:*

2 tbsp ginger–garlic paste
½ onion, ground to a paste
1 tomato, chopped
¼ cup curd (or yoghurt)
½ tsp haldi (turmeric) powder
2 tbsp dhania (coriander) powder
¼ tsp garam masala powder
chilli to taste
salt to taste

*Whole spice garam masala:*

2 bay leaves
¼ tsp peppercorns (around 4–5)
2 cloves
2 green elaichi (cardamom)
1 medium onion, sliced finely

**Method**

1. Soak the soya nuggets in hot water for 30 minutes.
2. While the soya nuggets are soaking, prepare the marinade by combining all the ingredients in a bowl. Once the nuggets have been soaked, squeeze out the excess water and add to the marinade.
3. Boil the soaked rice with salt, a bay leaf and a whole onion, adding extra water as necessary to top up the pan. Once the rice is tender but still firm (i.e. parboiled), remove from the heat and drain. Set aside the rice in a bowl covered with a cloth so that any excess water is absorbed. The onion is added to the cooking rice to ensure the rice grains do not stick together.

4. Mix together the bay leaves, peppercorns, cloves and elaichi for the whole spice garam masala. Heat 2 tbsp oil in a pan and add the garam masala. Next, add the sliced onion and fry until golden brown. Remove and leave to drain on a paper towel.
5. Add the marinated soya nuggets with the marinade to the pan. Fry until the masala is well sautéed and the oil has separated.
6. In a non-stick pan, add a layer of rice followed by the nuggets, then topped with another layer of rice.
7. On top, add some of the fried onions (saving the rest for the garnish), green chilli and mint sprigs.
8. Mix the food colouring or saffron strands in warm milk. Pour the mixture over the top of the rice. Cover and seal the pot with dough.
9. Put the pot on dum using a griddle pan or tawa (i.e. with the pot placed on top of the griddle on low heat – to keep it away from the flame). The dish is ready when the dough used to seal the pot is cooked.
10. Open, garnish with the remaining fried onions and serve immediately.

# The Lost Kitchen Cabinet of Bhopal

*Sikander Malik*

My fragrant childhood memories of Bhopal have contributed significantly to my culinary leanings. I was the first surviving child of my parents. Ammi was barely twenty when I was born. A few days before the due date, my parents were asked to move out from my uncle's house. Ultimately we landed up at gali number 2 in Retghat, near the iconic landmark Shakeela Bano ki building, which was the residence of the famous female qawwali singer.

Jameel Ahmed saab, our landlord, was of Syed descent and his wife Saulat Durrani was a Pathan. Their six children included three daughters and three sons. Jameel saab and his wife were like grandparents to me, and I called them Abba and Amma. Their house was built in the 1940s around an aangan and dalans (fully open and semi-open spaces). The southwest corner of the open space always remained under the shade of a large bihi tree (the guava is known as bihi in Bhopal), which kept the busy kitchen under it cooler. The reason the kitchen was in constant use during the day was that it catered to the food joint Odean Hotel. Sabra and Karim, the two servants, were always in the kitchen, doing chores for the hotel and simultaneously cooking for the family.

Abba, who passed away three years ago, was a gastronomic aficionado. He inherited his love of food from his father, the late Rafiq Ahmed. Also known as Rafiq Roosi, this man was a freedom fighter from the group of Bhopalis who, in 1919–1920, walked all the way to Russia with the aim of securing support for Indian Independence. Rafiq was said to have eventually met Vladimir Lenin and participated in the Russian Revolutions and Civil War.

Later in life Rafiq was employed by the last Nawab of Bhopal, Hamidullah Khan (ruled 1926–1949), as the head accountant of the entertainment department (mehmankhana). As part of its remit, the department managed the art deco Lakeview Hotel. During his service Rafiq supervised some great cooks, because of which he too became equally adept in producing the best of delicacies. Abba learnt cooking techniques from his father as he was little inclined towards academic study.

Even today the pasanda, bheja, qeema meethi and dibba gosht from the Odean guarantees a taste which can easily sideline big-name chefs and five-star restaurants. The food is prepared at home following signature recipes handed down by Rafiq Ahmed, offering great flavour in an array of dishes.

I grew up eating them with pleasure. My favourite was the kabab mix. Hearing the sound of the grinder that Amma used to prepare the fine paste for the kababs, I would run at full speed to relish the kababs even before the final product was ready.

Amma taught Ammi, my mother, how to prepare the same kind of kababs. They are referred to as the gupchup shami – those shami kababs that contain secrets. Bhopal's gupchup shami have a lot to say about Bhopal's history and the development of the city's refined palate.

These shami kababs are made out of minced qeema instead of meat pieces or the long-cut parchas which are primarily used for pasandas. The qeema is then boiled with red chillies and garam masala. Roasted chickpea dal (chana dal) is put into the mixture instead of a chickpea flour. Small quantities of roasted and finely ground dhania, or coriander seeds, are added to make the shamis lighter and less taxing on the digestive system. When the combination is ready, a small quantity of curd is added. At the end of the process, raw eggs make their way into the mixture, which is then left to rest before it is transformed into circular tikiyas. This egg ensures that the individual pieces don't break while they are being deep-fried.

The gupchup, or secret, that goes into the belly of the most coveted shami kabab is the kachumber, which consists of finely chopped onions, mint and green chillies. There are several reasons for putting kachumber in the shami, the primary one being to add volume and increase the number of kababs. What is more, the age-old trusted hakims of Bhopal, who stand behind much of the evolution of Bhopali cuisine, advised adding roughage to every non-vegetarian preparation in the city.

I grew up at the Ahmeds' eating these shamis from several plates. My favourite was a big plate, dark in colour, which I later realised was an unusual one, with something embossed or written in its centre. More recently, when I sat down with Amma during one of my seasonal visits, she revealed that the plate was a piece from the early twentieth century.

It came to the house draped in heerakani, a shimmery celebration cloth, bearing ladoos. This plate of mithai was intended to mark and celebrate the wedding of Mehr Taj Princess Sajida Sultan, the second daughter of the last Nawab of Bhopal to Nawab Iftikhar Ali Khan of Pataudi. The plate still bears the wedding date on it, 29 April 1939.

As a child I never thought that later in my life I would do extensive passion-driven research on the erstwhile royal family and the history and anthropology of Bhopal. Amma always says that I owe my loyalty to Bhopal and Nawab sahib's family because of that plate and every morsel I ate from it.

Over the last twenty-five years of my exploration, I have discovered Bhopal's rich history. We Bhopalis are the inheritors of an unparalleled legacy which came from fourteen generations of rulers and subjects of Bhopal state.

The Bhopal ruling family was of Afghan origin from the valley of Tirah in Afghanistan. The native population of Bhopal was tribal, mainly made up of Gonds, the indigenous peoples of central India who lived in forests surrounded by greenery, lakes, rivers and fertile land. It was next to Bara Talab, Bhopal's iconic lake, that one night in 1721 after a tiring goose hunt, Sardar Dost Muhammad Khan (the founder of Bhopal dynasty and an adventurer), is said to have made a decision to honour a dream experienced by his favourite wife, Fateh Bibi. He constructed a fort and dedicated it to his wife, calling it Fatehgarh. Dost Muhammad later extended the fort into a citadel, which had eight gates as points of entry and exit.

Six of these eight gates were named after days of the week to indicate the occurrence of haat, the local market in the gates' vicinity. Imami gate was named after Saturday, when the week started, and ran to Jumerati, for Thursday when the weekend began. Friday was like Sunday to Bhopalis in those days, with no bazaar or haat – and thus no gate was named after it either.

Since then, Friday has been the meatless day in Bhopal. As a result, most Bhopalis inevitably eat kadhi, a dish made of curd and besan, or chickpea flour, with vegetable fritters (pakora or bhajia), on Friday to this day – though some replace the bhajia with meatballs. Another legacy of our founding father is dining in a military way – by which I mean that the leader or commanding officer sits in a head position, but dines with the rest of the army, eating the same food. Dost Muhammad is said to have dined with his family, allies, advisors and generals – in fact, nearly all the prominent people of the entire basti, or settlement.

Even now we Bhopalis always spread out a long cloth which can host an entire basti. The cloth piece laid today to serve meals in Bhopal is still called bastani, while other notable Nizams, Nawabs or members of the Muslim nobility across the country limit themselves to the use of smaller dastarkhwans (table cloths).

Great disturbance followed the founder's death. At that time, many people from Bhopal thrived on natural produce from the forests and the surrounding areas, just as the native tribal peoples had long done. Primarily there's a plethora of bhajia (made from green leafy veggies), which became delicacies like kulfa, patarchata, methi, sarson and chana. Other products from the jungle, including wild fruits like mahua, khirni, kamraq and mainer made achars, chatnis and murabbas, or preserves.

Strict rationing also contributed to the creation of such dishes. At times when a basic ingredient was scarcely available, it was substituted for an available item with a similar taste. The siege of Bhopal by the Marathas for nine months in 1813 is one historical event which gave rise to the idea of making taste flexible. Such flexibility guaranteed survival even in the toughest of times. The famous Bhopali gutka, a mouth freshener made out of seeds, is an invention from those days.

The genesis of modern-day Bhopal can be attributed to the Begums of Bhopal. These were four successive women rulers who ruled the erstwhile princely state almost continuously for 107 years (1819–1926). This period was the age of zarda (tobacco), purdah (veil) and garda (dust) in Bhopal. Their reigns are metaphorically remembered as the days of a well-managed kitchen. The state was run with the help of only two ministers, who were part of the Begum's retinue and were therefore described anecdotally as 'the kitchen cabinet'.

The first reference to a great meal appears in a biography of Qudsia Begum (regent, 1819–1837) penned by her great-granddaughter, Sultan Jahan Begum. Titled *Hayat-i Qudsi*, it describes the first Begum's wedding feast. Hunting animals on foot was then a tradition started in Bhopal by Nawab Sikandar Begum (regent 1844–1860, ruled 1860–1868), who believed in giving the beast a fair chance. Dishes like parinda-i lashkar, labiri ka qeema (salted biltong) and filfora (a quick minced meat with negligible spices) were born then. Fishing was and continues to be treated as a passion in Bhopal. Over twenty recipes for the preparation of fish are described in various cookbooks from the princely era.

Making dining a grand affair, the third Begum of Bhopal Nawab Shah Jahan Begum (ruled 1868–1901) ordered crystal crockery from F&C Osler, the famous glassmakers from Birmingham, England. She wanted this glassware for Jashn-i Taj Mahal, the housewarming party for her new palace. Later in her life she also started celebrating the changing of the seasons. She ordered separate crockery for each season, with dinner sets of different colours being prepared for the various seasons and festivals. Pink was used for Jashn-i Gulabi in the winter and green for Jashn-i Haryali during the monsoon. Even the menus were designed keeping the colour scheme in mind. Shah Jahan Begum also commissioned a book, *Haft Khwan-i Ne'mat*, to be written about Bhopali cuisine by her cousin, Nawab Yar Muhammad Khan Shaukat, in 1875. The book's author was probably the poet Ghalib's last student, and I intend in the next few years to transcreate his work.

Nawab Sultan Jahan Begum (ruled 1901–1926), who I describe as my dearest Sarkar Amma, became a custodian of her mother's legacy. She documented Bhopali culture in several books written or commissioned by her. Sarkar Amma also undertook trips to Europe, in 1911 and later in 1925, during which she recorded the European food which she saw and tasted there. A cookbook of European cookery was published as *Matbakh-i King George* (1921). During her trips she also collected fine china, silver cutlery and scores of kitchen appliances. The better-quality items from this collection continue to make seasonal appearances among her descendants. A butler named Badcock even came back with her from England and lived for the rest of his life at the palace, photographing and filming in his free time. He was always seen standing beside His Highness Hamidullah Khan, the last Nawab, when he dined.

The Begums modelled Bhopal as a progressive state with a strong administration, which helped to create a flourishing economy. Bhopali society became culturally and aesthetically inclusive, which encouraged people from various backgrounds to come and settle in the state. From time to time we were also influenced by alliances less political and more matrimonial.

Several notable families from north India married in Bhopal. The last two Begums and even the last Nawab were married into non-Bhopali families.

These in-laws who settled in Bhopal contributed to influencing the Bhopali lifestyle and that helped the local cuisine to keep reinventing itself. In this way some amazing flavours were born which are specific to Bhopal. However, the exchange has largely been one-way and the flavours were hardly shared outside the state. This is one important reason why the delicate aromas of Awadh gain more attention than the overwhelming tang of the Deccan plateau. Our local flavours have not been well documented and information is being lost by the day, but the dishes still demand attention as an art form from a different era.

After Sarkar Amma's reign ended in 1926, His Highness Nawab Hamidullah Khan and his two Begums, Maimoona Sultan and Aftab Jahan, kept alive the tradition of subtle yet splendid *mehman nawazi*, or hospitality. Bari Begum saab (Senior Begum) picked up the family's culinary traditions exactly where Sarkar Amma left off, while, in the Independence era, Junior Begum saab organised parties. An interesting item I came across in my research was the weekly meal schedule of Junior Begum saab, dating from 1946 to 1947. Apparently, His Highness was a frugal eater, who loved aloo gosht, methi ki bhaji, mash ki dal and an evening tea with laung ke khare (a chickpea-based savoury snack).

His Highness kept a large kitchen with an area of more than five thousand square feet. The in-charge of the kitchen was Syed Yaqub Ali, popularly known as Yaqub sahib and more formally called Muhtamim Bawarchikhana. This chef was given a register with heirloom recipes which also had kitchen tips and quick fixes. Alas! The register is lost and at present can't be traced, though I am working on recovering it.

Visiting dignitaries to the palace enjoyed picnics by rivers, lakes and in the jungle. The ever-popular Bhopali shikar parties started by His Highness continued as a tradition even after his death until the Wildlife Protection Act was passed in 1972.

Among His Highness's three daughters, the eldest daughter and his heir, Princess Gohar Taj Abida Sultaan, was a great connoisseur of food and organised sumptuous dawats or formal dinners at her Palace Noor us Sabah. Her guests loved the sherbets and especially the matka kulfi served at her table.

As she migrated to Pakistan after Independence, His Highness was instead succeeded by his second daughter, Mehr Taj Begum Sajida Sultan. She became the last Begum of Bhopal recognised by the Government of India in 1961. She singularly worked towards keeping up with traditions and patronage. Unfortunately, trying circumstances and family feuds over inheritance led to the loss of that intangible legacy from the inestimable cuisine of Bhopal. After her passing in 1994, Bhopali pasanda, rezala, aloo qatli and a special delicacy, jahazi stew, were cooked and served at the Flagstaff House in Bhopal and the Pataudi House in Delhi by her son and cricket legend Nawab Mansoor Ali Khan Pataudi.

Bhopal has lost nearly all those devoted to its essence. Today the palace kitchen is not in use any more and its cabinets lie empty. Yet legends of the innovations made by the so-called kitchen cabinet governments of the Begums of Bhopal echo through the years in written and oral histories. As such, I still harbour a hope that the stoves of its palace kitchen will be lit again.

## Gupchup Shami Kabab

These shami kababs are part of the culinary evolution of Bhopal. They can be prepared with any kind of meat. In the Nawabi era, game meat was preferred, but now they can be made from mutton or beef. They are tender, crispy and come with a twist.

For this recipe, I have incorporated modern adaptations, like the use of a pressure cooker.

## Ingredients

*For the shami:*

1 kg mince from lean meat, mutton or beef. (If mutton is used, 2–3 tbsp of curd will also be required.)
2 onions, medium-sized, finely chopped
200g chana dal
2 eggs, beaten
1½ tsp ground garam masala
10–15 whole red chillies
1 tsp saunf (fennel seeds), roasted and ground
2 tsp ginger–garlic paste
½ tsp coriander seeds, roasted and ground
½ tsp cumin seeds, roasted and ground
salt to taste
Oil to fry

*For the kachumber:*

2 onions, medium-sized, finely chopped
green chillies, finely chopped, to taste
mint leaves, finely chopped, to taste

## Method

1. Wash the mince at least twice to clean thoroughly.
2. Rinse the finely chopped onions in water.
3. Rinse the chana dal in water.
4. Add mince, chopped onions, chana dal, garam masala and red chillies to a pressure cooker with approximately 1½ cups of water. Cook on a low flame with a closed lid until there are five whistles. Let the mixture release its steam and settle after which the lid can be opened to allow the mixture to cool. It is important that any excess moisture has evaporated.
5. Once the mixture is cool, grind it into a paste. The consistency should be thick and not too fine.

6. Add ground fennel, ginger–garlic paste, ground coriander, ground cumin and salt. Blend thoroughly. Add curd, if using mutton.
7. Add eggs to act as a binding agent and blend.
8. Once the mixture has rested, shape medium-sized shami kababs (dumpling or tikiya) using the palm.
9. Make the kachumber, then use it to fill the belly of the shami.
10. Heat the oil in a heavy-based frying pan on a medium heat. Fry the filled shami in batches for 2–3 minutes each side, or until golden brown and cooked through.
11. Enjoy as part of a meal with pulao.

# Food Myths and Unani Remedies

*Mobeen Hussain*

Many South Asian women remember being given dietary advice by family and friends about how to improve their skin's *rang aur roop*, or colour and glow. This advice, often trickling down from generation to generation, is commonly imparted to pregnant women too, to ensure that children are born fair and light-skinned. It contributes to the rife colourism, or discrimination based on skin tone, that is ubiquitous in many South Asian cultures. Milk-based concoctions like haldi ka dudh (milk with turmeric) continue to be popular in the region, thereby intertwining the beneficial properties of haldi into a mythology of skin colour.

Many mythologies around food and skin tone can be found in late colonial-era novels, domestic literature and periodicals. These were influenced by the racialised and caste-based superiority myths perpetuated by Aryanism, European colonialism, Mughal pasts and Persian lineages. The beauty myths also connected to modern notions of how to be healthy and hygienic. Some of this advice also derived from, and was embedded in, indigenous medical systems within Urdu domestic health manuals that targeted middle-class women – like Unani Tibb. A Greco-Arabic-based medical system, Unani Tibb (or 'tibbi' as a descriptor) is based on humoural balance and sees spiritual and physical health as two mutually dependent states.

In domestic health manuals, health and beauty advice was transmitted by linking culinary advice to optimum colour, health and strength. Writers tapped into ritualised activities as well as the science around food quality and nutrition emerging in the early twentieth century. One manual of this genre is *Hifz-i sehat* (Preserving One's Health), published in 1916 by Sultan Jahan Begum, ruler of the princely state of Bhopal. Another is *Tabib un-nisa* (Women's Medicine) by Hakim Doctor Kazi Mohammad Azimullah, published in Lahore in 1934.

Both manuals targeted elite and middle-class Urdu-speaking women as homemakers, harnessing Unani and Western biomedical knowledge. For women who had migrated with their husbands from mofussils and small cities to larger urbanising and port cities across India, these kinds of instructional manuals functioned as substitutes. These women no longer had ready access to the domestic knowledge customarily passed down from elders.

Sultan Jahan's *Hifz-i sehat* was the second volume in a two-part series. In the first book, *Hidayat az-zaujain* (A Guide to Marriage), the Begum discussed how sharia laws on spousal rights enabled the 'household to be run better'. In the second volume, she framed her teachings on health as core values: 'the principle of health is the principle of nature'. Specifically, she related rules around the preservation of health for 'coming of age' women. Finding women's health (*sehat*) and strength (*mazbuti*) lacking, her manual sought to redress this situation so that women could maintain 'pleasure and happiness' in their homes.

The manual included sections on waste, purity, household and personal hygiene, clothing, exercise and diet. By addressing each body part in turn, the Begum followed the style of nineteenth-century Unani literature. Her focus on easy improvements was couched within traditional Islamic authority and *akhlaq* (etiquette). But it was also linked to a modernising discourse of sanitation propelled by British public health initiatives – for which she was grateful. Sultan Jahan also sought to prove the authority of her manual as a tibbi medical text by reassuring her readers that a well-known Lahori hakim had cast his eye over the whole essay.

*Tabib un-Nisa*, on the other hand, is described as providing 'Brief Urdu Tibb knowledge' and is categorised as 'a family pharmacopeia'. Employing the titles of both 'Doctor' and 'Hakim', Azimullah prescribed two traditions of medicine, often in collaboration with one another, to prove his credibility. The author continuously repeats that his advice was based on his Western learning and his experience with native illnesses. The manual includes sections on gynaecological problems, anatomical differences between men and women, advice for curing common ailments, and guidance on exercise, nutrition, bathing and beautification.

Azimullah was part of the new Unani of the late nineteenth century. Those hakims who were not from established hakim families gained their authority from colonial medical institutions. At the same time, they adhered to Unani as a separate and increasingly Muslim healing practice. Such associations were strengthened by references to Prophetic tradition and by interacting with older Persianate forms of akhlaq. Many Urdu manuals of the period, including that by Sultan Jahan Begum, made connections between inner health, spirituality and morality.

## General food advice

In *Hifz-i sehat*, Sultan Jahan Begum promoted a comprehensive programme of preventive health underscored by bodily discipline. She emphasised the importance of health, stating, 'Mothers who are careless with their health become ill and make their children [ill]' (*mayai ka janbuje kar bache ki sehat se galfat karna ya'ni khud bimar ho-kar bache ko bimar bana-dena*). She thus instructed, in list form, on the six elements that were necessary to 'keep health firm' (*sehat qa'im rakna*): air, diet, sleeping and waking, cleaning the body, exercise and clothing. This advice derived from tibbi recognitions of six lifestyle factors that affected bodily temperament: air, food and drink, physical activity and rest, emotions and feelings, sleep and wakefulness and fluid retention and evacuation.

*Hifz-i sehat* and *Tabib un-nisa* also show how regimenting giza, meaning diet and nutrition, was vital to household and communal (*qaumi*) strength. Sultan Jahan criticised the excessive daily consumption of tea and cocoa in middle-income households, encouraging moderation to avoid damage or loss (*nuksaan*). She advised that food should always be kept simple as food preparation and quality was key to bodily health and beauty. Eating sweet and oily items in abundance, for instance, robbed the face of its glow. Conversely, consuming fruits enhanced facial glow (*ronak*), improved digestion, invigorated the heart and brain and assuaged hunger.

Azimullah also recommended that food be simple. He exalted fresh air, milk, roti, butter and eggs over fruit jam and the excessive consumption of rich curries. In fact, many Urdu manuals of the period employed the language of ronak and roop to indicate health, beauty and colour (or tone), describing beauty and skin colour as mutually dependent factors.

## Balancing extremes

Tibbi treatments are generally premised on the balancing of the humours: hot and moist *dam* (blood), hot and dry *safra* (yellow bile), cold and moist phlegm, and cold and dry *sauda* (black bile). Balancing the humours depended on bodily cycles and the environment. In many colonial-era Urdu domestic health manuals, this humoural principle was applied to skin colour as connected to physical and mental health. Sleeping late, morality, mental deficiencies, physical excesses, ruined blood and internal discords (mental states) all affected rang (complexion or colour). For instance, poor blood circulation could deform kidney function and, in turn, damage rang.

The other two major elements of Unani teaching, evident in both manuals, were emphasis on individual circumstances, and balancing physical and mental equilibrium. Commonly, hakims would prescribe unique medical treatments and advice dependent on an individual's physical and mental state. In *Hifz-i sehat*, Sultan Jahan implored her readers to use their own intellect since some foods 'might be advantageous to one woman but harmful to another'. 'Everyone's natures and habits are different,' she explained. Consuming sweet and oily foods was dependent on body size: 'an obese woman should abstain or take caution against sweet and oily foods and in contrast the woman who is sickly thin should eat those things that a large woman should abstain from'.

Many health manuals of the early twentieth century also urged moderation in food consumption. This approach was in line with indigenous medical practice – both Unani Tibb and Ayurveda – as well as a popular globalising language of nutrition and diet. Nawab Sultan Jahan Begum and Hakim Doctor Azimullah instructed their readers on how to balance their diets, while regulating erratic consumption and intermittent indulgences. Tapping into her authority, privilege and global knowledge, the Begum's manual was diverse in its cross-cultural influences. For instance, she described stories of longevity and moderation from American and French lifestyles. Azimullah also employed his knowledge of Western and Unani Tibb conceptions of bodily anatomy to explain: 'the stomach like other limbs of the body needs rest; if you are always eating or munching on something or other, how can the poor stomach rest' (*ma'dhe ko bi jism ke sutre a'za' ki tarha aram ki zarurat he – har waqt kuch na kuch kahte aur muh marte rehne se gharib ma'dhe ko keshe aram mil saktati hai*). He advised women to limit rich and stimulating food and eat 'fine and fixed amounts' in the morning, midday and in the evening. Sultan Jahan also instructed women to 'control themselves to eat at the correct times' – in other words, not to snack between mealtimes.

Hakim Azimullah warned women that a damaging diet could cause lasting illnesses. He simultaneously advised against dieting, encouraging women to visit a tibbi scholar (*fazil*) if they continuously suffered from a lack of appetite. For Azimullah in particular, bodily health and nutrition concerns were all the more potent because of the effect on female reproductive capacity.

According to Unani advice, a varied, wholesome and healthy diet was key to balancing corporeal and mental equilibrium. Looking after and sustaining the soul was also part of this. In *Hifz-i sehat*, Sultan Jahan Begum reminded her readers that if women wanted strength and health to show on their faces and bodies, it was necessary that the mind was unburdened and stress-free. Any work or activities should be undertaken with a pious heartfelt intention. This advice was inspired by Prophetic teachings which had come to influence the transmission of Unani medicine in the Indian subcontinent over time.

The Begum expanded on how to work on *rang ki hifasat* (preservation of colour) by analogising a person's face to a mirror which displays the state of one's strength. The effect of having limited exercise and cleaning, bad digestion and the habit of excessive sitting, she claimed, affected the face's glow and created marks. The interlinked causes of constipation and poor facial health included lack of exercise, weight and blood-related ailments, using spoiled cosmetics and 'perpetual glumness'. Clearly, an individual's physical state was intimately connected to and dependent on their mental state.

Related to this, Urdu manuals increasingly advocated specific exercise regimes as essential for maintaining health, strength and beauty at a time when purdah – in terms of both dress and confinement in the home – was coming under attack as unhealthy, unsanitary and antithetical to progress.

## Ideal skin colour

Popular manuals in various Indian languages also included recipes, or *nuskhas* – a word first used for prescriptions dispensed by hakims or vaids – for homemade skincare, beautification and cleansing concoctions. Recipes were often compiled from other manuals, newspapers and magazines. Some nuskhas were passed down intergenerationally by word of mouth until they were compiled in manuals at the time when this genre and mass printing were becoming popular in the late colonial period.

Nuskhas combined popular household food items such as chickpea flour and lemon juice with new kinds of chemicals available in the bazaars alongside Unani health advice. In *Hifz-i sehat*, the Begum of Bhopal reminded women that 'good colour is nature's gift' but can be influenced by strength, exercise, easily digestible foods and sleeping early. All were part of recommended tibbi treatments for maintaining good health and staving off ailments.

However, Sultan Jahan also suggested various resources or implements (*asbab*) that could help rectify blemished skin and transform flawed colour to become *khushnama* – in other words, pretty or pleasing to the eye. Her main two resources revolved around food. The first involved eating plenty of fruit, vegetables and milk, while avoiding too much spice. The second recommended homemade mixtures to 'clean or cleanse colour' and 'improve bad colouring'. These last two phrases were often deployed as euphemistic ways of expressing techniques to lighten skin colour. Although these terms had numerous meanings as Urdu developed colloquially, such euphemistic uses came to include suggestions for correcting *beronak* (unbecoming) skin in favour of *achha* rang (good colour), or methods for *chehra ka rang saaf aur safed karna* (cleansing or whitening the colour of the skin). Recipes included mixing milk and the whites of eggs into an ointment; mixing drops of jasmine oil with white wax and dissolving it before massaging the concoction into the face so that it glowed; washing the face with chickpea flour (besan) to cultivate a shine; and kneading powder of wheat into egg whites and applying it to the face to produce lustrousness and remove dark spots.

Keeping true to Unani medical practice while also borrowing from colonial science, many manuals provided detailed nuskhas with precise measurements as treatments. These were presented alongside advice about how to maintain healthy lifestyles. Homemade recipes also answered concerns about the cost and quality of skincare ingredients at a time when branded health and beauty products were increasingly available in a globalising marketplace.

Such recipes and skincare mythologies still hold sway across South Asian cultures – and even find new outlets in the age of social media and rapid communication. The phenomenon of the extended family WhatsApp group in particular has become a popular medium in which to share this kind of advice widely. As I have shown here, such remedies are rooted in domestic manuals from the early twentieth century.

## Three Recipes for Glow and Lustrousness

These instructions for cleansing the colour of your skin (*rang saaf*) have been summarised and translated from *Hifz-i sehat* (1916) by Nawab Sultan Begum of Bhopal.

1. Mix milk and honey with the whites of eggs into an ointment and apply it.
2. Mix drops of jasmine oil or iris oil with white wax, dissolve it, and massage the face with it, so that the face glows.
3. Knead chickpea flour (besan) or the powder of wheat into egg whites and apply it to the face or rub it in with cotton. This produces lustrousness and removes dark spots. Add onion, but avoid its use if skin feels like it's burning. This is also beneficial for removing of a visible unbecoming redness on the face.

# SEPARATED AT BIRTH

## Rampur and Bhopal Cuisines

*Tarana Husain Khan*

Mamma's reasons for the impromptu Bhopal trip were, in her opinion, perfectly sensible. She had to get away somewhere before a possible Covid third wave; she might die without visiting an important former princely state. With her roots in Rampur, another erstwhile Nawabi territory, Mamma has a penchant for historical places and crumbling Nawab-era royal relics. I ranted, argued and gave wild excuses – the parent's emotional invite had the effect of reducing a rational, middle-aged woman to a whining teenager.

'You can study Bhopal's cuisine. You will like it once you get there,' remarked She-Who-Must-Be-Obeyed as she reeled me in.

Resigned, I started reading up on Bhopal and realised that the common Pathan culinary roots shared by Bhopal and Rampur could make a fascinating study. Qamar, my travel-enthusiast husband, also decided to join us. Thus, armed with two extra sets of discerning Rampur taste buds, I started feeling excited about my gastronomic holiday.

Bhopal and Rampur were both princely states – semi-independent kingdoms under British imperial suzerainity – and shared in common an Afghan–Pathan cultural ethos. The Nawabi principality of Bhopal traces its establishment to an Afghan chieftain, Dost Muhammad Khan, in 1724. Rampur was also founded by an Afghan chieftain, Faizullah Khan, who established the state fifty years later in 1774. The chieftains with their families, allied tribes and soldiers brought their Pathan traditions with them as they settled in the two geographically diverse regions. Interactions between the two states were regular – as attested by letters from Nawab Sultan Jahan Begum of Bhopal writing to Nawab Hamid Ali Khan of Rampur on the occasion of his divorce in 1922. Diplomatic and personal ties between the states might have led to culinary as well as cultural exchange. I thought it would be interesting to note the similarities in cuisine and tastes after nearly three centuries of Afghan flavours mingling with local cuisines and those of other principalities.

Around the mid-nineteenth century and especially after the 1857 rebellion, the cooks and artists from the fallen states of Delhi and Awadh had found refuge among and sponsorship from the Nawabs of Rampur. This had led to an era of culinary integration and innovation in Rampur, where Awadhi and Mughal cuisine granted an elegant sheen to the rustic Afghan–Pathan Rampuri foodways. Bhopal's cuisine was also introduced to Awadhi cooking styles when the third Begum of Bhopal, Nawab Shah Jahan Begum (ruled 1868–1901), employed cooks from Lucknow in the royal kitchens. This process might have started with her mother, Nawab Sikandar Begum (regent 1844–1860; ruled 1860–1868), who was said to have visited Awadh and to have bought properties there.

Matrimonial alliances also had a significant influence on the evolving culinary culture. Nawab Shah Jahan Begum's second husband, Siddiq Hasan Khan, was from Kannauj, but had settled in Bhopal with his family upon gaining employment there. Nawab Sultan Jahan Begum (ruled 1901–1926) was then married to Ahmad Ali Khan from Jalalabad, and the influence of the United Provinces' Doaba culinary traditions found their way to Bhopal. The continued migrations from Afghanistan – Nawab Hamidullah (ruled 1926–1949) was married to Maimoona Begum from Shah Shuja Ahmad Shah Durrani's family in 1905 – ensured the base note of Pathan food traditions.

Sikander Malik, a local historian who organises heritage walks in the city and has also contributed to this collection, says that the founder of Bhopal, the Afghan adventurer Dost Muhammad Khan, enjoyed meat preparations, especially of game birds, and instructed his soldiers to avoid sweets and eat a meat-heavy diet for strength. A later French colonial influence is seen in the unique rectangular-shaped sheermal flavoured with cloves, which looks more like a loaf than Indian flatbread. According to food writer Vir Sanghvi, the city's outstanding vegetarian fare is the result of the significant presence of Jain traders in Bhopal. Other local influences from the Rajputs, the Gonds and the Kayastha communities may also have contributed to Bhopali foodways. Possibly reflecting these food traditions, Bhopal cuisine today is a gastronomic culture which has innovative vegetarian dishes along with meat preparations; echoes of Afghan cuisine are still evident in the kababs and pulaos.

We stayed at Jehan Numa Palace Hotel on Shamla Hill. The hotel belongs to the descendants of Nawab Sultan Jahan Begum's second son, Nawab Muhammad Obaidullah Khan, and is known for its preservation of heirloom recipes of Bhopal's Nawabi cuisine. It is regarded as the best place to discover royal Bhopal flavours.

I was especially intrigued by two new dishes with exotic and unusual names – the rezala and the filfora. Rezala is a chicken or mutton preparation known for its subtle taste and aroma. It is a popular dish in West Bengal and Bangladesh. There are several Bengali versions of rezala, some using simple yoghurt, poppy seeds and cashew pastes as the dominant notes, while others add turmeric and chilli powders. As no such dish is found in Awadhi cuisine, credence seems to attach to Bengali gourmands' claim that the dish was first created in Bengal. Oral history suggests that Bengali converts to Islam started cooking rezala, a simple dish amalgamating the local flavours with Awadhi and Mughal cuisine, after it was introduced by Mughal governors and later Nawab Wajid Ali Shah's establishment at Metiaburj. Sikander

Malik asserts that the rezala came to Bhopal when officials were hired from Bengal by the last two Begums of Bhopal, Shah Jahan and Sultan Jahan. Today the dish is only prepared in West Bengal, Bangladesh and Bhopal.

We met over tea with Princess Niloufer, granddaughter of Nawab Muhammad Obaidullah Khan from the Jehan Numa or Shamla hill branch of the royal family. An ardent foodie and grand old matriarch of Bhopali royal cuisine, the princess narrated the oral history around the origin of Bhopali rezala. According to her, the Bhopali style of rezala was innovated by Nawab Shah Jahan Begum. The Begum loved celebrations and royal events curated around colour themes. Thus, a jashn-i gulabi and a jashn-i hariyali celebrated the colours of pink and green respectively. Everyone dressed in the given colour, and the decor as well as the cuisine highlighted this tone. Thus, a dull beige rezala curry was granted coriander to make it green, and the Bhopali rezala was born. Another interesting gastronomic twist was the use of fried onions and turmeric to enhance the taste. The Bhopali rezala served at Jehan Numa and at other eateries in Bhopal combines copious amounts of coriander in the curry, lending it a dull green hue and a fresh taste, though the base is still yoghurt, poppy seeds and cashew.

Bhopalis apparently prepared rezala from peacock meat until hunting peacocks was banned. The story of filfora, a unique mincemeat preparation, is also rooted in the shikar or hunting traditions of Bhopal. During the colonial era, the region was known for game, and royal hunting parties would go with their cooks on shikar expeditions in the surrounding jungles. Princess Niloufer explained that the word 'filfora' comes from the language of the aboriginal Gond peoples and can be translated as 'quickly' Upon the killing of an animal – usually nilgai, deer or gazelle – its meat was coarsely chopped or sliced into slivers while still warm, and immediately fried with some basic ingredients on a campfire. The fat from the meat and the juices cooked into the meat with salt, chillies and oil was the most rustic and satisfying meal for the hunters. Today this hand-chopped mincemeat, cooked with ginger–garlic paste, turmeric, chillies, onions, yoghurt and the culinarily omnipresent coriander, is the popular filfora. It corresponds to a favourite quotidian mincemeat dish from Rampur – the darra qeema. Whereas Awadhi connoisseurs cringe at the prospect of rough-cut mincemeat and assert that fine mince is essential to absorb the flavours, the Rampuris and Bhopalis love their rustic mincemeat cooked without garam masalas.

The two baseline notes of nearly all traditional Bhopali dishes are fried onions and coriander. This reminded me of an old Rampuri khansama telling me that he can cook the best qorma and kababs just by using fried onions and green cardamoms. As in Rampuri cuisine, the Bhopal dishes rely on basic spicing and there is a near absence of the aromatics – mace, cinnamon, nutmeg, all-spice, star anise – favoured by Awadhi cuisine.

Princess Niloufer was married into the Rampur royal family and her sister-in-law Bano comes from an Aligarh family. Both the ladies have worked to refine and innovate the Jehan Numa Palace repertoire. Today the chefs and sous chefs working at Jehan Numa restaurants are trained by the family cooks under the supervision of the two women. The resulting amalgamations served at their Under the Mango Tree and Under the Jamun Tree restaurants are an epicurean delight. Saleem Qureshi, their head of marketing and a foodie, continues the culinary refinement as Jehan Numa hosts food festivals, inviting cooks from Rampur, Lucknow, Hyderabad and Delhi. They also host Bhopali rezala masterclasses to popularise this neglected culinary marvel.

The Bhopalis, like the Rampuris, favour the yakhni pulao – with the rice cooked in lightly flavoured meat stock – over the spicy biryani. The Bhopali yakhni pulao that we tasted had the familiar light aroma. Mamma and Qamar, like most Rampuris, are qorma–pulao–kabab snobs, and I awaited their comments as we were served the Jehan Numa Palace delights. The qorma passed muster. It was slow-cooked on coals and, in their view, had just the right consistency with an accurate balance of spices. Mamma remarked that there was a floral aroma to it, which turned out to be rosewater combined with kewra. Though rosewater is never used in Rampur curries, it was pronounced pleasing by the two gourmands.

The seekh kababs were thick and golden, their lavish dimensions matching the Rampur seekh kababs, and were approved by my discerning mother. It was further observed that Rampuri kababs have a more uniform and creamy texture than the Bhopali. Rampuris collectively disapprove of the overuse of papaya tenderiser and aromatics, which according to them tend to make the Awadhi and Kakori kababs too dark and mushy with a garam masala aftertaste. The Jehan Numa cooks use basic masalas, and there is a dominance of meaty tastes. The same reticence in the use of spices was found in their chapli kababs. These are flat, round kababs made from marinated mincemeat, fried over large skillets. They have their roots in Afghani and Peshawari kababs and take even fewer spices than the seekh kababs. A garnish of finely chopped onions, green chillies and coriander is mixed into the mincemeat before frying, which lends a crunch to the smooth taste. Princess Niloufer aptly describes the flavours of Bhopal as 'earthy' – not spice-heavy like Mughal cuisine, and not as delicately aromatic as the Awadhi cuisine. I could broadly define Rampuri cuisine in similar words.

Fish is an important part of Bhopali cuisine as good quality freshwater fish from the lakes is available all year round. We ventured to Sadar Bazar for its famed Afghani kachchi machli. There are several Afghan restaurants in Sadar Bazar whose proprietors claim descent from the original Afghan settlers. Kareem Khan, the proprietor of the highly recommended New Afghani Restaurant, looked every inch a Pathan with his grey beard and grand gestures. Meeting fellow Pathans from Rampur, he lit up and we were given a tour, interspersed with stories, of his hotel and restaurant. He explained that the Afghani kachchi machli is marinated in curd and masalas for three hours. The curry is cooked over four hours and the marinated fish is simmered in the curry. Since the fish is not fried before cooking, it is called 'kachchi', or raw. By now we knew Kareem bhai well enough to halve the cooking and marination time. Notwithstanding his hyperbole, the fish was delicious and freshly caught from the lake. Rampuri fish curry always carries a redolence of fenugreek. We cannot dream of tempering our fish without methi seeds. Most Rampur cooks mount a war against the fishy smell by scraping, cleaning and washing it obsessively with mustard oil, lemon juice or vinegar, sometimes with all three of them. Frying the fish is an important part of the process. Kareem Bhai told me that since the fish comes fresh from the lake, they don't have to do much washing. For Rampuris masher and sanwal are the best freshwater fishes; Bhopalis are also devoted to sanwal fish.

We also sampled mutton stew in the chowk area at another Afghan restaurant. Indian meat stew has its roots in the British cuisine and dates back to colonial times. Sometime in the culinary history of the subcontinent, the English stew – with its oldest recorded representation in the Burdwan stew containing meats, onions, various vegetables, butter and red wine – underwent drastic changes at the hands of the Indian cooks. The Burdwan stew was a favourite colonial stew cooked in Calcutta since at least the beginning of the nineteenth century. As the stew made its journey across India from the kitchens of the British colonial masters to the Indian elite, we put in whole garam masalas, threw out the seasonal vegetables and the red wine and cooked the ginger–garlic–onions into a thick mush along with the meat. Rampur stew even discarded the tomatoes because we are not too fond of cooking the vegetable in our meat preparations. The Bhopalis have a different version of the stew. They have added turmeric, coriander leaves and green chillies, making the dish look more cheerful. Our communal Rampur taste buds cringed at the culinary blasphemy. For us, the sharp tang of the turmeric destroyed the expected smooth blandness of the Indian stew.

Loaded with stories and food, we returned home. Still intrigued by rezala, I tried making a Bhopali rezala from the recipe kindly shared by Jehan Numa's owners. I also cooked Bengali rezala from an internet recipe and we debated the rival tastes of the two dishes. Qamar was all for the Bengali version while Mamma felt that the latter was too sweet to be called a curry. She preferred the spicier Bhopali rezala. As we sat there critiquing the remembered flavours, I hit upon the idea of taking Rampur khansamas to Jehan Numa, and busied myself reconnecting with Saleem Qureshi and making plans to organise a Rampur food festival at their hotel.

Mamma smiled. 'I knew you would enjoy Bhopal.'

## Bhopali Chicken Rezala – from the Jehan Numa Palace Hotel

### Ingredients

1 kg chicken, washed, cleaned, cut into bite-sized pieces
100 ml vegetable oil
100g onions
3 tsp ginger paste
3 tsp garlic paste
1 tsp turmeric powder
2 tsp coriander powder
7 cups coriander leaves, chopped
100g green chillies
2 tsp poppy seeds (khus khus), soaked, finely ground into a paste
1 tsp garam masala
1 cup yoghurt, whipped

1 egg, hard-boiled, peeled, halved
juice of 2 lemons
Salt to taste

**Method**

1. Heat the oil in a pan and fry the onions to a golden brown. Drain the oil from the onions and set aside.
2. Add ginger and garlic pastes, turmeric powder, coriander powder and salt to the oil. Fry until the mixture turns golden brown, sprinkling water if necessary to stop burning.
3. Add the chicken pieces and continue to fry until the liquid dries out and the chicken turns golden brown.
4. Add the chopped coriander leaves along with the fried onions, green chillies, poppy seed paste, garam masala and yoghurt. Cook on medium heat until the oil rises to the top.
5. Serve garnished with the halves of hard-boiled egg and a squeeze of lemon juice on top.

*Recipe reproduced with kind permission of Jehan Numá Palace Hotel, Bhopal.*

# The Foodscape of Manipur's Pangal Community

*Md Chingiz Khan*

It is only after settling into a comfortable acquaintance that I tell my friends that I'm a Pangal – a term used for the indigenous (*yelhoumee*) Muslims of Manipur. Invariably the admission draws a blank stare, polite smiles or curious questions. One of those queries is often: What do you eat? Sometimes I invite my friends to a Pangal meat curry, a sajouthongba meal which they say tastes a lot like their qorma. Several Pangal dishes have Manipuri names – which my friends, with some effort, try to learn. This challenging nomenclature reflects that Pangal cuisine has evolved from the eating habits and cooking procedures of the Meitei community – an ethnic group local to Manipur – superimposed over eastern Bengal Muslim food cultures through four centuries of living together.

The Pangals began settling in Manipur during the first half of the seventeenth century. At that time they received grants of local women, land and servants from the king Khagemba (1597–1652 CE), for their permanent settlement in the state. Despite this fact, some local scholars make unhistorical and mythic claims about their settlement in the state before the seventeenth century. What is without doubt is that the Pangals have contributed substantially to the society, economy, culture, polity and administrative affairs of the state of Manipur.

Certain local dishes appear to have been adopted by the Pangals from the Meitei community. These include eromba, which is a vegetable mash. Eromba is made up of boiled potatoes and vegetables which are then mixed with ground red chillies and ngari (fermented fish). The mixture is flavoured with onion, coriander leaves and garlic. This popular food makes for one of the most mouth-watering dishes. Not only did the Pangals adopt eromba, but they also adapted it, by way of innovations in the preparation. Particular kinds of eromba eaten by the Pangals include the Pangal chanam eromba, mathak eromba and makha eromba. The first two are usually only made by the Pangals, while the last recipe is cooked by all the communities of Manipur state. Mathak eromba is created from a mixture of ground leafy vegetables and boiled potatoes flavoured with turmeric powder, chilli powder, onions and garlic, which are fried in oil. Makha eromba, in contrast, is fashioned from a mixture of boiled red chillies, boiled green vegetables, potatoes and ngari (fermented fish), but is not fried. Pangal chanam eromba is made from a proportionate amount of boiled chanam (garlic) and chillies, onion and salt. Sometimes turmeric powder is also added. It is garnished with fresh coriander leaves. The Pangal elders believe that chanam eromba is beneficial for one's health, particularly among those who have low blood pressure. Most Pangal family members used to eat it, but nowadays it is rarely consumed.

Other famous dishes include moroksingju (a type of salad), ngari (fermented fish made from a sundried non-salted dry fish called phoubu or *Puntius sopore*, usually imported from Bangladesh and the Brahmaputra valley of Assam), and soibum (bamboo shoot). These repasts are enjoyed by the Pangals after perhaps having been adapted from the Meitei community. Soibum is lavishly procured from particular villages like Andro, Kwatha and Noney. In some remote villages and even in urban areas, soibum plays an essential part in eromba and fish cooking by the Pangal community. Manipur's various communities particularly use it in their festivals, a key example being Ningol Chakouba of the Meitei community, when married women return to their parents' house to revive family traditions.

An important ingredient in Manipur is pennywort (peruk), a medicinal herb with the scientific name *Centella asiatica*. Peruk Singju, a dish consumed by most Pangal families, is a mixture of ground peas, cabbage leaves, pea shoots, ngari, red chilli paste, coriander leaves, spring onion, garlic chives, mayangton/mayangba (lemon basil) and tokningkhok (heartleaf plant). Another staple is thangjing (foxnut) singju, which is eaten in every Pangal family just as it is in the counterpart Meitei community.

Another well-known dish of Pangal cuisine is hentak. This is a side dish which we Pangals often use as a condiment with rice or curry. It is made from small fish called ngasang in the Manipuri language. The fish is exposed to the sunlight and then crushed to a powder in a sumban (a wooden mortar to pound grains) by adding incremental amounts of the stalk of *Alocasia Macrorhiza*. After that, onion, garlic and ginger are also crushed and added for their taste. Next, oil is added and the hentak is created in a ball shape, which is kept in an earthenware pot. This ball is to be kept for one week of fermentation.

Hawaichar/hawaijar (fermented soyabeans), ooti (a black lentil) and Pangal tal (made especially from ground black powder rice, chakhao) have been used by the Pangals since their settlement in Manipur. However, the Pangals' way of preparing hawaichar and ooti is somewhat different from that of the Meitei community. Hawaichar is, in fact, one of the distinctive foods of the Pangal community. The preparation involves the seeds of medium and small-sized soyabeans being boiled, washed with hot water and packed tightly into a small bamboo basket. Atop this basket is a lid, and below is a base layer of *Ficus hispida* (asseeheibong) or banana plant leaves. The basket is then kept near a stove or in a layered gunny bag to keep it slightly above the normal temperature. The palatable stage of fermentation in the soyabean is noticed within three to five days, with an ammonia odour and the production of mucilage fibre. Scientific studies have suggested that fermentation increases the protein content and other antioxidants in the soyabean, such that hawaichar can be used to combat malnutrition and even prevent degenerative diseases and type 2 diabetes.

Ooti and yamthakpa are prepared with leafy vegetables, particularly peas, ginger leaves, ground rice and salt. After slow-cooking, pea roots are burnt to ashes and then added in. Later on, baking powder is used in the making of ooti. To make yamthakpa, the same process is followed as with ooti, except that baking soda is excluded. Pangal tal is a uniquely Pangal dish made from black powdered chakhao rice (a kind of black rice) prepared in a round shape. It has to be fried in oil. Its ingredients include many proteins, which are beneficial for diabetic patients trying to avoid carbohydrates.

Last but not least, the Pangals' most notable and highly acclaimed food, and a favourite of my Delhi friends, is the Pangal sajouthongba. This is largely prepared for consumption at weddings and serni (a feast carried out thirty to forty days after a person's death) along with sagol hawai (urad dal) thongba (literal meaning: 'to cook'). To make Pangal sajouthongba, first of all a traditional earthen oven is chosen and dredged based on the size of the pan. Halal meat is placed in an enormous pan containing hot oil. Added to this are chilli powder, turmeric powder, salt, tejpatta (bay leaf) with a crushed paste of ginger, onion and garlic. Then some mukthrubis (known as prickly winged leaf) are thrown in. *Myristica linifolia*, called sa in the Manipuri language, is used in the sajouthongba. For cooking, a medium-sized stick coated with iron and made from bamboo (called sa khabei in Manipuri) is used by the two expert chefs needed to create this elaborate dish.

My eighty-five year-old grandmother used to make tamphut, a distinctive food of our community. It is constructed from flour, wrapped in a banana leaf and then boiled in a pot for a while. It is still cooked in rural areas but because of the tedious labour most Pangals have stopped cooking it. Another dish is ngangkok, which is also made from flour but involves a very different process than tamphut. This dish too is only infrequently cooked by the Pangals nowadays.

The culinary evolution of the Pangals reflects our peace-loving temperament and our syncretic and acclimatising nature. We have maintained idiosyncratic food cultures, sometimes making dishes typical to the region but adapting them to halal prescriptions. Other preparations were newly introduced by the Pangals to the state. What is cooked in our Muslim kitchens distinguishes the Pangal community, but our cuisine also ties us to our neighbours.

## Eromba

### Ingredients

1 powa (250g) green beans. Remove the stringy edge of each bean and cut into two pieces. Green beans can be replaced by another green vegetable, like cabbage.
2–3 potatoes, medium-sized, each cut into quarters
3 ngari. This fermented fish from Manipur can be bought from specialist and online retailers.
5 dried red chillies
1 onion, sliced finely
6 garlic cloves, sliced finely
salt to taste
coriander leaves for garnish

### Method

1. Wash thoroughly the beans, potatoes, dried red chillis and ngari.

2. Boil the green beans, potatoes and dried red chillies in a pot for 10–15 minutes.
3. Fry the ngari for 2–3 minutes in another pan. You can also steam the ngari by placing them in a bowl on top of the potatoes and beans while they are being boiled.
4. Remove the boiled red chillies and place in a bowl with the fried ngari. Add salt to taste, then add a small amount of water. Mash the chillies and ngaris with a steel tumbler or some other implement.
5. Mash the boiled potatoes and beans.
6. Mix all the mashed ingredients together using a medium spoon.
7. Garnish with sliced onion, sliced garlic and coriander leaves to taste.

# The Hunza Diet and the Secret of Prolonged Youth

*Ashok Malhotra*

In a lecture delivered to the University of Pittsburgh in 1921, a colonial medical researcher in British India named Dr Robert McCarrison first made reference to a 'Himalayan' people he had encountered. According to him, this group of people had exceptional physiques and low susceptibility to illness, leading them to live for an unusually long time. Later that year, McCarrison published *Studies in Deficiency Disease*. In the book, he confirmed that the Himalayan people he was discussing were the Hunzakuts (henceforth 'Hunzas', but these days referred to as the Burusho people) who lived in Gilgit, northwest India (now Pakistan). McCarrison attributed their longevity to the region's traditional diet, which he claimed was made up of 'grains, vegetables, and fruits, with a certain amount of milk and butter, and goat's meat only on feast days'. Crucially, the Hunzas consumed simple foodstuffs, unlike the processed and mass-produced food which McCarrison asserted to be commonly eaten in Britain at the time. By McCarrison's reckoning, this diet prevented the 'tribe' from suffering the kinds of ailment to which supposedly 'civilised' peoples were prone.

Dr Guy Wrench, a British doctor and advocate of preventative medicine, was inspired by McCarrison's work to pen *The Wheel of Health* (1938). Never having visited Hunza himself, he relied upon McCarrison's claims to espouse the supposed health benefits of organic vegetables and to warn against industrialised food production. He also drew on selected European travel accounts and second-hand anecdotal evidence to make complementary claims regarding the Hunzas' physical strength, endurance and intelligence. Like McCarrison, he claimed that these traits stemmed from their dietary choices and agricultural practices.

Wrench averred that the Hunzas were predominantly lacto-vegetarians who consumed large quantities of fruit, wheat chapatis, pulses, vegetables, dried apricots, milk and milk-based products. Moreover, they either ate vegetables raw or ensured that they did not overboil them, gaining the maximum minerals and vitamins from the plants. Hunzas, according to Wrench, did not consume foodstuffs and beverages like tea and sugar which were popular in Britain. A common thread running through Wrench's account is that the Hunzas did not consume foods that had been imported from elsewhere or had undergone any mechanised process or chemical adulteration. Such processing, he believed, would have diminished the food's nutritional properties. Wrench deployed the Hunzas strategically to argue that Britain and other Western industrialised nations should return to the unprocessed and unrefined diets of yesteryear, in order to obtain a higher standard of health for their populations.

The Hunzas, in Wrench's account, were traditional agricultural practitioners. They collected their own faeces and manure from their cattle, and returned them to the soil to ensure its fertility. In this respect, *The Wheel of Health* resonated with the embryonic organic movement that was developing in Britain at this time. Leading figures from this movement, such as the writer and politician Gerard Wallop and the aristocrat Lord Northbourne, as well as the agricultural scientists Albert Howard and Eve Balfour, subsequently hailed the Hunzas as a people who testified to the benefits of holistic farming practices and organic diets.

The idea was also picked up by Jerome Rodale in the United States of America, who repeated many of the same claims in his *The Healthy Hunzas* (1948). Rodale's narrative, however, was further influenced by James Hilton's novel *Lost Horizon* (1933), which depicted a fictional mountainside location in Tibet where people lived on average several hundred years in a state of contentment, peace and perfect health. Rodale constructed Hunza as a veritable Shangri-La where its people experienced similarly high standards of physical health. In addition, Hunzas were said to suffer from none of the social or psychological problems that prevailed in the USA, such as crime, divorce, juvenile delinquency and anxiety. Rodale attributed this, once again, to the Hunzas' dietary habits and farming practices.

In the 1960s came a series of travel accounts by North American authors. These writers were inspired to visit Hunza and spill much ink about this Shangri-La. Book-length examples include *Hunza Land* (1960), *Hunza Health Secrets for Long Life and Happiness* (1964), *Hunza: 15 Secrets of the World's Healthiest and Oldest Living People* (1968), and *Yoga: The Art of Living: Hunza Way to Health* (1969). All these narratives confirmed the notion that Hunza was a paradise on earth, and progressively more exaggerated claims were made during this period. Indeed, the books claimed some of these Hunzas as the oldest inhabitants of the planet. Renee Taylor in *Hunza Health Secrets for Long Life and Happiness* even stated that she encountered a 145-year-old man energetically playing volleyball. She also asserted that the Hunzas were consummate meditators, expert breathers and yoga practitioners.

It is important to remember that these travellers all came under the sway of the Mir of Hunza Jamal Khan, who ruled Hunza as a semi-autonomous kingdom between 1945 and 1974. Jamal Khan hosted them and supplied them with information during their stays in Hunza. They were always chaperoned during their tours by a member of the Mir's family or his entourage. Since they could not understand the native language Burushaski, they were dependent upon their accompanying translators when seeking to obtain information.

The Mir was keen for his own reasons to keep an eye on foreign visitors. Although the North American authors presented the Mir as firmly in control of Hunza, his situation was actually more precarious in postcolonial Pakistan. In 1947, when India was partitioned, Mir Jamal Khan opted to join the State of Pakistan as a semi-autonomous kingdom. However, he was also conscious after Pakistan's Independence that the Pakistani central government would seek to exert greater control over Hunza and take away more of his powers. Yet Jamal Khan was keen to maintain control and autonomy in the wake of external pressures. Consequently he was invested in catering to the orientalist preconceptions of these North American authors that Hunza was an idyllic region uncontaminated by the deleterious effects of modernisation. Indeed, he sought to promote the notion that any interference from outside could threaten this supposed Shangri-La. On a personal level it would have been also personally flattering to the Mir to have himself seen by a variety of sycophantic and naive Americans as a benevolent and wise ruler of an idealistic state, who had all the solutions to the problems that existed in modern Western industrialised societies.

Renee Taylor, a lifestyle guru and yoga instructor, and Dr Jay Hoffman, a medical practitioner of geriatrics, created sections wholly devoted to Hunza recipes in their respective works. Taylor's chapter entitled 'Recipes from the Rooftop of the World' consists of recipes supposedly provided by the Mir's wife, the Rani of Hunza. As reported by Taylor, most of these were instructions for 'original Hunza dishes', while others the Rani had collected 'from around the world'. Out of a total of 103 recipes provided, only eighteen loosely resemble Indian dishes. Indeed, the 'Hunza Mutton Curry' lists curry powder as one of its ingredients, rather than the wider variety of spices and herbs usually associated with South Asian cooking.

The rest of Taylor's recipes feature standard North American dinner party dishes of the time, such as 'Cold Shrimp Hors D'oeuvres' and 'Avocado Cocktail'. The ingredients necessary for these particular dishes, including pineapples, avocados, mayonnaise and cold shrimp, make it unlikely that they could be prepared in a remote mountainous area in Gilgit, Pakistan during the period. The recipes were more likely composed by Taylor herself and designed to appeal to cosmopolitan consumers in the US. The Hunza label for many of these recipes is tenuous and the claim that the majority were authentic Hunza dishes is problematic. Nevertheless, the labelling aimed to tap into consumers' desire for an alternative to the North American fare of the 1960s, even if the recipes themselves, in many cases, offered little substantially different.

Hoffman's Hunza recipes differ from Taylor's in key respects. His recipes consist of such dishes as 'Hunza green leafy vegetable', 'chapatti green vegetable', 'apricot breakfast', 'cheese bread', 'curd bread', 'potatoes with apricot nuts', 'wheat pudding', 'barley pudding', 'turnip bread' and 'mulberry soup'. The recipes are entirely devoid of eggs, sugar, meat or fish. They limit their ingredients to wheat, apricot nuts, vegetables, fresh fruits and milk-based products (milk, cottage cheese and homemade yoghurt). No seasoning is offered apart from salt. Thus, while Taylor's recipes had a range of cosmopolitan ingredients, Hofmann's recipes are bland even by the standards of North American cuisine of the day.

It should be noted that Hoffman was a devout Seventh-day Adventist. Moreover, he was influenced as a medical researcher by the writings of the famous breakfast cereal entrepreneur and anti-masturbation crusader Dr John Kellogg (also a Seventh-day Adventist). This meant that he was affiliated to a theological and medical tradition which recommended vegetarian and plain foods precisely so as not to stimulate sexual desire or to aggravate the bowels. Hoffman's version of Hunza recipes certainly chimed with these aims. What is apparent in Taylor's and Hoffman's differing recipes is that the Hunza diet was heavily adapted to suit the particular interests and agendas of these North American authors.

It is difficult to reconstruct a completely accurate sense of what the average Hunza family might have eaten in the 1950s and

1960s. Various European and North American travel accounts of the twentieth century all state they consumed curd (soured milk), as well as a range of fruits, nuts and vegetables. Apricots were a key component of their diet, whether in the form of apricot oil used for cooking, apricot kernels, dried apricots or ripe apricot fruits. They most likely did not eat meat regularly simply because of the lack of availability, rather than through choice. Moreover, they probably often consumed stuffed chapatis. It would, however, be reasonable to assume a wider range of mountain herbs and spices would be available to them than were displayed in either Hoffman's or Taylor's recipes.

The Hunza state was opened up to the rest of Pakistan by the Karakoram Highway, which was completed in 1979, allowing for a greater variety of foodstuffs coming in from outside. In YouTube travel videos and Hunza-themed websites that have recently been uploaded on the internet, contemporary Hunza recipes consist of the range of spices common to South Asian cooking. Moreover, meat seems to be widely used. This is evident, amongst others, on the *HunzaBytes* website, authored by Naveed Alam, a local Hunza man seeking to promote Hunza cuisine to Australia and the rest of the world.

It is significant that *HunzaBytes* displays recipes that did not feature at all in those provided earlier by Hoffman and Taylor. For instance, there is 'Daudo Soup', which is a noodle soup consisting of wheat flour (used to make the noodles), beef, brown onion and a range of South Asian spices. There is 'Chap Shuro' (Hunza meat pie), which consists of ingredients such as mincemeat, spring onions, tomatoes, green chillies, flour and a range of spices. At the same time, though, the website draws from an earlier discursive tradition inherited from British and North American representations, which valorised the Hunza diet for being holistic and unprocessed. *HunzaBytes* claims that the Hunza diet is 'seasonal, wholesome, and free from preservatives, artificial colourings or flavourings'. It promotes staple ingredients of Hunza cooking such as wholegrains, fruits, nuts, apricot kernels and apricot oil. What is more, Alam states that the 'people of the Hunza, a hidden valley high in the Himalayas' are a testament to the age-old proverb 'you are what you eat'. Internationally, the peak period of fascination with the Hunza diet was the 1960s. However, it is still evident that certain Hunzas today, as the Mir of Hunza did previously, are for their own purposes advancing claims to Western consumers about the Hunzas' diet and physical prowess. Thus, while there might be more ingredients that have now been added to the Hunza recipes which are promoted abroad, the healthy Hunza diet narrative is a powerful one that still resonates today.

## Hunza Rice with Apricots or Nuts

This recipe has been reproduced from Renee Taylor's *Hunza Health Secrets for Long Life and Happiness* (1964). It gives a sense of how the 'healthy' Hunza diet was being substantially adapted to the tastes and agendas of her North American audience.

### Ingredients

2lb (roughly 1kg) brown rice
½ cup butter or apricot kernel oil
¼lb (roughly 100g) apricots or nuts
¼lb (roughly 100g) raisins
4 large onions
salt to taste

### Method

1. Cook rice in the usual manner.
2. Brown onions in a skillet in butter or apricot-kernel oil.
3. Sprinkle browned onions over rice, then add chopped apricots or nuts, as well as raisins.

# *part three*
# Survival and Revival

# On Kashmiri Food and Authenticity

*Aliya Nazki*

The other day when I was scrolling through my Instagram feed, I came across a couple of posts from one of my favourite food accounts. One of them was about sweet and savoury scones, which I loved. The other was about a chicken rogan josh. It turns out that a rogan josh made with chicken instead of lamb I'll forgive, but a recipe that calls for tomatoes and calls itself a rogan josh, I most certainly won't.

What did I do? I of the strict 'no-comments-on-public-posts' rule, what did I do? Obviously, I commented (almost), eloquently expressing my righteous outrage. I believe the comment started with the following words: Oh for the love of god!

All very calm and measured. You know.

But it got me thinking, again, about why I get so cross about these things – tomatoes in rogan josh, or bay leaves or garam masala powder in what claim to be Kashmiri recipes.

I'd like to think that I'm a fairly tolerant person. I've always embraced change. I've lived in different cities, become intimate with and fervently admired various cultures, celebrated the coming together of disparate and even opposing points of view. So why do I find it so hard, impossible even, to shrug my shoulders and say, 'Oh well, makes for a change', when I see people making nun chai tarts (from Kashmiri green tea) or Kashmiri biryani? Why does every bay leaf, every tomato, every spoonful of sugar in nun chai feel like a personal attack? Why can't I be more like my Punjabi friend, who once took me to a paratha stand in Delhi that made and sold, of all things, chicken chowmein parathas, and respond with undisguised glee?

I also know that I am not alone in feeling like this. It's a very Kashmiri thing. Kashmiris are extremely protective of our food, the way it is cooked, served and eaten. The slightest change, especially if it comes from outside, is often perceived as a direct attack, an insult. And there's outrage: It's not authentic! That's not how it's supposed to be! Or as I so movingly put it under that Insta post, 'Leave rogan josh alone!'

Palestinian people, I find, are much the same, as are some Jewish people. All are fairly obsessed with preserving the authenticity of their food.

But really the question should be: what is authentic? Authenticity-bashing is on point these days, after all. I have by now engaged in more than a few conversations on various social media platforms where people – intelligent, well-informed, often well-intentioned people – will routinely and passionately dismiss the concept of authenticity. This dismissal is especially impassioned when it comes to food, but also adheres to some other markers of identity.

Nothing is authentic, they say. And, by extension, everything is. Your version of your favourite food is as authentic as mine, even though the two of them may be wildly different from each other. Often, these naysayers argue, our versions or definitions of authenticity are formed by our childhood introductions to those foods, clothes or other markers. It's the way a particular dish was made in your parents' kitchen that automatically becomes your idea of the authentic version.

So, no one can claim theirs is the definitive authentic version. And by extension everyone can claim theirs is. Authenticity as a concept is thus inherently false and meaningless.

Very good points all of them. And yet, and yet…

Food, like language, is one of the most important and obvious markers of cultural identity. And food, like language and culture, is intensely political. Authenticity, then, is not just a nice, catch-all term. For some, it becomes a matter of survival. Let me elaborate.

In fact, let me go back to my Punjabi friend, the one who loves chicken chowmein parathas and I'm sure would not blink even if I suggested we eat momos with makki ki roti. I love her, obviously, but I also envy the self-assurance with which she navigates the world. She is so sure of her place, the place of her culture, her language, her clothes, her food in the world she inhabits that she is open to everything. Nothing is a threat.

By contrast, to someone who comes from a people torn apart by conflict for generations, someone who is unsure of everything, including whether or not they will return home alive in the evening, everything is a threat. Every time someone tries to add a bay leaf to 'my food', it feels like a direct assault precisely because so much of what comprises 'my identity' is already under threat. Kashmiris often talk about their identities being diluted through an erasure of everything that makes them distinct. This includes their language, what they wear, how they sing, celebrate and mourn, what they write, how they read, and above all what they cook and how they eat.

When I was growing up, Kashmiri wasn't taught in schools, though I understand this has changed now. Pherans had given way to shalwar kameezes, and brides wore lehenga cholis on their big days. But one thing that has not changed is our food. It has sometimes been stripped down, as it was during long curfewed months to be sure, but the essentials are still the same. The rogan josh I make in my tiny little kitchen in London is exactly the same as my mother made in her various kitchens, in Kashmir and outside, and her mother made on a wooden stove in hers. It's mine, ours, and I'm sorry but you cannot add tomatoes, bay leaves and garam masala powder to it. Thanks.

And sure, of course food, like every other marker of identity, evolves over time. It must, if it wants to survive. My grandmother cooked over a mud stove fired by wood. My mother on a gas stove attached to a cylinder. My little kitchen in London has a gas hob and an electric oven. And sure, of course there were times, especially when we no longer lived in Kashmir, when my mother had to improvise – regular chillies instead of Kashmiri chillies, brown cumin instead of black, onions instead of shallots – something I end up doing too.

What is also true is that there are regional variations in how Kashmiri food is cooked. Sometimes the same dish will be cooked somewhat differently even in the same region. Kashmiri Pandits and Muslims will use different spices for the same dish.

The point is that variation, improvisation, innovation even, is not a problem as long as it comes from within. As far as most Kashmiris are concerned, all of these variations and versions are authentic.

I have had conversations with some of my Palestinian friends about why it is important to preserve exactly how a particular dish is cooked, and the parallels and the echoes are fascinating.

And of course while there is much that's different between Kashmiris and Palestinians, and their respective situations, in a world where they seem to have such little control over their individual and collective lives and lands, where from their point of view, every marker of their identity seems to make them a target, food is one thing they still have control over. One thing they can reject. One thing they can preserve. One thing they can pass on to future generations.

So, although my son was born and has lived all his life in London, even he knows that there are no tomatoes in rogan josh. Because that wouldn't be authentic. And at this point authenticity is the only thing we have.

## Rogan Josh – Our Family Recipe

### Ingredients

1 kg lamb (You could use any cut, but chops are great – meat, fat, bone. Oh yeah.)
3–4 shallots, medium, finely sliced
3–4 fat cloves of garlic, minced
1 inch ginger root, minced (optional)
400–500g yoghurt
Oil for cooking (I use olive oil but vegetable oil is fine. As is ghee. Whatever rocks your boat.)

*Whole spices:* (*Note:* Kashmiri cooking is all about whole spices)

5 black cardamoms (because odd numbers are better than even. Yup.)
5–7 green cardamoms
2–3 black peppercorns
1 clove
1–2 tsp cumin seeds
1 inch stick of cassia

*Ground spices:*

1–2 tsp fennel powder
1–2 tsp turmeric
1–2 tsp Kashmiri red chilli powder
salt to taste

**Method**

1. Use a thick-bottomed pan, big enough for the amount of lamb. Once the pan is hot, add a generous amount of oil. Add the shallots and cook on a high flame for a few minutes until they are soft and translucent.
2. Add the meat and fry until golden brown.
3. Add all the whole spices and fry until it all smells gorgeous (around 5–6 minutes). If you, like my son, don't like 'seeds' in your curry or prefer a slightly more intense flavour, then all you need to do is dry roast the whole spices (except cassia) and grind them in a pestle and mortar before adding to the meat. Boom.
4. Next, add all of the ground spices to the pan and fry. Add garlic and ginger. Stir well, making sure to coat all of your meat with the spices.
5. Now is the time to start adding the yoghurt to the pan, a little at a time, making sure its cooked down completely before adding more.
6. Once all the yoghurt is added and cooked down, add a cup of water and bring the pan to a boil. Add salt to taste. Let it cook on a high flame for a couple of minutes before turning the heat right down.
7. Put the lid on and forget about it for about an hour and a half until the meat is terribly tender and falling off the bone, and the gravy is rich and thick and beautiful.
8. Garnish with fresh coriander and serve with lots of steamed white rice.

# Preserving Traditions of Love among Odia Muslims

*Sheikh Intekhab Alam*

I always felt annoyed, walking through the village lanes to some relative's house, lugging the bakhra – a large tiffin wrapped in shiny cloth – my new, pristine white, Eid kurta pajama in imminent danger of getting soiled. Our parents sent us children to distribute food, a practice in our Odia Muslim community which had the benefit of acquainting youngsters with their relatives and learning appropriate social behaviour. Children were taught what to say and what not to say, how to make sure the bakhra remained intact, and other niceties. Food was also sent to the houses of relatives with whom we had some misgiving. It was thought that when they saw the children with food, their hearts would melt. They would accept the food, maybe give Eidi and hopefully the bakhra would serve to revive relationships. Sometimes the offerings were turned away by irate relatives and we had to know how to conduct ourselves in such a fraught situation. Especially elaborate dishes were sent to the houses of the girls from our family – aunts, sisters and daughters – because of the fragility of those relationships. We were also sent with bakhra to the homes of those with whom we wished to foster new relationships, perhaps with a view to sending a marriage proposal later on. We were told that we were entrusted with the duty because we were intelligent enough to restore or reinforce the delicate balance of relationships.

At the centre of every relationship was the all-important food offering – the bakhra. Bakhra, a cultural practice unique to Odia Muslims, is a custom of making and distributing food during festivals and other important family events. This custom is attributed to Islamic teachings, because in many hadiths the distribution of food to relatives is encouraged. The process would include almost every member of a household – men would make sure all the ingredients were available on the set day, while women would be responsible for cooking it, and we children would be assigned the duty of distributing it.

A typical bakhra consists of a full meal, including dessert, being sent to families and friends, especially during such festivals as Eid ul-Fitr, Eid ul-Adha and Eid Milad un-Nabi, as well as for weddings and family celebrations. Even in the month of Muharram, which is essentially a time of mourning, dishes like haleem and maleeda are prepared and distributed. The focus here is on the distribution and not just the preparation of food. Even today, Odia Muslims consider this custom so crucial that no event is complete without it.

My father told me that for the relatives living far away, professional bakhra carriers were engaged in our village, who then traversed rivers on boats to convey the precious bundle safely. Odisha frequently experiences heavy rains and floods. Notwithstanding these treacherous climatic conditions, people use special means, like palm tree leaves, to protect the food from rain. The loved ones would feel that they were remembered on the special occasion and would find themselves drawn into the ambit of familial affection.

The practice of showing gratitude by feeding others in order to achieve *barkat* or prosperity is so integral to the Odia Muslim community that Ammi continued it after our family migrated to Delhi. We would be asked to give bakhra to our neighbours, the tiffin carriers reflecting the size and appetites of the recipient family.

The bakhra offering was prepared with care. The eating habits and dietary requirements of each family member had to be taken into consideration when it came to the choice of dishes and spices. The bakhra would be lavish for the son-in-law's family even after years of marriage. The tiffin and wooden utensils would be wrapped in a special ostentatious cloth. Both the food and its attractive packaging reflects respect and love for the receiver.

One dish that is often included in the bakhra is a chicken curry. To prepare it, a whole chicken is chopped into pieces and put in warm water to make it easier to pluck out the feathers. The chicken pieces are then roasted in a wood-burning chulha until they turn a golden brown; haldi (turmeric) is then applied to the meat. Odia cuisine uses the basic spices so that the taste of the meat is not overwhelmed by the masalas. We strongly advocate the preparation of the haldi and other spices on a sil-batta, or grinding stone, to retain the best taste. Of course, pre-packaged ground spices are readily available in the market – and are used sometimes for ease – but, for a special occasion, the sil-batta is the only way. Elders would often comment on the lazy daughter-in-law if store-bought masalas were used in the curry.

Odia Muslims are either immigrants from Bengal – settling into the region during the period of the Bengal Sultanate – or converts from the local population. Oral history says that there was large-scale migration from Murshidabad after the defeat of Siraj ud-Daulah at the Battle of Plassey in 1757. Even today, we Muslims speak a style of Urdu at home which is called *Murshidabadi mahal ki zuban*, the courtly language of Murshidabad. Odia Muslims residing in Odisha are currently about 2 per cent of the total population concentrated around the cities of Bhadrak – which is near my village – Cuttack, Jajpur, Khurda and Bhubaneshwar. An important feature of Odia Muslim cuisine is a shared food culture across socio economic strata – all eat the same types of food, with non-vegetarian dishes featuring alongside vegetarian ones – as well as the adaptation of local foodways.

In Odisha, everyone – Muslim and non-Muslim – takes their fish very seriously. Though the fish eaten is from the sea, those from a *pokhar* (pond) or a *nadi* (river) are preferred as they are considered more delicious and healthier than seafood. Like Bengalis, our favourite fish is hilsa. However, my mother started cooking rohu when we shifted to Delhi as it was easily available and had fewer bones. Prawns, lobsters and other seafood are also found in Odisha's coastal areas – indeed, these days, they are even farmed. Though they are expensive, they are boneless and tasty. Seafood is more expensive in Delhi and a rare family treat. Muslim households prepare prawns and lobsters in a distinct manner; due care is taken in shelling, removal of the head and cleaning the stomach. As with the other Odia dishes, the cooking of these foods is quite simple, meaning that they can be prepared almost instantly. Especially when preparing fish, a small amount of spices is used so as to ensure that the fish does not lose its original taste. Fish and seafood is either prepared with gravy or simply fried. Wooden utensils were used to fry the fish as it was considered to retain the taste. This practice has now declined even in the villages.

For dessert, zarda pulao, or sweet rice, is a food common in Muslim households throughout the length and breadth of Odisha. It is prepared for various festivals and weddings. That said, as Odisha food is incomplete without a generous helping of dessert, many other sweets are prepared and consumed. Some sweets are particular to festivals and observances, which include various types of halwas and maleeda made of wheat flour mixed with ghee, jaggery, dried fruits and nuts.

With its geographical location on the east coast of India, it may be surprising that Odisha cuisine has Arab influence as well. A particularly delicious dish adapted from Arab cuisines is taraza, also known as sukha gosht. Taraza is basically dried meat, which is marinated in zeera (cumin), garlic, mustard seeds, fenugreek seeds and mustard oil and then fried. What is distinctive about this dish is that it can be preserved for a long time without a change to the taste, making it ideal for a long journey. We don't get this meat in Delhi – so, when our relatives used to come from our village, they would bring taraza with them and Ammi would cook it for us.

Pakhal bhat prepared from soaking the leftover rice overnight in madh (rice water) and water is the staple breakfast dish across all communities. It is a simple meal often accompanied by taraza and aloo chutney or a vegetable chutney. Rice used to be eaten thrice a day in our homes because it was considered to have a cooling effect on the stomach. In Delhi we sometimes enjoy pakhal bhat during the summer months. Gradually we have started eating wheat rotis, which has changed the texture of the meal completely. While rice required several gravies and chutneys, roti can be eaten with a single gravy or dal.

My Ammi had to make major changes in the way she cooked food in Delhi. The bainthi had always been Ammi's go-to item of food cutting equipment. The bainthi required her to sit and cut – a practice she continues to this day – but she had to stand and cook using the gas stove. Another important tool is the pathri or grinding stone that is used for making chutney – for example, mirch ki chatni, methi ki chatni, aloo ki chatni, sukhe huye gosht ki chatni, sukhe huye machli ki chatni ... the list goes on! On our roof we still have a mud chulha like the one she had in the village, and we use it during the winter. Prepared food items used to be stored in a neymat khana or a wire mesh cupboard to protect them from pests and insects. There is no place for the neymat khana in our Delhi kitchen. Our dining table has taken the place of the neymat khana, and we barely have enough space to eat our meals.

We Odia Muslims used to eat on the dastarkhwan, often serving food – rice and chutneys – with our bare hands when eating with family members. Moreover, after moving to live in colonies and apartments, Ammi had to be careful about not offending her neighbours by cooking strong-smelling food like dried fish. We rarely cook such foods in Delhi. Every year, around the time of Dussehra, our parents would buy dried fruits and spices like alsi, kalonji, ajwain and hing from Balli Maran spice market in Old Delhi, because being from a coastal region we are all susceptible to colds. We often shop for our kinds of fish, vegetables and spices at the C. R. Park markets which cater to Bengalis. Ammi and Abba miss the various leafy saags we used to eat in the village. We tried unsuccessfully to grow them in pots. Ammi attempts to get her favourite red saag from the vegetable vendors; sometimes she gets lucky. The vendors haven't seen or heard of most of our saags which used to grow so plentifully in every house in our village.

Our visits to the village have become rare over the years. Despite this, we still initiate friendships, maintain relationships and express our love and respect with the elaborately packed, sumptuous bakhra offering.

## Butter Garlic Prawns

**Ingredients**

1 kg prawns
250 ml vegetable oil
1 tsp ginger paste
1 tsp garlic paste
2 tsp mustard seeds paste
½ tsp garam masala
2 large pieces of chopped onion
100g butter
salt to taste

**Method**

1. Clean and wash the prawns and apply some salt to them. Set aside for 5 minutes, then wash.
2. Marinate the prawns with ginger–garlic paste, mustard seeds paste and salt to taste for 10–15 minutes.
3. Heat oil and fry chopped onions in a kadhai (deep pan or wok) till golden brown.
4. Add the marinated prawns on low flame and shallow-fry.
5. Turn over the prawns and make sure that they are well fried on both sides. When they change colour, switch off the flame. Add butter and garam masala.
6. Serve hot in a bowl and garnish with coriander leaves.

## Odia Prawn Curry

**Ingredients**

1 kg raw prawns
200 ml mustard oil
3 tbsp turmeric and salt paste
1 large onion, chopped
1 large onion for paste
2 medium tomatoes, chopped
2-inch piece cinnamon
4 cardamoms
1 tsp turmeric powder
2 tsp coriander powder
1 tsp cumin seeds
3 tsp ginger–garlic paste

salt to taste
a handful of coriander leaves to garnish

**Method**

1. Clean the prawns and wash thoroughly.
2. Marinate prawns in turmeric and salt paste for 15 minutes.
3. Heat mustard oil in a kadhai (deep pan or wok) on a medium flame.
4. Add chopped onion and fry until golden brown.
5. Add cinnamon sticks and cardamom.
6. Add turmeric powder, dhania powder and zeera powder.
7. Add ginger–garlic paste.
8. Add chopped tomatoes, mix thoroughly and sauté all ingredients in the pan together.
9. Add enough boiled water to the pan to cook the tomatoes well. Sauté until the oil starts to separate.
10. Add prawns and fry on low heat for around 10 minutes.
11. Spoon the prawn curry into a dish and garnish with coriander leaves.
12. Serve hot with steamed rice.

# An Ode to Street Food Vendors

*Sadaf Hussain*

I was standing outside my house in Ramgarh, Jharkhand, when Raju Bhai walked up. On his head, as always, was his pani puri khomcha and on his left shoulder a wooden stand. His pani puris, what we called gupchup, were delicious but that wasn't the only reason I admired Raju Bhai. He also had enviable knife skills. Before serving pani puris, he would teach me how to dice onions.

To a great extent, I have learnt cooking from small dhaba owners and street vendors like Raju Bhai. Each time I visit the Chindian noodle or samosa-jalebi seller near my home, I learn how to make sweet batter or stuffing or something unexpected. Besides delicious food, they create permanent memories and flavours that reside on the palate forever.

I always loved street food but my respect for it grew when I moved from Ramgarh to Delhi. In the lanes of Malviya Nagar and Purani Dilli – two places that offer a range of street food, from Mughlai and Afghan to Bihari, Punjabi and Kashmiri – I became a student of it. I began to see patterns. I saw that urbanisation and migration had left inexorable imprints on food in the megacity. In Purani Dilli, Lucknow's nimish or makhan malai was being prepared by a migrant from Bihar or Madhya Pradesh. In Chittaranjan Park, the ghugni served by a Bengali migrant used the same yellow matar that was used in chhole kulche by another migrant in another part of the city.

Another common thread I found was history. A lot of the street food we enjoy today in Delhi can be traced back to the time Shahjahanabad was built. Muslims, Baniyas, Jats, Gujjars and others were settling in the walled city, and erecting stalls to serve their traditional food. The result was a panoply of cuisines. The term 'street food' – 'ready-to-eat food and beverages sold and sometimes prepared on the streets' – may have been first agreed upon in 1986 at the FAO Regional Workshop on Street Food in Asia. However, according to Chef Davinder Kumar, Vice President F&B Production, Le Meridian in New Delhi and President Indian Culinary Forum:

> The roots of street food can take us way back into history. It is believed that as the first distribution point of street food, small fried fish were sold on the streets in ancient Greece. Street food was widely consumed by poor urban residents of ancient Rome whose tenement homes did not have ovens or hearths. In ancient China, where street foods generally catered to the poor, wealthy residents would send servants to buy street foods and bring meals back for their masters to eat in their homes. Urbanisation and street food go hand-in-hand. Historically, in places such as ancient Rome, street food was purchased because urban poor did not have kitchens in their homes.

In an article for the *Hindustan Times*, columnist Vir Sanghvi wrote: 'In most cities, street food originated as a way for poor people to feed themselves or as a means of providing sustenance to those who worked odd hours.' This is why it is so easy to find street food outside offices and factories.

## Fruits of creativity

The rich often have a bias against street food – they think it something cheap meant for blue-collar workers or that it is a class of foods classified as chaat. Neither could be further from the truth. Just take a trip to Purani Dilli. You'd be surprised to see how many people with different sartorial styles and bank balances queue up to gorge on scrumptious parathas, kababs, butter chicken, biryani. In fact, several old institutions of Delhi – Karim's, Moti Mahal, Aslam Butter Chicken, Old Famous Jalebi Wala, Hira Lal Chaat Bhandar, Kuremal Kulfi, Roshan Kulfi Wala and many others – started out as street vendors. Today, people from all over the world queue up at these places.

I find street food refreshingly creative. In Old Delhi, Kuremal Mohan Lal Kulfi Wale cores fruit and pipes in kulfi to create an all-natural ice cream. In Old Delhi too, you can find a blend of Rooh Afza, milk and watermelon called mohabbat ka sharbat (love potion). Street foods like these have inspired numerous chefs, including Anahita Dhondy, Vineet Bhatia, Vikas Khanna, Atul Kochar and Saransh Goila. A while back, I asked Kalyan Karmakar, author of *The Travelling Belly*, why restaurants in India serve 'elevated street food'. He said these dishes do not travel in the globalised world, but well-travelled diners with urbane palates demand these flavours, which pushes restaurants to curate them. I agree with his hypothesis.

I asked Kalyan to suggest a city for a fantastic culinary experience. His reply: it has to be Kolkata. He made me understand the flavours of the city by listing the people who have made the beautiful city their home – from the Chinese and Armenians to Muslims and the British. Every culture brought its own recipes, which, in my opinion, can now be collectively termed Bengali Zaika (Flavours of Calcutta).

The main rule for eating Indian street food is to unlearn fancy food etiquette. Touch and feel the food, become aware of how it smells and feels, thank the creator, create a bond with them, and then use your hands again to feel the soul of the food.

## Qeema Samosa

### Ingredients

*For the qeema filling:*

500g ground meat, lamb or mutton (80 per cent meat: 20 per cent fat)
½ cup curd
¼ cup ghee

*Spices:*

2 tbsp ginger–garlic paste
1 tbsp coriander, roasted and powdered
1 tbsp cumin, roasted and powdered
1 tbsp red chilli powder
1 tsp garam masala powder
½ tsp turmeric powder
1½ tsp salt, or to taste

*Other ingredients:*

2 cups onion, finely chopped. Only measure after squeezing out excess onion water.
½ cup spring onion, finely chopped
¼ cup green coriander, chopped
4 tbsp mint leaves, chopped
2 tbsp lemon juice
4–6 tbsp green chillies, finely chopped
28 samosa patti (spring roll wraps)
extra water to seal the edges
oil, to deep-fry

**Method**

1. Mix curd with all of the spices. Taste to ensure there is a balance of flavour.
2. Add the ground meat. Mix well and set aside for 30 minutes.
3. In a deep pot, heat some ghee and add the marinated meat.
4. Cook for 20–25 minutes on medium heat or until everything is well cooked and the water has evaporated. Remove from heat.
5. Immediately add all the remaining ingredients, including onion, spring onion, green coriander, mint leaves and green chillies, to the hot qeema. Mix thoroughly and then leave to cool.
6. Fill and fold the samosa with prepared filling and seal the ends with water. Try to make a triangle.
7. Fry the samosas over medium heat for 3 minutes until they are golden and crispy. Ensure there is enough room in the frying pan.
8. Once cooked, place the fried samosa on a paper towel to soak up any remaining oil.
9. Serve hot with green chutney.

# Dishoom!

*Claire Chambers*

To enter an Irani cafe in Mumbai is to enter a bygone era. These cafes may not be as popular as they were in their heyday in the mid-twentieth century. Moreover, their numbers have declined dramatically from around 350 in the 1960s to scarcely thirty. But they remain as spaces of geniality. You can still visit them for a cutting chai with snacks like khari biscuits and buttered buns without ripping a big hole in the wallet.

Interest in Irani cafes has grown in the British South Asian diaspora because of the outrageously popular restaurant Dishoom. The doors of the first Dishoom opened in London's Covent Garden in 2010, and the restaurant was refurbished for its tenth birthday in 2020. Its growing popularity over the past decade led to the setting up of four more establishments in various districts of London, each with its own style and imagined backstory, but all paying homage to the Irani cafe. This success also prompted a migration to other British cities: Edinburgh, Manchester and now Birmingham.

Dishoom opened its 'godown' in a cavernous former railway building at King's Cross in 2014. I discovered it as a place to while away a few hours as I waited for the train back to my home in the north of England. However, it quickly became my happy place.

Why do I find Dishoom so pleasing? It starts with the name, an onomatopoeic word for a punch or smack. Then there is the food, always flavourful and well presented. Bringing the idea together is the decor: tiled floors, an imposing station clock, vintage luggage scales and references to Indian cinema on the walls. Lounging on Dishoom's rattan chairs recalls languorous punkahs turning in subcontinental homes, and an ice-cold glass of nimbu pani on sweltering afternoons.

I am reminded of the probably apocryphal story of the early refugees from Iran coming to India and stirring sugar into milk. These would-be settlers had been sent an overbrimming glass of milk by local authorities to indicate that the area was full and they were not welcome. The Parsis stirred in the sugar to respond that they would blend in, but also sweeten and improve society. I've always thought that this is a beautiful story with much to say about migrants, hostility and hybridity.

In the British establishments, a nostalgia for the Bombay Irani cafe of the 1960s is at once poignant and humorous. Signs speak to the diners in Indian English or exuberant Devanagari script. The King's Cross establishment is lined with dark wood and warm 'Chilli-man-green' walls, making it easy to forget the all-too-British wind and rain outside. Hole-in-the-wood toilets are another reminder of the subcontinent.

## Father's approval

The team behind Dishoom – cousins and co-CEOs Shamil Thakrar and Kavi Thakrar, alongside their head chef Naved Nasir – published a book in 2019 entitled *Dishoom: From Bombay with Love*. As a recipe book, this would have been exciting enough, for it divulges the secrets behind Dishoom signatures from akuri to their cocktail, the East India Gimlet. Yet, as its title suggests, the volume is also a love letter to the western metropolis of Mumbai or Bombay.

In an interview, Uttar Pradesh native Nasir told me his story. He had been making a name for himself as a chef in Aurangabad,

Maharashtra, when in 2009, a colleague introduced him to the Thakrars. He made the life-changing decision to move to London to work in the new Indian restaurant they were setting up because as an ambitious chef, he 'wanted to perform on the world stage'.

An anecdote is recounted early in the book about Nasir's reservations about the restaurant's name. When I ask why at first he wasn't convinced, he tells me that he and his friends had laughed about it and thought Dishoom didn't make sense. The trend at the time was to name restaurants after spices: saffron (kesar), cumin (zeera), cinnamon (dalchini) and so on. But now he believes the place lives up to its brand name, given its palpable affection for Bombay and the golden age of Hindi cinema.

Nasir never meant to be a chef. His father was a doctor and wanted his son to continue in the family profession. The young man dutifully enrolled in medicine and, failing that, went to college to become a pharmacist. Unfortunately, he soon found he couldn't progress in the world of healthcare. His mother made her peace with his subsequent decision to go to a catering school in Delhi. Yet the father was so upset that he never shared another meal with Nasir in the years before his death in 2012. Despite the chef's successes – the awards, magazine articles and interviews – he felt a failure as a son. Even today, Nasir laments, 'I let my father down big time.'

His mother comes from an aristocratic family with roots in a village near Meerut in Uttar Pradesh. When they would go back to the ancestral home for holidays, his maternal relatives had three cooks who between them were experts in most Indian cuisines. One of them was a ninja at making shami kababs and koftas. From a young age, Nasir would watch him and help for hours with pounding meat and mixing it with spices and other ingredients.

He finds it impossible to identify a favourite recipe from the book, declaring that to do so would be like choosing between your children. However, he acknowledges that Dishoom's slow-cooked and creamy black dal (the restaurant's name for dal makhani) is close to his heart. Whenever he visits one of the restaurants' kitchens, he has to check this pan first, since the dal is his barometer of everything being in order.

When the conversation veers to his preferred regional cuisine, Nasir tells me that north Indian food is underrated, unrecognised and often misunderstood. Its gustatory culture is more complex and, for want of a better word, cooler than the grand, meat-heavy 'Mughlai cuisine' most people automatically associate with it. He points to the wedding feast in north India as an example, describing with relish the savoury biryani mixed with sweet zarda rice, and the elaborate qormas which guests are routinely served at these celebrations.

In some of the closing lines to *Dishoom: From Bombay with Love*, the authors write:

> We can offer no guarantee that this highly subjective and personal guide has covered the important bits of Bombay, or the most important parts of its history. Some will point out things that we've missed, dishes that we just had to eat but didn't. Others may tell us that it's all a bit incoherent, a mish-mash of stories, foods and cuisines; still others will say that it is all too rose-tinted a view of a challenging city. Perhaps it is.

While the British Asian Thakrars look at Bombay through the rose-tinted spectacles of visits to their grandmother's home during childhood holidays, Nasir's memories are more current and reflect the city's challenging side.

After catering college, he worked in one of Delhi's (and India's) most famous restaurants, Bukhara at the ITC Maurya Hotel. From there, he moved to Bombay, maturing and growing as a chef. At first, he hated the Maharashtrian conurbation, missing home and the north of India, which he could only afford to visit once or twice a year. He recalls the tribulations of travelling in Mumbai and, out of frustration, attempting the long commute on foot.

However, in the second half of his time in Mumbai, Nasir got bitten by the bug of this enchanting city and began 'to see past first impressions'. After finishing his shift at 2 a.m., he would ride together with a friend on his motorbike, revelling in the empty roads, to go and sit in front of the Hilton. He would give fifty rupees to some chaiwallahs and ask them to keep refilling his glass till sunrise. Then he would head for home and a few hours of sleep before the next cooking period began. 'Those were the most beautiful memories of the city.' He confesses that he cried when he moved away.

Now he happily finds himself back there at least twice a year. Dishoom takes everyone who has been promoted or worked in the restaurant for five years for Bombay Bootcamp. This is a foodie's tour of the megalopolis led by Kavi Thakrar, as well as Nasir himself. Initiates discover that Mumbai is a city of contradictions. Here the rooftop terraces of five-star hotels and fine dining restaurants frequently overlook slums.

## Culinary connections

Nasir never thought much of Irani cafes when they were plentiful. But with time, things look sweeter. He remembers a place in Malabar Hill that served superb food and afforded a spectacular view of the Queen's Necklace or Marine Drive, that road tracing part of the Arabian Sea coastline. This cafe may be gone today, 'but we have our memories'.

The loss of India's rich food heritage is painful. The Dishoom team was left bereft in 2019 at the death of Boman Kohinoor, the founder of Britannia & Co., at the age of ninety-seven. For them, the main focus of any visit to the Ballard Estate restaurant was a conversation with its proprietor. It is uncertain what will happen to the restaurant now. Such places sit on prime real estate, so often younger generations have no financial incentive to continue their legacy.

There exists nothing like the very organised French cooking schools when it comes to Indian food. As a result, a wealth of knowledge is lost when each senior khansama dies. Nasir himself learnt under the tutelage of master chef Imitiaz Qureshi (born 1931). Once he is gone, Nasir worries, the nonagenarian's knowledge will die with him – especially his encyclopaedic understanding of north Indian food from the days of the British Raj. Younger chefs don't have the patience for traditional epicurean rigours, preferring instead the safety of fusion and fast food.

In the book's introduction, there is a discussion of celebrating Ramzan and Janmashtami together at Dishoom. Nasir insists that food helps people to get past religious and cultural divisions. Partaking in a communal dining experience creates a remarkable opportunity to bridge divides and foster connections among individuals. This is especially important in settings where social hierarchies and religious customs hinder close interactions. Nasir drew this valuable lesson from Olympia Coffee House, one of his favourite Mumbai Irani cafes, whose four-chair arrangements at round tables are often occupied by strangers from different religions.

Back in London, when Dishoom puts on its Eid celebrations, half the people who turn up are non-Muslims. Similarly, for Diwali, a majority of attendees are not Hindu. The world, especially India and Britain, needs this kind of culinary conviviality now more than ever.

## DISHOOM'S BLACK DAL

### Ingredients

300g urad dal (whole, not split – or, if unavailable, I use beluga lentils)
4 litres cold water
12g garlic paste
10g ginger paste
70g tomato puree
8g fine sea salt
⅔ tsp deggi mirch chilli powder
⅓ tsp garam masala
90g unsalted butter
90 ml double cream
chapatis, to serve

### Method

1. Put the dal into a large bowl, cover with water and whisk for 10 seconds. Let the dal settle, then pour out the water. Repeat three or four times, until the water is clear. Tip the dal into a large saucepan and pour in at least four litres of cold water. Bring to a boil and cook steadily for two to three hours. Skim off any impurities that rise to the surface, and add more boiling water as required to keep the grains well covered. The dal grains need to become completely soft, with the skins coming away from the white grain. When pressed, the white part should be creamy, rather than crumbly. When cooked, turn off the heat and set aside for 15 minutes.

2. In a bowl, mix the garlic and ginger pastes, tomato puree, salt, chilli powder and garam masala into a paste.
3. Carefully pour off the dal cooking water, then pour on enough freshly boiled water to cover the dal by 3–4 cm. Bring to a boil over a medium–high heat, then add the aromatic paste and butter. Cook rapidly for 30 minutes, stirring regularly to prevent the mixture from sticking.
4. Lower the heat and simmer for one to one and a half hours more, stirring regularly to prevent it from sticking, and adding a little boiling water if the liquid level gets near the level of the grains. Eventually, the dal will turn thick and creamy. The creaminess must come from the grains disintegrating into the liquid and enriching it, not from the water being allowed to evaporate, leaving only the grains behind.
5. Add the cream and cook for a further 15 minutes. Serve with chapatis or other Indian breads. When reheating any leftover dal, you may need to add a little more liquid; use cream or cream and water, rather than just water alone.

# Kabul Night in Berlin

*Razak Khan*

*Az tu duram manu divanah vu madhush-i tu am*

I am far away from you,
Driven mad by longing, I am not in possession of my own self

It was a lazy, sunny July evening in Berlin. After months of Covid restrictions, I decided to go for a leisurely walk around the beautiful Rehberge park in the district of Wedding. I headed back through the sunburnt grass fields to the U6 Seestrasse train station, crossing the 'African Quarter' (*Das Afrikanische Viertel*), with Kameruner Strasse and then Kongostrasse and other German colonial remnants commemorated in the street names of the neighbourhood. I could not help but wonder about the social life '... of the colonised, the refugees and migrants in contemporary Berlin.'

Lost in my thoughts, I was distracted by the velvety voice of the legendary singer Ahmad Zahir issuing forth from a newly opened Afghan restaurant, Kabul Night, on Müllerstrasse. 'Az tu duram' is an iconic Dari song memorably sung by Ahmad Zahir for the album *Shab-i hijran* (Evening of Exile). I spent the rest of the evening listening to Zahir's melodious love songs while sipping safran chai and eating Afghani food in the restaurant. I wondered if the longing in the song 'Az Tu Duram' was also about love-torn yearning for Afghanistan and not just for the beloved left behind. I sat under the chandeliers and bright lights of Kabul Night on even glitzier Afghan furniture surrounded by old German-Afghan families and young Afghan refugees. They have been gradually turning this new restaurant into a hub of Afghan socialising in Berlin.

In what follows I will explore a history of forgotten food, longing and healing with the culinary heritage of Afghans in Berlin. Taran Khan has written about the 'map of arriving' of Afghan refugees in Germany. I wish to add food geographies to these histories of arriving, making home and departures in Germany. In the process, I hope to connect food history to the history of migration, refugees and belonging in exile in Berlin.

When I moved to Berlin from Delhi in 2010, the Wedding district was pitched as the next hipster part of the city. A decade later, this remains an unfulfilled prophecy. Wedding may have a dearth of the bio kale brunch places or craft beer bars found in Kreuzberg and Neukölln. Yet what it lacks in ever-changing, contemporary, on-trend food consumerism is more than compensated by its rich history and legacy of subaltern migrant food culture. Historically a working-class district, Wedding remains a truly multicultural space of what I call 'post-German speaking' Berlin. Already in the 1920s, Weimar Berlin attracted Arab, Turkish, Indian, Iranian and Afghan students, modernists and revolutionaries. Layers of post-war Turkish and Kurdish Gastarbeiter (guest worker) migration followed by refugee resettlements have made Wedding home to Kurdish, Sri Lankan, Iranian, Pakistani, Afghan and Syrian migrants. Each migrant community has added new flavours to these geographies of food and memory. My focus in this essay will be on the Afghan eateries Kabul Night restaurant and Barakat restaurant and food supermarket on the historic Müllerstrasse of Wedding district in Berlin.

Sahil Warsi, in his affective ethnography of Afghan refugees in Jangpura, Delhi, writes about how food provided not just nourishment but also emotional comfort and a feeling of sociality and solidarity (*hambastagi*) to Afghan migrants in Delhi.

Hambastagi is an important political, cultural and emotional concept that one also encounters among Afghan migrants in Berlin. I heard this word both when dining in restaurants and at political protest marches as well as in Afghan refugees' mental health support and healing group meetings in Berlin. Indeed, Hambastagi is the name of a global Afghan solidarity and resistance party and movement against the Taliban. The politics of protest provide a shared emotion of solidarity on the street; a shared meal does the same in a restaurant. Food not only has a history but also connects with contemporary politics, particularly among Afghan refugee communities.

How do displaced people and communities make home again? What are the everyday new emotional concepts and practices through which they adapt to their new environment and culture that are different from and often at odds with their cultural inheritance? How does a person rediscover the emotional ties with the culture and country that they left behind? I found the archives of such an affective history in restaurants and food markets, which provided one among many rich arenas for mapping the history and politics of migration and food.

## From Herat to Berlin: Food as archive and history of migration

I have known Reza Ahmadi, who manages Kabul Night restaurant, for over four years now. We developed a quick friendship as I was one of the earliest visitors at Kabul Night. We spoke informally during this time. A formal interview was finally conducted with his permission over safran tea on 26 September 2021.

Reza Ahmadi was a young boy when his parents moved from Herat to the Netherlands as refugees. He grew up in the small Dutch town of Schagen near Rotterdam but retained his memories of Herat, especially the food. When Reza decided to pursue a career in the restaurant industry, he knew he wanted to eventually open his own Afghan restaurant. However, he began working at an Indian-Pakistani restaurant and learnt about South Asian cuisine, developing a taste for spicy biryani and curries. He carried these accumulated culinary memories when he moved to Berlin to be with his Afghan wife (who also brought with her memories of Afghan food and culture) and to build a new home and restaurant together.

Reza stressed this mixed history of Afghan origins, a European upbringing and his love for Indian food as guiding influences on him. He articulated a lot of thoughts (*bisiar fikr mikunam*) and took advice (*mashvarat*) before finalising the menu of his own new restaurant. The results reflect this careful attention to detail.

Ahmadi used the word for pleasant memory (*yaad*) to convey the joy of remembering food from Afghanistan. He carried a nostalgia for his childhood food as his guide. He consulted his parents, relatives and extended-family members in the diaspora and also visited Afghanistan several times. These deep emotions and sincere ideas underpinned the making of the eclectic menu of Kabul Night. The restaurant focuses on traditional food from various regions of Afghanistan, with specialties from Herat like okra and pumpkin curries (bamia kadu) as well as from Kabul, Mazar-i Sharif and Jalalabad.

I enquired about Iranian influences in the menu. While Reza admitted to an influence, he insisted that the same dish is available in Iran and Afghanistan, with Afghan variations such as berries rice (zirishk pulao/palu) and vegetarian dumplings (ashak). When it came to Indian cuisine (ghaza-i Hindi), he emphasised a shared culinary heritage but highlighted the differences in the making of meat broth (yaqni and paya), while also noting the influence of minced meat (qeema). Reza insisted that he aims to be authentic and yet adaptive (*man flexible daram*).

Qabuli pulao or ghabeli polow, translated into German by the Barakat restaurant as *Afghanishes Reisgerichte* (Afghan rice dish), is particularly interesting for its ingredients. It requires rich long-grain basmati rice, raisins, dried fruits and sheep meat from South Asia. Qabuli pulao separates and makes Afghan food distinct from the boiled rice and meat plov of Uzbekistan, safran rice of Iran and the greasy rice pulau of north India. I have always found dry rice biryanis overrated, and I value a nicely done boiled pulao rice. As Tarana Husain Khan has written about the migrant Afghans or Rohilla food culture in Rampur, India is famous for its legendary pulau and not for biryani. Pulao carries these shared and distinct migrant affective archives and global histories of Afghans.

Reza pointed out that increasing numbers of German diners prefer vegetarian and vegan options and less spicy, soupy options. Since Afghan food is typically dry, he improvised some plant-based options with curry. The result is a hybrid Afghan menu with an Indian touch but less spicy for the German palate. The Sunday brunch offers varieties of vegetarian options alongside non-vegetarian ones. Similar efforts went into the curation of the restaurant's aesthetics, including its photographs, chandeliers, utensils and the male leisure and music space (hujra, mausiqi khana). Careful selection provides not just the feel but the multisensorial atmosphere of Kabul Night in Berlin.

I asked Reza Ahmadi why he had named the restaurant Kabul Night. He paused and explained that he did it to honour his two mothers (*Madar-i man du-ta hast*): the one who gave birth to him and the other the land of his birth. Kabul Night monumentalises his bond with Afghanistan's capital city. A picture of an Afghan girl child in traditional costume adorns the wall of the Kabul Night restaurant. Ahmadi informed me that she was his daughter who studies in a German school. This prompted me to ask for his thoughts about German national integration. He shared his opinion that language integration is important for dialogue, but that openness is also important. It is with this view that he also serves European foods. At the same time, he maintains cultural and religious distinctions about halal food and non-alcoholic drinks. National integration should not come at the cost of cultural and religious difference and diversity.

This attention to cultural diversity and food norms quickly made the restaurant very popular among the Afghan diaspora as well as with the wider Persianate communities, including Indians, Pakistanis, Tajiks and Iranians, in addition to with Germans and other Berliners.

## Longing and belonging

The adaptation, transformation and persistence of Afghan food in Berlin attests to the value of studying migrant food as an affective archive. Specifically, while exploring culinary historical and political strands, it is equally important to understand that food is also a site of the affective. The concept of hambastagi is interesting and crucial precisely because it encapsulates the historical, political, cultural and emotional dimensions of this process. Hambastagi provides a new repertoire of social cohesion beyond the statist integration discourse and policy.

The emotionally turbulent summer of 2021 with the sudden Taliban takeover has been especially traumatic for Afghans – not just in Afghanistan, but also those who left the country decades ago. Many of my Afghan friends spoke to me about revisiting this trauma with mental and emotional distress. We also participated in a community help group for young migrants and in our workshop, asking people to write down words to encapsulate their feelings. The word hambastagi (a feeling of togetherness and solidarity), naan (Afghan bread), mausiqi (music) and Dari (an Afghan language) were among the many articulations of feelings of loss, helplessness and longing for Afghanistan in Berlin. This is an affective archive of loss but also of survival and healing. Food is central to thinking about the history of emotions, particularly home-making practices and physical and mental wellbeing in migrant communities. Food places also serve as sites of emotional nourishment.

I run a Dari language and Afghan music group, also named Hambastagi, in Berlin. During the particularly distressing time with the ongoing chaos in Kabul in 2021, we visited Kabul Night for an evening of comfort food. The dishes were both delicious and a source of solace and hope for many of my Afghan friends. This evening also helped us to connect on a deeper emotional level by sharing food.

Food often serves as the everyday archive of emotions, especially the longing for a time and place that many immigrants miss dearly. Food and not words can provide for this sense of loss. It seems to me that food carries not just the flavours of spice but also the flavours of place.

Food has a history, but it is also an archive. Kabul Night forms both a geography and a history of migration and homemaking in Berlin. And of longing and belonging in Berlin.

## Afterword and Recipe from Marjan Wardaki

The migrant labour force in diasporic restaurant kitchens is a well-studied phenomenon, but few accounts focus on the migrant's own engagement with food. Taste, smell and meal preparations as a practice can conjure up memories of a distant home and frequently serve as a tool to connect detached generations to a place their parents called home.

Growing up in such a migrant home, it was my grandmother's small kitchen that brought together a variety of different generations, genders and even new non-Afghan family members and friends to her small apartment in Bonn. Duties ranged from chopping and stirring to simply stealing food, all the while listening to the adults fervently discussing ongoing political developments in Afghanistan. I developed my foundation for cooking in this house and, as I grew up, felt confident enough to experiment with every possible recipe. Until this day, my kitchen table features Japanese and Korean as well as Indo-Afghan cuisine. What you find in this recipe, too, bridges traditional Afghan ingredients with French searing techniques borrowed from Julia

Child. Such customisation featured here allows the cook to lock in the meat's juices and maximise its flavour.

Similarly, in reducing the cinnamon, I have customised my own six-ingredient masala-yi pulao yielding a much more savoury flavour, rather than the usual warm and sweet one. In many ways, this is a recipe that reflects what we migrants do best, which is to learn to draw on our experiences and foundations to exist in the new and amorphous.

## Qabuli Pulao

**Ingredients**

cooking oil (I use avocado)
3–4 small cups white rice (my preference is Royal Basmati Rice or Aahu Barah Basmati Rice)
1.5 kg lamb or chicken pieces, on the bone (for lamb, you can use shoulder or leg cut into large chunks of approximately 2 inches/ 5 cm or shanks. For chicken, thighs and drumsticks work well.)
2–3 onions, medium, preferably red, minced very finely
1 whole head of garlic, peeled and minced
4 tsp masala-yi pulao. This powdered blend of spices includes: green cardamon, black cardamon, cloves, cinnamon stick, cumin and black pepper. It can be bought in any Afghan store.
salt and pepper to taste

*For the topping:*

carrots, thinly sliced
raisins
½ tsp sugar

*To do the night before:*

1. Thoroughly wash the rice in water and then place in a shallow dish. Cover well with fresh water. Add 2–3 tablespoons of salt to the rice and gently mix.
2. Leave the rice to sit overnight. The objective is to let the rice grains expand in the salt water to achieve elongated grains, rather than sticky rice.

*To do on the day:*

*Preparing the meat sauce:*

1. Dry the lamb or chicken with a paper towel and then lightly sprinkle with salt and pepper.
2. Heat up a large Dutch oven or a deep stainless-steel pot that can go in the oven. When hot, lightly coat the lamb or chicken pieces with oil and sear it on all sides. To ensure a nice brown crust, do not overcrowd the pan. If cooking with lamb, you can use the base of a pressure cooker to sear the meat. Once seared, set the lamb or chicken pieces aside.
3. Add 2–3 tablespoons of oil to the same pan and add the minced onions. There should be enough oil to barely cover the onions. Sauté the onions on high heat while constantly stirring until you achieve a golden-brown colour. The darker the onion, the deeper the colour of the rice, but it is important not to burn the onion.
4. Add the seared lamb or chicken pieces to the same pot and cook on medium high heat for 2–3 minutes. Add the minced garlic and keep stirring for another 1–2 minutes. Add 3 tsp of the masala-yi pulao powder and 1 tsp of salt to the meat and keep cooking for another minute or two. Lower the heat to low-medium.
5. If you are using lamb, all ingredients will need to be cooked in a pressure cooker from this point. Add 1½ cups of warm water and cook the meat for 20–30 minutes. If you are using chicken, it may be cooked in a regular deep pan. Add ½ cup of warm water, cover with a lid and leave it to simmer for 25 minutes.

Once cooked, the meat should not fall off the bone, but it should be somewhat soft. The onions should be cooked down to a nice saucy consistency. The meat should taste quite salty as it will later be diluted with rice.

6. Remove the lamb or chicken pieces from the pressure cooker or pan and set aside. Leave the sauce in the pan.

*Preparing the toppings:*

1. Heat half a teaspoon of oil in a wide skillet. Add the carrots and sprinkle them with sugar, cooking them in the oil for 2–3 minutes.
2. Turn off the heat and add the raisins. Cover with a lid and set aside.

*Preparing the rice:*

1. In a separate deep pot, add the rice with the saltwater in which it has been soaking. Cover it with a lid and let it come to a boil on high heat.
2. Stir the cooking rice constantly with a slotted spoon for about 5 minutes. During this time, you should keep checking the rice to see if it is done. It will be done when the grain is soft on the outside and firmer inside. Depending on the rice, the water may not fully come to a boil.
3. Reserve a cup of the water in which the rice has cooked, then drain the rice through a fine sieve to ensure the grains don't fall through the holes.

*To assemble:*

1. Preheat the oven to 200°C/180°C fan/400°F.
2. Add the rice to the pot still containing the meat sauce, carefully folding the sauce into the rice. Add more oil (to get a glossy effect on the rice) and more salt if needed.
3. Once mixed well, pile the rice into a mountain, poking random holes in it for steam evaporation. Add some of the rice water – there should only be about one inch of water surrounding the mountain.

4. Assemble the meat pieces around the mountain of rice, then sprinkle the remaining 1 teaspoon of the masala-yi pulao on top.
5. Place the raisins and carrots inside a parchment paper pouch or foil, then nestle it gently inside the mountain of rice.
6. Cover with a lid, then cover the lid with foil or a clean damp cloth.
7. Place the pot in the preheated oven. After 15 minutes, reduce the temperature of the oven to 150–175°C/300–350°F and cook for another 40 minutes.

*To serve:*

1. Arrange the lamb or chicken pieces on a larger shallow platter. Cover with rice, then sprinkle the raisins and carrot.
2. Serve with an Afghan salata, minty yoghurt and pickled vegetables.

# The Quest for Tilak Chandan

*Tarana Husain Khan*

After the dizzying rounds of marriage ceremonies, dinners and introductions were over, my first task as the lady of the house was to make a monthly grocery list based on my mother-in-law's recommendations. At the top of the list, the *saude ka parcha*, were three rice varieties in varying weights: Tilak Chandan, Hans Raj and Indrasan. The list with pulses, spices and other items was to be procured from the local mandi, my mother-in-law giving instructions about how to ensure that the servants brought old rice rather than tricking us with broken rice. I was told that the long-grained Hans Raj was to be kept for pulaos, Indrasan for daily khushka (plain boiled or tempered rice) and Tilak Chandan to be used for winter urad dal khichri. Of these, Tilak Chandan was the only freshly harvested rice. The names, though not the usage and points of identification, were familiar to me because my Rampuri grandparents living in Aligarh, where I had grown up, never ate any rice other than the traditional Rampur varieties. During the 1990s, the fertile 'terai' rice belt of northwestern Uttar Pradesh – earlier corresponding to Rohilkhand centring on Rampur, Bareilly, Moradabad and Bijnor – was dominated by these three heritage varieties. It was the redolence of Hans Raj that announced that pulao was on dum as we returned from school or college.

While I followed the set pattern of grocery lists through the 1990s – even sending for these specific rice varieties and spices when we moved away to Allahabad – the beginning of economic liberalisation in India heralded a dramatic change in our lives. Concomitantly there was a gradual, unobserved change in the landscapes around us. The village huts with roofs of long-stalked hay gave way to brick structures; short-statured hybrid rice and wheat plants dominated the countryside and their produce flooded the agricultural mandis. My grocery list now began with Pakistani basmati and sharbati hybrids or sometimes the indifferent roz marrah ke chawal or daily rice because the traditional varieties were now often unavailable in Rampur mandis. Things were being gained while others were being lost. But this was something only noticeable by taking the time to look, and back then my life had a dizzying speed.

It was when I moved to Rampur and started writing on my ancestral town's obsession with khichri, the humble rice and lentil savoury porridge, that I realised that Tilak Chandan, an essential element of our rice palette, had disappeared. Before the era of liberalisation, khichri had always been cooked with newly harvested crops of this highly aromatic, small-grained local variety. People would wait for the harvest to start cooking the 'real' khichri.

The longer gestation period, higher water requirements and lower yield of Tilak Chandan had given the advantage to hybrid varieties. These hybrids were disease-resistant, required less water and ripened quickly, with the effect that farmers could manage two rounds of rice cultivation in a single year. Needless to say, the heritage varieties were hedged out by this mass conversion to hybrids. Some farmers still cultivate heritage grains for the connoisseurs in small plots and sell it at double the price of hybrids – but the crops often fail. Flooding by the monsoons at the right time is critical for the Tilak Chandan to flower. The climate, especially the levels of precipitation, has undergone a sea change since the mid-twentieth century, contributing to the abandonment of the water-hungry Tilak Chandan and other varieties. Today oral history recalls a culinary memory of the aromatic Hans Raj and Tilak Chandan. 'When Hans Raj was cooked, the whole mohalla (neighbourhood) could smell the pulao' is the oft-repeated remark, a food legend which provokes bemused disbelief in the young ones.

Hans Raj, the traditional basmati rice generally used for pulao and the sweet rice zarda, is also on the verge of extinction. With fewer types of rice available, the flavours, textures, historical contexts and social meanings of many of the prized dishes of Rampur cuisine have been forever altered. As hybrids dominate, the smell and taste of heritage rice recede from our daily consciousness – a sensory amnesia. They exist only in the affective memories of the older generation. Even the visual aesthetics of the countryside have undergone a gradual mutation with this conversion; short, uniform, quickly maturing fields have replaced the measured and evolving shades of rice plants gradually ripening until the early winter harvest festival of Diwali. We barely notice these changes as we speed by in our cars, insulated by the air conditioning.

My writing on Tilak Chandan and Rampur cuisine evoked the interest of historian Siobhan Lambert-Hurley from the University of Sheffield, one of my fellow editors for this collection. As we connected over our shared interest in food histories, I expressed my concern over the near extinction of local rice varieties. Since the rice and the 'forgotten' dishes were a part of the region's foodways just a generation back, there seemed to be a strong case for the resurrection of Tilak Chandan and Hans Raj.

Our project, 'Forgotten Food: Culinary Memory, Local Heritage and Lost Agricultural Varieties in India', has at its core the revival of historic recipes and resurrection of lost rice varieties – what plant scientist and our collaborator Duncan Cameron calls the 'democratisation of rice' through crafting hybrids. We hope that the hybridisation of Tilak Chandan and other heritage varieties will ultimately make the variety more disease-resistant and higher-yielding, thus increasing its appeal to local farmers and alleviating hunger with local foodways. We decided to work towards growing Tilak Chandan and Hans Raj and to showcase dishes made with heritage rice varieties at a food and culture festival we planned to curate at the end of the project. In honour of a historic festival in Rampur, it was to be called Jashn-i Benazir.

The first step, however, was to locate original Tilak Chandan seeds. The food historian Jayeeta Sharma offered to help. She flew to Kolkata, took a train and finally walked to Rayagada in Odisha to connect with Debal Deb, a renowned rice ecologist who preserves and sows nearly fifteen hundred heritage rice varieties at his Basudha research farm and Vrihi rice seed bank. Amongst these were the original Tilak Chandan and Hans Raj, which Deb permitted us to use on condition that we deposit back double the seeds into the seed bank after the harvest. But while we were planning the logistics of procuring and sowing the rice varieties in Rampur and in labs at the University of Sheffield, Covid-19 burst into our lives. There was no way that we could take the journey to the farm or manage a courier from there. Everything was under lockdown.

Rampur is predominantly an agrarian economy, and there are still pockets of heritage rice that have survived the onslaught of the hybrids. My friend Birendra Sandhu, who runs the Benazir farms, fulfilled my quest: a farmer friend of his in nearby Bilaspur claimed to have original Tilak Chandan seeds. We sent images of these seeds to Duncan, as the project's plant scientist, who confirmed that they had all the physical characteristics of Tilak Chandan. Yet, without DNA tests there was no way to prove it definitively. Rather than wait another year, we decided to take our chances. In the pandemic's full throes of 2020, we requested Mr Sandhu to plant the seeds on about two bighas of farmland. The Benazir farm used to sow Tilak Chandan and Hans Raj until about fifteen years ago, sometimes only on a small plot for their own consumption. It was important to grow the seeds every year or the variety would not be reproduced. Somewhere along the way they, like every other farm in the region, had lost the seeds.

As someone who has spent her life in towns and cities, I never truly appreciated the beauty of sowing rice. Standing on the edge of the inundated field in the sweltering monsoon June heat, I watched the planting of rice paddy up close for the first time in my life. I could hear the squelch of their bare feet as the six workmen walked with batches of saplings and set them into the mushy soil. In all it took about an hour.

Four months after the planting, I sent pictures of the Tilak Chandan plants standing at their full height – more than four feet, each stem bearing only one ear of precious seeds. Duncan was delighted at their unapologetic stature and unevenness. The real challenge was to save the vulnerable plants from the 'gundi bug' infestation. We had to resort to some minimum pesticides or risk the harvest.

As November came around, the plants continued to ripen at a leisurely pace under the winter sun and I waited with excited impatience for my first harvest. Even after nearly six months, the grains were still slightly green, prompting Mr Sandhu to postpone the harvest until after Diwali. Every day's delay meant more risk to the harvest. Sudden unseasonal rainstorm could spell disaster – the tall plants are prone to collapse in strong winds and the wet sheaves of grain would rot. The hybrids, being short, can't carry this burden.

The night after Diwali, unexpected rainclouds gathered and the deluge began. I used to love sudden dramatic downpours, completely apathetic to agrarian rhythms. Now, with our own harvest at the mercy of nature, I watched the incessant, steady raindrops with foreboding and prayed for a miraculous clearing of the dense clouds.

The next morning, a quarter of the plants lay supine, but Mr Sandhu was optimistic as the sun came out and the sky became a promising blue. He assured me that the field would dry up in the strong sun. Two days later, as the swish of sickles rang quick and crisp, his predictions were confirmed; even the flattened plants had dried up. Tying up my scarf, I tried my hand at harvesting, much to the amusement of the farmers. The sickle felt warm and heavy in my hand as I bent low, clutched a plant and tried to cut with one swish, mirroring the actions of the harvesters. Gathering the crop wasn't as easy as it looked and I soon had to squat down to ease my aching back. I had come a long way from the woman who only wrote about rice. My efforts in the field were brief – after about half an hour the professionals took over – but I was proud of the sheaves I had cut.

After five hours of intense labour by the workmen, our precious rice bundles lay drying. There were further rhythms to be followed – threshing, shelling and polishing – before this fading rice could be brought back to life on our platter. Mr Sandhu told me that there was a specific time to polish the rice. If the grain was too dry the rice would break.

The harvest from our two bigha was just ninety kilograms of rice, a minuscule proportion of the average yield of about 1800 kilograms for the same area. Moreover, the whole cycle of sowing from the nursery to the final threshing was about six months. During this time Mr Sandhu harvested two crops of the rice hybrids. However, there was a market for heritage varieties and the connoisseurs brought that at five times the price of hybrids.

We shipped about two kilogrammes of Tilak Chandan seeds to Sheffield with the aim of growing them in a lab environment mimicking the environmental and soil conditions of 1930s Rampur. This was the era when, according to historical records, Tilak Chandan was a dominant variety of the region. Everything from the quality of soil to the air parameters and the angle and brightness of the Indian summer sun was to be recreated in the labs in the hope of producing rice that replicates the historic flavours as closely as possible. Heartbreakingly, despite many attempts, the rice seeds wouldn't germinate in Sheffield, perhaps due to the fumigation process necessary for import. We were in for another setback the next year. In 2021, Mr Sandhu sowed the rice again, but unseasonal rains flooded the fields and all but destroyed the crop. We could only save about a handful of seeds.

Meanwhile I had a precious harvest of Tilak Chandan to keep safe until we planned to conduct some blind taste tests to gauge if the diners found a perceptible difference between the flavours of Tilak Chandan and hybrid rice. As a literal taste of what was to come, I prepared Tilak Chandan khichri alongside hybrid rice khichri for an informal taste-test with my family and friends. As the Tilak Chandan khichri simmered, I caught a whiff of something forgotten, an aroma of my childhood and youth. It was a smaller and plumper grain than the hybrids, making the khichri a completely different texture from the one to which we had become accustomed. When I served the Tilak Chandan khichri with dollops of clarified butter, each grain was completely coated in a way that the long-grained hybrid rice in the other khichri could not aspire to. My friends – all except one – far preferred the Tilak Chandan khichri over the other khichri, and went gaga over the aroma. The hybrid rice khichri was left uneaten.

After a few months I took a peek into the sealed plastic container to check on our Tilak Chandan and was horrified to find tiny black ghun insects – a kind of weevil. Mr Sandhu laughed at me – surely, I knew that the rice had to be regularly sunned and winnowed? At my grandparents' place in Aligarh, rice and wheat used to be stored for the whole year in ten to twelve feet tall aluminium cannisters lining the storerooms. The maidservants would clean the rice and wheat working with their soop (cane baskets) – throwing the grain up in the air and catching them expertly – to sift and pick out blackened grains and ghuns. It used to be a whole day's work. At some point, we had given up the whole ecosystem and started buying flour and rice from the stores. Houses had become smaller and we didn't have so many servants. The cannisters had rusted and were dismantled.

An old woman came to sort out my rice, sieving and winnowing until we got rid of the bugs. Mr Sandhu advised me to use turmeric roots and dried neem leaves to prevent another infestation and to be sure to repeat the procedure again after monsoons.

Meanwhile we were making all efforts to find Hans Raj seeds to grow in the last season before the culmination of the first phase of our project. A farmer near Bareilly was selling what he claimed was Hans Raj. He refused to collaborate, and so we instead bought freshly harvested Hans Raj from him in the hope of germinating the rice in Debal Deb's lab. The experiment failed when Debal Deb informed us that the farmer, like other traders, had mixed about ten percent of some aromatic rice with the hybrid basmati to fool the buyers. Once again Mr Sandhu came to our rescue with his relentless quest for Hans Raj. Through his farming connections in Chandigarh and Jammu he got the information that Hans Raj was being grown in Jammu valley. But the farmers had moved away due to chaotic political disturbances, and the seeds were probably lost. His farming connections finally found the Hans Raj seeds in a village called Chakroi about three hundred metres from the Pakistan border. It was miraculous that the seeds reached us just in time for the sowing season. Mr Sandhu asked me to peel off the husk and chew on the rice. It had a distinct aroma.

As I write now, Hans Raj is thriving at Benazir Farms, in the shadow of the ruins of Benazir Palace of the Nawabs of Rampur. We hope to bring in a full harvest. It is one step in the long journey to bring back our peerless heritage rice varieties to our food palettes and grocery lists.

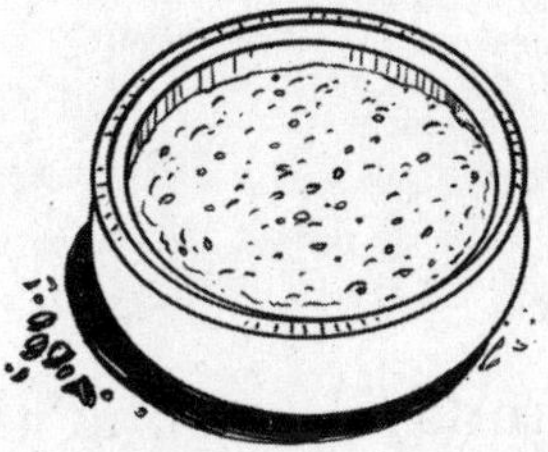

## Rampuri Urad Dal Khichri

You can see me producing this Rampuri khichri with rice from our Tilak Chandan harvest at: https://youtu.be/tGizT8jbpGE.

### Ingredients

1 cup rice, preferably Tilak Chandan
½ or ¾ cup black split urad dal
2-inch piece of ginger, julienned in thin long strips
5–6 dried red or yellow chillies, broken into half inch pieces
salt to taste

### Method

1. Wash and clean rice and lentils. Mix together.
2. Add ginger, chillies and salt. Add water. A simple measure to check the quantity of water is that it should stand about an inch over the rice.
3. Cook until rice and lentils are soft but not mushy.
4. Serve hot with garlic and red chilli chutney and radish pickle.

# Sunday Lunch at the Mahindra Sanatkada Lucknow Festival

*Noor Khan*

The Mahindra Sanatkada Lucknow Festival has become an important event in Lucknow's cultural calendar. From small beginnings, targeting a local audience, it now attracts visitors from outside the city and even the country. The five-day festival, held at Safed Baradari in the first week of February, includes a Weaves & Crafts Bazaar, literary events, cultural performances, craft demonstrations, walks and tours and much more.

One of the most popular events of this festival is the Awadhi Home Cooked Food Festival. As the name suggests, the food is not professionally cooked – rather, it is prepared by a team of volunteers, or 'home cooks', in their kitchens using old family recipes. The idea for the Sunday lunch came out of a realisation that there was so much more to Lucknow food than the popular street fare which had, for so long, passed off as representing Awadhi Cuisine. We wanted authentic food to be brought out of Lucknow homes and served to a discerning audience, not simply as an afternoon lunch but as an entire gourmet experience.

The dynamics of the Awadhi Home Cooked Food Festival change every year. After much deliberation the menu is decided. To add novelty, new dishes are introduced each time. Care is taken not to be repetitive, although some popular dishes from previous years may be included. There is always a variety of salans, such as mutton or chicken qorma, aloo gosht, shab degh, nahari or methi machli ka shorba. Dry meat dishes on the menu can include mutton raan, seekh pasanda or mutton stew. There are endless combinations of kababs to choose from – shami, galawat, boti, gole ke kabab, patili ki tikiya. Qeema dishes can vary between hara bhara qeema, qeema sem ke beej and lal mirch stuffed with qeema. Roomali and tandoori rotis are served hot from a common cooking area. And there are steaming platters of yakhni pulao and dum biryani with smoked raita or a fresh tomato chutney.

The Mahindra Sanatkada Lucknow Festival celebrates diversity, so there are regional representatives on the menu, such as the Bundeli thali and UP thali. The festival theme also influences the menu. At one festival, the theme was the many communities that had made Lucknow their home. These community archetypes included the Marwari thali, Parsi dhansak and Bengali mustard fish curry, to name just a few.

Much thought is given to the vegetarian section as well. A glass of kanji makes a platter of makki ki roti, gur and sarson ka saag more interesting. Soya variations of popular meat dishes are popular with the festival-goers, and the Marwari thali is invariably the first to be sold out. For people looking for more basic, simple fare, there is always kadhi chawal, matar pulao with chutney, sukhe aloo, sagpaita with zeera chawal.

Rounding off the menu are traditional Awadhi sweets such as shahi tukra, firni, shakarkand ki kheer, qimami seviyan and gajar or chane ki dal ka halwa. Shahi tukras and firni are popular sweets that are served all year round at local weddings. Shakarkand ki kheer is a seasonal sweet, which can be cooked only in winter months when shakarkand (sweet potatoes) are in season. Halwas are rich because they are cooked in large quantities of clarified butter and so they are best enjoyed in winter. The Mahindra Sanatkada Lucknow Festival is always held in the first week of February, so winter vegetables and sweets are often an essential part of the Sunday Food Festival.

New volunteer cooks are added to the team every year, and they invariably introduce exciting new dishes. The hara bhara qeema was added to the menu by Ashar Jamal in 2020. Ashar is an educationalist by profession, and her family of ulama and hakims have lived in old Lucknow for seven generations on record. Even today, the extended family lives within walking distance of each other. Ashar picked up the recipe from her bua, an old family retainer who would occasionally cook her own dinner in the family's woodfired kitchen. Often this one-dish meal was chunky bits of meat cooked with coarsely-pounded ginger and garlic, stewed in its own fat and garnished with generous quantities of green coriander and chillies. Ashar recreated and refined the recipe from childhood memories, replacing the animal fat with mustard oil and fatty flesh with lean minced goat meat. She is an instinctive cook and does not feel the need for written recipes.

Farzana Shahab's family came to Lucknow in the mid-1950s from a farming community in the Bundelkhand region. Farzana, an artist by profession, served aloo gosht at the Sunday Food Festival, a recipe that has been used by four generations of women in her family. She picked up cooking by helping her mother in the kitchen and has started the practice of recording her family recipes in a recipe book. She shares these written recipes and gives cooking demonstrations with her daughter Anam, who lives and works in London.

Another of the festival's home cooks is Zarine Viccajee. She is an educationalist and the president of the Awadh Educational Society, which runs Avadh Girls' Degree College in Lucknow. Her great-great-grandfather, Nowrojee Damkawala, came to Lucknow in the mid-nineteenth century to trade in silks and pearls with the Nawab of Awadh. Gradually, a Parsi community settled in Lucknow. Parsis adopted the language, dress, food and mannerisms of Lucknow. In return they gave Lucknow the seedha palla, gorgeously-embroidered saris and borders, and delicious Parsi dishes, the most well-known among them being the dhansak. Zarine does the cooking herself, but this recipe was passed down orally by her mother to her trusted cook, Lal Mohammed, who in turn shared it with Parvati, the current family cook. It was Lal Mohammed's version that was shared for the first time in 2020 at the Sunday Home Cooked Festival. Zarine's niece, Sanaya, has now written down the recipe and cooks it just the way her grandmother did.

The Awadhi Home Cooked Food Festival has acquired an adda-like status of a carnival. Families eat together, friends meet up and share a meal, rounding it off with a sikora of hot chane ki dal ka halwa. The senior cooks double up as hostesses and mingle with the guests, suggesting different combinations from the menu and ensuring that everyone is comfortable and satisfied.

The festival can throw up some surprises. The chocolate orange cake, a new entrant in 2020, was the first to be sold out. Who would have thought of that, when the long-standing demand has always been for traditional Awadhi sweets!

As we learn and grow, our customers learn along with us. No one asks anymore what a khichra or the feminine-sounding koftee–pulao is. Everyone has learned that the former is mutton cooked with lentils and rice, and the latter is a colloquial term for a bite-sized mince kofta layered with green peas and fragrant rice. It gives us immense joy when we hear that some of the dishes we introduced have become part of common fare. Khichra and nargisi koftas are more visible now on menu cards in popular eating places. One loyal customer told us that she had eaten qeema with lal mirch at a wedding in Delhi but it was not as good as ours. Discerning audiences have learned that the Awadhi style of cooking meat and vegetables together creates delicacies that are to be appreciated for their subtle flavours and pleasing colours. The golden potato halves simmering in a dish of aloo gosht, the red of the beetroot enhancing the colour of chukandar gosht, or the dhania and green chillies lending their name, flavour and colour to the fiery hara bhara qeema are combinations to be savoured and appreciated. The festival journey is more than a decade old and the idea has been to share and spread awareness about Awadhi food. We feel we have been successful.

## Qeema Karela

My father's family belonged to Amethi, a small qasba adjacent to Lucknow. My grandfather settled down in Lucknow in the early 1900s. Lucknow has been my home for almost five decades, and the city has a tradition of good food served with the utmost care and a genuine sense of hospitality. I am an educationalist by profession, but, over the years, I have developed an interest in cooking. Here I am sharing my paternal aunt's recipe for qeema karela, or minced meat cooked with bitter gourd. My aunt died before I was born, but her daughter, my cousin, shared her mother's recipe. This recipe is about seventy years old, shared only through memory. It will be added to a family recipe book that I started writing about five years ago.

**Ingredients**

500g minced meat, washed and set aside
6 karelas, medium
3 large onions, sliced lengthwise
2 medium onions, finely chopped
1 tsp ginger, finely chopped
1 tsp garlic, finely chopped
1 tsp haldi (turmeric) powder
1 tsp red chillies, coarsely pounded
1 cup mustard oil, smoked and cooled
½ cup karaunda (Bengal currant), halved and deseeded
salt to taste

*For the dry spice mix:*

1 tbsp saunf (fennel seeds)
½ tbsp zeera (cumin seeds)
½ tsp methi (fenugreek seeds)
All should be lightly roasted and then coarsely pounded. Then add ½ tsp of kalonji (nigella) seeds to this mixture.

*For the garnish:*

pudina (mint) leaves, whole green chillies, browned onions

**Method**

1. Scrape the skin of the karelas. Slit, deseed and cut into rings. Add ½ tsp of salt and set aside for half an hour. Wash thoroughly and pat dry.
2. In a wok, heat the mustard oil. Add the sliced onions and cook until they turn golden brown. Set aside half of the onions.
3. To the remaining onions add the coarsely-pounded spice mix, minced meat, turmeric powder, pounded chillies, chopped ginger and garlic, finely chopped onions and salt. Mix well, cover with a tight lid and leave to cook on very low flame. Continue cooking until all the liquid has evaporated. Stir until the oil separates and the mince is brown and well cooked.
4. Add the karela rings and karaunda halves. Add a cup of water and cook on very low heat until the karela and karaunda have softened but retain their shape.
5. Serve garnished with pudina leaves, green chillies and brown onions.

*Note:* This is a summer dish as that is when karelas and karaundas are in season. Chopped pieces of raw mango can be substituted for karaundas if karaundas are not available. Karaundas and raw mangoes are souring agents and combine well with the slightly bitter taste of the karela. Take care to retain the shape of the karaunda and karela. This enhances the finished look of the dish.

# Celebrating the Ganga–Jamuni Tahzib with Allahabad's Sanchaari

*Samina Naqvi*

As a child, I loved vacations in Allahabad with my aunt, Dr Rehana Bashir. My fondest memories are of garden parties during winter afternoons or evening teas where the proud hosts would showcase their perfectly manicured gardens lush with vibrant seasonal blooms. But what I carried in my heart all these years were the varieties of home-cooked delicacies that followed later in the day. I guess it is these memories that I nurtured until they culminated in a food festival on Allahabad cuisine, Dil Ek Khane Anek, decades later. At the festival, we would invite local denizens to participate with home-cooked food representatives of their community.

The rare quality of the Ganga–Jamuni tahzib, imbibed through generations of living together, resides in the souls of the people of Allahabad. The simplicity of having chaat from a roadside vendor, churmura at Civil Lines, hanging out at Cozy Nook, eating tikka at Meals on Wheels – the city's first takeaway food joint – are the shades of the quintessential Allahabad foodie's life.

My passion for gourmet food grew exponentially when I got married and settled in Allahabad. My husband would probably say that the first love of his life was food and, only after that, came all of us. His passion for food prompted me to brush up my skills and, much to my own amazement, I could cook better than I had presumed. Food in my family meant planning, presentation and combination – even the colour of the vegetables was discussed at length before they were laid on the table. My husband's verdict is still spelled out with grave finality after every meal. I attribute my daughter becoming a professional chef to the overwhelming importance given to food in our family.

## The Allahabad pace

Over the years I witnessed myriad changes in the social life of Allahabad. The pragmatic would say that the changes were inevitable, but it hurt me merely to be a mute spectator. I had been drawn into the city, meeting people and discovering dishes and haunts as an insider–outsider. In the heterogeneity of this historic metropolis, there was once an exquisite social fabric of intricately woven threads that created a colourful tapestry of people from different communities bonding over music, classical and modern, culinary delights and conversation about books and thoughts. Every house provided a journey into a startlingly beautiful culture of language, values and practice.

Sadly, the education system in which I worked – as a teacher in the Boys' High School – prompted schools to concentrate on churning out robots programmed to achieve impressive mark sheets for their parents to flaunt. The young ones were completely detached from the inherent beauty and soul of their city. It is a great irony that many of my students returned to explore Allahabad only when they heard or read about their own city in some other part of the world.

As I began to explore what had been lost, Allahabad unfolded itself to me with its refined social norms – a rich culture and heritage narrated by friends and acquaintances. People shared anecdotes of poetic evenings with Firaaq Gorakhpuri, Mahadevi Verma, Sumitra Nandan Pant and Suryakant Tripathi Nirala. Women had magic in their fingers for creating culinary delights.

Street food – dahi jalebi at Hira Halwai or chaat at Nirala or kachori dum aloo at Netram and fruit cream at Loknath – was liked by everyone.

This enriching journey became the driving force behind our organisation Sanchaari. I shared my idea of starting a movement or organisation that would celebrate culture, literature, food and heritage with Pallavi Chandel, a trained historian, who also felt deeply for the city and its rich heritage. We approached Lalit Joshi, an academic historian by trade and a musician by passion, who became our guide, mentor and inspiration on our journey. Naresh Roy, whose family runs the well-known restaurant El Chico joined in to cater to our food segment. One of my especially creative former students, Shlok, became our graphic designer. Saba, an assistant professor at Jamia University, my friends Anu, Sehar, Tahira, Pooja, Vasundhara and Shasya – people kept joining our enterprise.

Times changed the politics of the state, and the rapid influx of people from various districts altered the demographic pattern of society. Sanchaari took it upon itself to rebuild, recreate and relive the glory of the city, not only by recalling the past, but also by involving people in participating, appreciating and contributing to the city in the present. We amplified our heritage and connected with old-timers who had gone into their cocoons.

Allahabad food is a confluence of many cuisines, each influencing the other, yet retaining its distinct flavours. Allahabad has its own pace and any outing was mainly visiting people and sharing food. My frequent visits to my friend Sheila Varma's typically Allahabadi household were other enriching experiences of dwelling in fine tastes and exotic vegetarian food. Varma led me into a world of warm hospitality where kababs, fried parwal (gourd), methi chaman (cottage cheese with fenugreek), tomato paneer and seasonal vegetables were cooked in a distinctive style.

Allahabad has been home to a large community of Anglo-Indians since the time of British colonial rule. Though many members migrated to Australia and the United Kingdom sometime in the 1970s, the community still has sizeable presence in the city. My teaching job at the Boys' High School connected me to this community and their delectable cuisine: a mixture of Indian and British culinary heritage. I discovered the Goan dish vindaloo, Christmas cakes baked at Bushy's, and homemade mustard dips. Bushy's, a bakery run by a Muslim family since 1963, still bakes in traditional wood-fired ovens. It is the only traditional bakery in Allahabad and, come Christmas, all Christian families book a slot at Bushy's, lining up with their cake batter loaded with dried fruits soaked in rum.

I was delighted to discover dhansak, berry pulao and other food traditions of the tiny Parsi community of Allahabad. Mrs Harkoli, in contrast, prepared methi goli, a Kashmiri dish, for one of our Sanchaari festivals. Mrs Ghatak, a family friend, introduced me to fine Bengali cuisine – including the art of cutting vegetables, which contributed a great deal to the taste and flavour of the chingri machher malaikari, aloo posto and machher paturi. Enjoying these other cuisines, I was reminded of when I visited Allahabad as a child to spend time with my grandparents. There the Goan cook of a Mrs Banerjee tempted me with the most delicious fish mayonnaise.

The ann koot lunch, also known as the chhapan bhog, at a Khatri friend's house after Diwali left me enamoured with sumptuous dishes cooked without onion and garlic. The all-vegetable medley, sabzi ka saag, rice with khoya, homemade mithai – the dishes are endless and I look forward every year to the perfectly crisp kachoris with my favourite parwal ki sabzi made from the pointed gourd. The highlight of the meal is kanji, a drink prepared with mustard and fenugreek seeds soaked in water sweetened with sugarcane juice, the imli (tamarind) chutney lending tart tones, and dumplings floating with sublime elegance. Another winter speciality of Allahabad is nimona. Raw peas are peeled, crushed and cooked in a pressure cooker with spices, tomatoes and boiled potatoes. Nimona tastes best when the crushed peas are fried in methi (fenugreek) and onions with a bit of crushed ginger and dry masala.

## Sanchaari's initiatives

Sanchaari has now been in existence for just nine years and, in that time, it has earned a reputation for revisiting heritage and bringing forth hidden aspects of the city.

The guavas of Allahabad – the Allahabadi amrood – have always been legendary. Our poet, Akbar Allahabadi, referred to this fruit with a pinch of sarcasm:

*kuch Allahabad mein saman nahin bahbud ke*
*yan dhara kya hai ba-juz Akbar ke aur amrud ke*

There is nothing for salvation in the city of Allahabad
What is here anyway but for Akbar and guavas

We thus organised a Guava Festival, the first of its kind, amidst the guava orchards of Khusro Bagh – the gardens surrounding the beautiful mausoleum dedicated to the Mughal prince, Khusrau Mirza. To our amazement, most people who visited the festival had little knowledge of the variety of guavas, and few had ever visited Khusro Bagh. Sanchaari can easily take the credit for reviving neglected varieties of guavas and making Khusro Bagh a more popular tourist spot. Allahabad Tourism and the district administration joined us to make this an annual event, inviting local vendors to showcase their varieties and promoting the plantation of guava trees. Recently, there had been a decline in guava orchards with many farmers planting banana trees for quick returns. As part of our environmental initiative each year, we encouraged many to plant guava trees.

The Guava Festival has gained tremendous popularity and every year people come up with the most delectable delights to enter in competitions and exhibitions – from guava cakes, smoothies, shakes and kheers to salads. An elderly gentleman prepared guava cheese and jelly to sell, sharing some interesting anecdotes about having learned the craft from an Anglo-Indian lady. Guava cheese and jelly sell like hot cakes, and nostalgic Allahabadis from around the globe book these products in advance.

Our food festival, Dil Ek Khane Anek, truly resonates with the ethos of the city. Its focus is on inviting people to participate with their original home-cooked dishes, including those prepared for particular festivals and seasons. Food becomes a binding force between communities, with a medley created from bati chokha (stuffed wholewheat dough balls with brinjal mash), varieties of Bengali sandesh, tangy palar (a fermented curd drink with moong dal dumplings), Marwari thali with dal ki puri and sangiri (a green bean dish), and the green pea broth nimona. Another dish which deserves a special mention is the heritage recipe dum ka salan – the meat being marinated in spices and slow cooked in an earthen pot and served with khameeri roti.

During our yearly literature festival, we organised a heritage food walk to the narrow lane in Allahabad's old city known as loknath ki gali. There, we devoured hot kachoris and dum aloo followed by lassi with malai, or clotted cream. Sweet delicacies like lauki ke launj and khus khus gajak, kali gajar ka halwa and mompati were relished with great pleasure. Sweet anarsas, the traditional monsoon sweet, became part of our kajri musical events featuring folk and classical songs sung during the rainy season. Anarsas are prepared with crushed rice that is fried and dipped in sugar syrup and then rolled in sesame seeds. Kharcha (a fried maida snack) and aam (a mango-shaped sweet made with chickpea flour) eaten during Navratra fasts were showcased and shared with pride by Vineeta Singh in the food segments of the fest. Vinti Agarwal, a dear friend, would treat us to tasty mathris with a variety of sumptuous pickles. Dum aloo kachori, karonde ki sabzi, ladoo ki kheer, pati sapta – every household shared its homely specialty and tasted from other tables. In 2019, we invited the renowned food historian, Pushpesh Pant, to our food festival. He especially loved the mutton kofta curry served at my place, generously showering compliments while doing full justice to the dish.

In the same year, Sanchaari was honoured to collaborate with an editor of this collection, Siobhan Lambert-Hurley, and her team based at the University of Sheffield to host the opening event of their 'Forgotten Food' project as part of our Sanchaari Sanskritik Parv. Their project addresses challenges linked to local communities and food sustainability in India through oral history, creative writing and promoting local varieties of food grains – and thus chimes with Sanchaari's own aims. Like our group, the project also brings together academics, practitioners and community activists in collaboration. Though the planned workshop went ahead with participants from India and abroad, the associated food festival had to be cancelled due to a political situation that seemed too serious for a large congregation of people. The unexpected turn of events disturbed the flow of our festival, but not our energy: a lively gathering was still held at an impromptu venue with many inspiring exchanges on India's diverse food cultures underpinned by a rich culinary heritage.

## Nimona

### Ingredients

½ cup onion, finely chopped
½ tsp ginger, finely chopped
1 tsp garlic, finely chopped
2 green chillies, finely chopped
1 cup fresh green peas (approximately 150g)
½ tbsp mustard oil
1 bay leaf
3 cloves
½ tsp cumin seeds
1 medium tomato, finely chopped
1 pinch asafoetida (hing)
¼ tsp turmeric powder
½ tsp Kashmiri red chilli powder
½ tsp coriander powder
1 medium potato, peeled, cubed and parboiled or lightly fried (optional)
3 tbsp chopped coriander leaves
1.5 to 2 cups water – or add as required
¼ to ½ tsp garam masala
2 tbsp chopped coriander leaves (to garnish)

### Method

1. Grind onion, ginger, garlic and chillies into a smooth paste without adding any water. Set aside.
2. In the same container, add the peas and grind to a coarse paste without adding any water. Set aside.

3. Heat the mustard oil in a kadhai (deep pan or wok) and then add bay leaf, cloves and cumin seeds. Let the spices crackle and splutter briefly.
4. Add the onion paste to the pan. Mix well and sauté, stirring often.
5. Once the oil rises to the surface, add the finely chopped tomato. Mix well and leave the tomato mixture to sauté.
6. Once the tomato is soft, add asafoetida, turmeric powder, Kashmiri red chilli powder and coriander powder. Mix well and cook briefly.
7. Add the ground peas and cooked potato cubes (if using) and stir.
8. Add the chopped coriander, water and salt to taste, and stir. Cover and cook on a low heat for about 10 to 15 minutes, adding additional water as needed. Stir through garam masala to finish.
9. Serve with plain rice.

*part four*

# A Dish in Time

# Bihari Kabab and Other Stories

*Sadaf Hussain*

From the poets Mir and Ghalib to the rulers Wajid Ali Shah and Bahadur Shah Zafar, everyone loved a good plate of hot kabab with optional chutney on the side. Like biryani, rasgulla and a crispy cheese sandwich, the kabab invites controversy, yet you cannot confine it to one definition.

A dictionary would define kababs as meat cubes which are marinated and then barbecued alongside vegetables, often on a skewer. This description, however, is only a half-truth. How do seekh kabab, galawati kabab or shami kabab fit with this description? And, most notably, how can you define Bihari kabab, which is neither cubed nor cooked with vegetables?

In March 2001, my parents, brother and I were in Sasaram in Bihar at my grandparents' house. I was twelve years old, running around so much that I covered the length and breadth of the aangan (courtyard). I would often brush up against the mehndi shrub between the kitchen and kothri (dry pantry). You might be wondering why I was running. There are two reasons. I was a kid, and kids do such random things. Second, it was dawat, and a feast for Eid ul-Adha was planned for the evening. An elaborate menu was being designed with biryani and Bihari kabab, but the meal would not be limited to these dishes. Eid ul-Adha, or Bakr Eid, is a day when your fridge will have more meat it in than it will hold for the rest of the year. And, if you are creative enough, you will make the most of all that meat by creating different dishes that include multiple varieties of kababs.

But back to the Bihari kabab. On that day of Eid, we had fresh, chopped meat coming from a butcher who set up in an open space within the house. I was the one chosen to carry the meat on a huge tray from the butcher to my grandmother, mother and aunts in the main kitchen. Twelve-year-old me ran with a tray full of meat, trying to save my brighter-than-ivory fresh new kurta. The ladies of the house were sitting outside the kitchen opposite the kothri, watching this show and laughing, while ordering me to run and bring meat as fast as I could. A local blade, which we call baithi, was under the feet of one aunt. Bihari kabab neither asks for a big chunk of meat, nor is it minced. One has to slice the meat very thinly, just as it is for a pasanda – a cut known as parcha. The slicing needs precision and years of experience. Even after so many years, Abbi is the only one in our nuclear family who can weave the magic. I still have to learn this technique from him. Once he is done with the slicing, I step in to mix the meat in the marinade, and then, together, both of us will skew and put it on the sigdi, or grill, to cook. Indeed, Bihari kababs are not cooked in a tandoor.

Kababs have always been a rustic favourite. They are said to have been a prominent part of the cuisine of many rulers and dynasties, and not just the Mughals' (as per a widespread belief in modern India). The word kabab came into Indian languages from Arabic. For those from the Indian subcontinent, it means to fry, burn or cook on a skewer through grilling or cooking on an open fire.

Just as a barbeque or grill is among the main gastronomic attractions for an Australian and American, so too the kabab is quintessential on a Muslim dastarkhwan or table spread. At least, it is if I am hosting you. Be sure to stuff yourselves with some of this tiny deliciousness.

In August 2021, my whole family accompanied me on a road trip to Rampur to explore the local tahzib and flavours. We were hosted by one of this volume's editors, Tarana Husain Khan, in her luxurious home right by the main streets. Together, we visited the famous and lesser-known nooks and corners of Rampur, with a dastarkhwan waiting for us at home in the evening. A vast spread was laid out, but, unanimously, what we all loved were two kababs: one made of fish and the other of mutton. To call these kababs the show-stopper would be no exaggeration.

We finished the food, and thanked Tarana and Chef Suroor, who had graciously hosted and served us those beautiful dishes. The very next day, we were home – and, within a few days, it was my turn to host a table d'hôte dinner for friends and family. I told myself that this would be the best time to impress my guests by serving them kababs from Rampur contained within the Nawabs' stockpile of recipes. My thought was that there are two kinds of people: one who likes kababs and the other who simply doesn't exist. This is because I haven't met a single meat-eater who does not like kababs!

I reached out to Tarana, requesting her to share some recipes. Among the many dishes she wrote to me about, one of them was called Kabab Tarz Bazaar. I wondered why it had this exciting name when it included only dalchini (cinnamon), laung (cloves) and elaichi (cardamom), along with a lot of black pepper to give it a distinctive spiciness. Tarz means 'form or manner', while bazaar means 'market'. Hence, this kabab is not mahal ka khana, the food of the palace, but bazaar ka khana, the food of ordinary people in the market. In earlier times, ordinary people could not afford so many spices and so the flavouring in this dish was kept to a minimum. But when I made and ate this kabab, I fell deeply in love with it. The bare, minimal spicing worked so well for me and my diners.

But this experimentation does not mean that I can forget my absolute favourite, Bihari kabab! It is unfortunate that its distant cousins – seekh, chapli, boti and other types of kababs – have become more popular worldwide.

In 2019 I travelled to Patna for one of my food pop-up cafes. One of the restaurant managers took me to Sabzi Bagh to feed me exquisite Bihari kabab, nihari and baqarkhani. Having spent twenty years growing up in the lanes of Bihar and Jharkhand, this short trip to Sabzi Bagh was steeped in nostalgia for me.

Of course, Bihari kababs are just kababs in Bihar. One of the most popular shops in Patna is called Mahngu Ram in Naya Tola. This shop makes these delicious kababs with mutton meat, although in earlier times the real Bihari kababs were made from beef. Now, buffalo meat is more common.

Interestingly, Bihari kabab is not just popular in Bihar itself, but also in Karachi in Pakistan. After India's Partition of 1947, many affluent Biharis migrated to districts like Lyari and Orangi Town, becoming known as muhajirs. Legend has it that it was in these localities that the preparation of Bihari kabab first started in Pakistan. Now, however, you can find these kababs all over Karachi with many renditions and versions.

Wajiha Naqvi, a friend who is a vocalist and creative practitioner based in Karachi, told me that Bihari kabab is top of her BBQ list when she steps out to relish some meat. But for another friend, food blogger and vlogger Zia Tabarak of Street Food PK, Bihari kabab is not just a barbeque dish. Growing up in Gulshan-i Maymar in Karachi, he had neighbours who were Bihari and, every Eid ul-Adha, there was a ritual of grilling the thinly sliced meat. Both Wajiha and Zia specify that their choice of meat is beef, but, inevitably, you can now find chicken and mutton versions too.

Zia, who explores food for a living, says people perhaps love them because of the spiciness of these kababs; one can enjoy them by themselves or with rumali roti or parathas, chutney and freshly cut onions. He sometimes pairs these kababs with the deep-fried snack kachori.

I would go so far as to say that there's no nibble quite as fulfilling and delicious as Bihari kabab. You may well ask, what makes them so great? The thinly sliced meat marinates for twelve to fourteen hours in a mixture of mustard oil, papaya paste, various whole spices, dried coconut powder, poppy seeds and sattu or besan. Tell me: have you ever had such a kind of texture and marination? Furthermore, when you grill them on an open sigdi, you baste the meat with ghee to keep the kabab tender and moist on the inside, which also imparts a rich flavour. The use of poppy seeds, or posto dana, is common in West Bengal, but perhaps, because of their geographical proximity, there has resulted in a cross-cultural evolution of this dish, further enhancing its flavour.

I always turn to Abbi for his wisdom, banking upon his food memory. So, when I started the planning of this essay, I made sure to tell him about it over dinner. When you talk to him about food, he has the biggest smile from ear to ear! He may not remember the exact name of a particular shop, but he will give you all the stories. Growing up, he had a butcher, Qadar, whose shop was outside my father's house in Sasaram (and from whom I also remember buying meat). Even though my father agreed that Bakr Eid was a mauka, or opportunity, to grill Bihari kababs, that does not mean the family abstained from this dish for the remaining days of the year. He learnt how to make kababs from his mother. It seems this is a tradition; people are taught by their mothers and other matriarchs in the family. The way one makes the fine cut, or parcha, adds all the delicate flavour, which my father thinks the butchers of Delhi can't manage very well. They don't do justice to this kabab. I have noticed my father slicing the meat still thinner even after the butchers have given it their best shot. I guess, once in a while, you have got to take matters into your own hands. Abbi also enjoys it when the kabab masala is made on a sil-batta, or grinding stone, and not in an electric grinder. He says that the latter lacks originality and the characteristic flavour. This kind of detailing and care makes Bihari kababs the most rustic, yet delicate type to serve.

Many might come to you and claim kababs are easy to make, but I advise you not to listen to them. Kababs can have a subtle flavour and texture. You need to make them in the most painstaking way and live up to the dish's history. For my own family, Bihari kabab is what brings different qisse, or stories, together. It has become a tradition passed on from my nani to her three daughters. And now I too know how to make and serve these kababs as I have learned from my Ammi and Abbi.

Bihari kabab strikes me as being like a beautiful symphony, with the people that make these kababs as the conductors. The kabab's high notes of chilli and nutmeg are balanced by the lower tones of papaya and cinnamon powder, as well as the middle range of poppy seeds, cumin, garlic and more. In short, each spice has a role to play in this delicious grill. This kabab has a distinct tune blending with the local texture and aroma. Like a song from Coke Studio, the grill is rustic and bursting with soul and flavour.

## Bihari Kabab

### Ingredients

*For the Bihari kabab garam masala:*

12 dried red chillies
10 green cardamoms
6 black cardamoms
2 star anise
2 cloves
2 tbsp coriander seeds
2 tbsp cumin seeds
4 tsp whole black peppercorns
2 tsp kabab chini
2 tsp fennel
1 tsp mace
½ tsp nutmeg

*For the kababs:*

1½ kg beef or lamb (boneless), thinly sliced (parcha)
¾ cup yoghurt
3 tbsp raw papaya with skin, finely grated into a paste
¾ cup onions, fried
4 tsp ginger, freshly grated
4 tsp garlic, minced
2 tsp red chilli powder (or paprika), or to taste
1½ tsp cumin powder, roasted
½-1 tsp nutmeg powder
1 tsp cinnamon powder
2 tsp poppy seeds
4 tsp Bihari kabab garam masala
3 tbsp chickpea flour (besan)
¾ cup mustard oil (optional)
salt to taste
½ cup ghee, to baste kababs during cooking

**Method**

1. Dry-roast all of the whole spices for the Bihari kabab garam masala in a hot pan until fragrant. Then, grind it into a fine powder to form the masala.
2. Combine all the ingredients for the kababs, including 4 tsp kabab garam masala, mustard oil (if using) and besan, in a clean bowl. Make a smooth paste out of it and massage it into the meat thoroughly.
3. Allow the meat to rest for at least 10–12 hours.
4. Thread the meat onto an iron skewer and grill over an open flame, brushing with ghee at regular intervals until the kababs are done. If you don't have a grill (sigdi), you can cook the kababs in a regular pan.
5. Serve with fresh onion slices, lemon and green chutney.

# Memories of Awadhi Qorma

*Rana Safvi*

There were cooks of yore who specialised solely in cooking qormas. In *The Classic Cuisine of Lucknow*, there is an interesting anecdote. In 1925, Nawab Jafar Hussain – a descendent of the nawabi aristocrats of Lucknow – came across a cook named Mohammad Hussain, who belonged to a family of cooks from the royal period. When the Nawab sahib asked him what he could cook: 'He replied in the typical Lakhnavi tone of voice, "Sir, qorma and chapati. Besides this, what else is there in food? I will feed you only this. I do not know how to cook anything else."' Nawab sahib immediately employed him and he stayed with him until his death in 1931. Before you wonder at this, let me add what Nawab sahib pointed out: 'In the period of approximately five years, every day, for both meals, he cooked qorma and I never felt even a twinge of monotony.'

Though such artists are hard to come by, it is possible to cook a decent qorma if one uses the spices from scratch. That means you roast and grind all the fresh garam masalas, coriander, etc., just before starting to cook. There must be many people who remember the storeroom, with their mothers sitting in front of it, getting the masalas taken out and ground fresh daily. The khansamas would grind them on a huge sil (grinding stone) with a batta (stone). The garam masalas were dry-roasted, pounded separately in an imam dasta (mortar and pestle) and then strained. In those days, hardly any house used powdered masalas.

In my childhood, qorma was associated with guests, festivities and celebrations. Our daily meals consisted of qaliya, or mutton cooked with vegetables, to ensure the consumption of seasonal produce.

Though chicken qorma is popular today, chicken was not always the preferred meat. Those were also the days when chicken was quite expensive (weight-for-weight) compared to mutton, and it was thus a delicacy. Murgh ka qorma was the ultimate dish cooked for a guest. All this was before the late Padmashree Dr B. V. Rao revolutionised the poultry industry. He established Venkateshwara Hatcheries Pvt Ltd in Pune in 1971 and is still remembered as the Father of the Indian Poultry Industry.

To this day, I associate chicken with feasts. I even prefer the desi variety over the farm-grown, as the latter is too bland. The epicures of Awadh, too, probably found chicken bland, for Abdul Halim Sharar writes in *Guzishta Lucknow* (a book about Lucknavi culture first published in serial form between 1913 and 1920) that the chickens used to be fattened with musk and saffron pills until their flesh was scented with these two substances. Since nobody can afford musk- and saffron-fed chicken, to ensure that the meat is not bland, it is best to marinate it in a garlic, salt and yoghurt mix for a few hours and then sauté it in the masala before adding water for the curry, so that the spices seep in.

Chicken was not the only meat that was used for qorma. Game meat (especially venison, quail and partridge) was also very popular, as hunting was a popular pursuit of the landed gentry before it was banned. Now, farm-grown quail is available and bater ka qorma is gaining in popularity. But one must remember that quail is a very delicate meat, so the masalas have to be minimal in order not to drown out the flavour. Indeed, while cooking any qorma, it is essential to remember this fact. Too often, the meat in the qormas is overpowered by the masalas. The special taste of Awadh is in the delicate flavouring as compared to the robust taste of Delhi cuisine.

I was accustomed to using very minimal garam masala. When I got married, that turned out to be a boon – or I would have had to reinvent my recipes. My husband is allergic to cardamom, which almost led to a disaster. My wedding was held at home, as was usual in those days. Tents and shamianas would be erected on people's lawns, as hotel weddings were unheard of. The cooks were called from Lucknow. I remember the old khansama sitting near my mother a couple of days before the wedding and giving her a list of ingredients to be bought. When he presented the amount of cardamom that was needed, my mother said, 'That won't be added to any food, as my son-in-law-to-be is allergic to it.' I will never forget the look on the khansama's face when he replied, 'Begum sahib, had you told me earlier, I would not have come. What face will I show the world when they see that the qorma has no elaichi in it?' My mother had to coax him not to leave in a huff, persuading him that the taste was in his skill of using the right proportions, roasting the masalas, marinating the meat and not in the blighted cardamom! The khansama then took it on as a personal challenge and the qorma turned out to be superb.

There is rarely any cardamom in my kitchen even now. I believe that the taste of the dish comes from the amount of time spent in roasting the masalas well – not in drowning it in oil and garam masalas.

To come back to the qorma, a feast would be considered complete only when there were at least two types of qorma, the sweet rice zarda and pulao, as well as at least two varieties of kababs and sheermal (a flatbread). This formula also meant that at least three types of meat such as mutton, fish and chicken were offered. Again, there would be adjustment in the masalas depending on the meat. Ginger paste continues to be used for meats with a strong smell and those that are tough to digest. Fish, on the other hand, requires a delicate hand when using masalas.

Another important point to be noted is that the meat (if it is mutton) should be from the raan (leg). The pieces in Lucknow would be cut with artistry and called katoris (bowls) – for they did not have bone and would curl up into a round shape in the curry. Today, when we ask the butcher for boneless mutton, he tells me to show him a boneless goat. These butchers lazily chop the meat instead of cutting along the grain.

While cooking, special care must be given to ensuring that the onions are fried just right, as the base of the qorma comes from the paste of fried onions. If it is too brown, the curry will taste bitter and have a dark colour; if it is not fried well and left a little raw, the colour of the qorma will be pale. The trick of a khushrang qorma (the bright reddish-brown hue) is in the way the onions are fried and the masala is sautéed. I learnt these tricks as a young girl around the wood fire chulha in my grandparents' kitchen, while my grandmother would describe the cooking process. I share this family recipe for you to try. Of course, as you start cooking, you will learn to make your own adjustments.

## Awadhi Murgh Qorma – Our Family Recipe

**Ingredients**

1 whole chicken, cut in curry pieces (cleaned; no skin or offal)
(*Note:* marinate the chicken for at least 2 hours in 1 tsp salt, lemon juice and 1 tsp of ginger–garlic paste)
1 large onion, finely sliced
3 tbsp oil
3 cloves
¼ tsp whole peppercorns
2 green cardamoms
2 bay leaves

1 tbsp ginger paste
1 tbsp garlic paste
chilli to taste
1 tbsp coriander powder, lightly roasted on a griddle
2 tbsp curd
½ tsp garam masala, freshly ground or powdered
1 cup water
salt to taste
¼ cup fresh cream, well beaten
a few strands of saffron, soaked in 1 tbsp of warm milk

**Method**

1. Heat oil in a pan, and then add the cloves, peppercorns, cardamom and bay leaves. Toss in the onions and fry until golden brown. This takes about 4–5 minutes on low heat.
2. Remove the onions and spices from the oil, making sure the oil is drained back into the pot and set aside. Remove bay leaves. The rest should be ground to a fine paste.
3. Reheat the oil in the pan. Shake off excess water from the chicken before adding the pieces to the oil and frying lightly.
4. Add the ginger and garlic pastes, chilli and coriander powder to the pan. Sauté, adding dashes of curd at intervals to prevent the mixture from sticking or burning. This process will take at least 10 minutes.
5. When the oil separates from the masala, add the garam masala, salt, paste of fried onions and bay leaves. Stir for a minute. Add the water and cook until the meat is tender. Keep the flame low and the pot covered.
6. Strain the cream if you are using fresh cream from home, so that it is smooth in consistency. Add cream, saffron and let it simmer for two minutes.
7. Add 2 drops of kewra water (mixed in 1 tbsp of water) before serving.
8. When serving, do not garnish the dish with coriander leaves. That garnish is reserved only for qaliya.

# The Magic of Hyderabad's Nahari

*Ayesha Mualla*

Most Sundays at home are spent savouring a comforting daytime meal of warm sheermals dipped in the collagenous richness of nahari. Hyderabad's nahari is prepared with lamb trotters (paya), parts of the head (sirey) and a meaty delicacy, the tongue (zuban). *Nahar*, which translates as 'day', describes the diffusion of light throughout the day, from sunrise to sunset, in both Arabic and Persian. This explains why the dish is usually spelt 'nahari' in Hyderabad, rather than 'nihari' as in much of the rest of South Asia. The morning unfurls in an explosion of flavours, as the nahari reaches our palates soaked in the soft sheermal or crispy parathas.

Hyderabadi nahari, like that of the other regions, is slow-cooked overnight in large cauldrons (deghs) on wood. But with the changing urban landscape, and with indoor cooking and faster techniques, people have adapted to slow-cooking nahari in pressure cookers. At home, we start our cooking after fajr prayers, to be ready for a daytime feast. As the cooker reluctantly whistles, the aroma engulfs the whole house in a deep sea of meaty fragrance. This dish makes post-fajr sleep magical, with the subtle wafts of the broth's herbaceous aroma taking us into a dreamy otherworld.

'Time, tide and nahari wait for no one!' This is the ruling of my mamu-jaan or maternal uncle, a trained fighter pilot, as he lovingly cooks for us his version of the nahari with a generous portion of lamb tongues. This popular statement conveniently changes to 'Time, tide and ice cream ...' as we get closer to desserts at dinner time. But mamu-jaan is absolutely right. Much like ice cream, nahari doesn't like to wait on the table, and it needs immediate attention and care. It must be served and devoured while it is warm and before the gelatinous elements in the broth start thickening, at worst sticking to the inner creases of our fingers like an industrial-grade skin adhesive.

The instructions at home are always clear: no bone is to be spared as it is packed with juicy marrow. This marrow is to be sucked out, leaving behind a pile of calcareous remains. Those who are prone to unsolicited medical theorising believe that, upon ingestion, this coagulating collagen intoxicates us into deep sleep. Thus it is the source of the wonderful daytime siesta that follows the meal – making it the ultimate Sunday meal.

But before we get to the end, let us embark on a journey into all the things that complete the nahari. My ammi often repeats a popular Urdu proverb: '*harkat mein barkat*'. 'There are blessings in being active.' So, if you are a Hyderabadi, then prepping for nahari will make you traverse the length and breadth of the city, regardless of your location. No force in the world can stop you from acquiring the harkat (movement) mileage as you gather all the ingredients that unravel the gustatory and olfactory landscape of Hyderabad's cuisine. It is only to be redeemed as barkat (blessings) in the form of nourishment and good health.

## Meaty debates

People in Hyderabad often find themselves embroiled in endless debates on the preference for meat cuts and the animal itself, whether it should be sirey–paya or zuban of lamb, goat or beef. My parents have addressed this ongoing controversy by ensuring a good relationship with the butcher in the neighbourhood of Hussaini Alam in Old City. Butcher sahib unfailingly provides us with clean, succulent and lavish goat sirey, paya and zuban. Locating the right cuts and the best quality of sirey–paya is crucial and can be assured only by immersing oneself in the viscerality of the sights and sounds of a meat shop to make this feast worth it. This is a sentiment my father holds dear, as he unhesitatingly vetoes my plans of ordering paya online or over the phone from another local meat shop.

Many a time the sirey–paya procured from the butcher shop after the big sacrifice on Eid ul-Adha has remnants of hair and dirt. An important detail is to meticulously de-hair and clean the trotters by scalding them in hot water or scorching them on hot charcoal. The key is to ensure that the paya is not burnt or, worse, charred, as that will make the broth bitter. Alternatively, the trotters can be washed with gram flour to remove any remaining hair and smell. The exposure to the heat and careful brushing of the skin gives it a smooth texture. The subtle smokiness enhances the flavour of the nahari and adds layers to its richness. Before the spices are added, the cleaned meat is slow cooked for hours with a little turmeric, salt, ginger–garlic paste and fresh onions.

As a child, I remember being invited to the home of close family friends in Delhi, the Qureshis from Bhopal. The invitation was to relish home-cooked nahari for breakfast on a cold Delhi morning. As the dastarkhwan was laid out, fresh parathas emerged along with the nahari in a large serving dish made of the finest china. This was the first time I would see a nahari other than our 'own'. It was a beautiful dark reddish brown, with a thick layer of rogan, or oil. I was served a big chunk of the well-cooked meat, and the fibres just naturally unravelled as I touched it with my paratha. It was delicious, instantly warming and so different. It had a salan-like consistency and it was thick and spicy. I could not believe that it only had meat and no paya! This was my first lesson that all naharis are not the same.

## Bread talk

In Hyderabad, nahari goes best with sheermal that is baked across the city, the most flavoursome coming from the hot tandoors of Nampally and Purani Haveli. The bread is invitingly displayed in large glass cabinets to retain its warmth and to protect it from the roadside hustle. Much like Afghani breads, sheermals can last for days. In fact, my aunt in Oman is famous for storing sheermals for up to a year in the freezer. And yes, if you haven't guessed, gifting relatives a fresh batch of sheermals from Hyderabad is as common as presenting Hameedi's jauzi halwa, Subhan Bakery's Osmania biscuits or tamarind tuk from Deccan Achaars, specially packed for those travelling abroad.

The oldest naan shop is said to have been established in 1851 by Mohammed Hussain Sahab, known as Munshi Naan, named after his designation at the royal Asaf Jahi court. The Munshi family folklore suggests that the recipe was brought to Hyderabad from Delhi. Interestingly, the timing is said to have coincided with a period when chefs and scholars were migrating to safer states embedded in the Indo-Persian cosmos, escaping the colonial policies in the north and the hardships that came after the rebellion of 1857. Migrating chefs brought with them recipes and techniques and trained the local bread makers in the art of baking this soft and savoury bread, using freshly ground flour, khamir or yeast and milk.

I have not found anything similar to Hyderabadi sheermal in Delhi, even as the city has its own delectable version that is dense and sweet, sometimes flaky and topped with saffron. Many of the ones you find now are richly endowed with a layer of thinly sliced dried fruits, making this bread a meal in itself. During a recent stay in Dadri town in Uttar Pradesh, however, while staying at Shiv Nadar University, I found the small round kulchas at the local naan-bai closest to the sheermals of the Deccan plateau. Exhausted with the hostel dining hall food, I spent much of my Ramadan savouring these kulchas with a local speciality – kaju qeema.

## Dawasaz and the spice mix

Back with Hyderbadi nahari, it is safe to say that we have now arrived at the most critical part of this assemblage of flavours, which takes us straight to the doorstep of the local dawasaz: the Unani and Ayurvedic herbalists. As their name suggests, dawasaz make medicines, having been formally trained with university degrees in Unani and Ayurvedic medicine. At the dawasaz, one is overwhelmed by the bouquet of scents and meticulously organised glass jars and metal boxes, containing rare herbs (jadi butis), carefully named, numbered and often catalogued. The store presents itself as a library of spices, social relations and histories. Some even double up as clinics and host-certified Unani hakims and Ayurvedic vaids for the people to consult for specific ailments.

These shops have been traditionally owned by Marwari and Muslim mercantile families, with new entrants making their appearance each year. Despite competition from supermarkets and exclusive dried fruit stores, dawasaz have adapted and survived over time. These shops remain a lifeline for local communities in Hyderabad to procure herbs, resins, dried fruits, curative panjiris (powdered supplements), murabbas (like gooseberry preserves), medicinal tonics, organic cosmetics and, most importantly, potli ka masala.

The spice mix that is used to make the nahari is known as potli ka masala. The word 'potli' means a small round bag, referring to the muslin cloth that is used to hold the mix. This muslin potli is carefully dropped into the broth, richly suffusing it with flavours. It contains a unique potpourri of fragrant ingredients with healing properties. The warm, musky, woody and aged scents of the ingredients make it one of the most perfumed mixtures used in cooking.

Over time, the proportions and contents of the potli have been carefully crafted by local khansamas and Unani hakims, keeping in mind the alchemy and nutritive qualities of each ingredient to balance its warming and cooling properties. The principles that animate everyday Hyderabadi cuisine are the Unani discourse around food being healthy and nutritious. Food is medicine and should help nourish the body and the soul. It should smell good, taste good and should suit each temperament. It requires us to be cognisant of the weather and our geography in the food choices we make: what works in Hyderabad may not work in Chicago.

Delphine Roger, writing from Pondicherry in the 1990s, mentions several early Unani treaties patronised by the Qutub Shahi dynasty that ruled the Golconda Sultanate in the northern Deccan (1512–1687). She mentions two treatises in particular that were compiled in Persian: *Mizam ul-Tabaye Qutub Shahi* and *Zubdat ul-Hikam*. These compilations came to have an indelible influence on the hybrid cuisine of the region.

Mohammad Quli Qutub Shah (1580–1612), who is honoured as the founder of the city of Hyderabad, also established a Dar ush-Shifa (House of Healing) in 1595. The Dar ush-Shifa worked both as a hospital and a medical school, attracting several well-known physicians to settle and publish from the Deccan. Even with the changing political landscape after the siege of Golconda (1687) and the coming of the Asaf Jahi dynasty (1724–1948), the medico-culinary discourse remained an important part of Hyderabad's culinary ethos.

To date, hakims continue to recommend Hyderabadi dishes as prescriptions: meethi dal (yellow mung) for strengthening the back, bhindi for breakfast as a laxative, hareira for postnatal care, among others. Hence, the potli ka masala assembled in the Deccan is considered remedial and curative. The hakimi flavour is distinct, and the closest that comes to my mind from elsewhere in the country is the aromatic but subtle bitterness of Lucknow's most delicious tunde kabab.

## Unravelling *Amar Ayyar ki Potli*

For those who have read the *Tales of Amir Hamza* or attended some of the zestful dastangoi performances, nahari's potli is reminiscent of *Amar Ayyar ki Zambeel*. It is a bag that has infinite possibilities, holding endless stories and fables about healing, the origin of each ingredient, the mapping of diverse trade routes and the sensorial experiences of luscious tastes. These eclectic flavours tell histories of labour, scenic plantations and climatic zones. The heady aromas of the potli are steeped in tales of enchanting geographies and connections of historic bazaars, port cities and voyages.

And what is included in that potli? First of all, it includes cooling ingredients like dried vetiver roots (khus ki jad), a popular summer sherbet. Vetiver grass grows wild in damp swampy parts of northern India and is still used in the form of curtains or screens (*chilman*) lining the front porch (*pesh dalan*) of homes or modern-day balconies. Chilmans are frequently watered so that the house is well ventilated with cool fragrant breeze.

Other cooling elements include dried rose petals, rich in vitamin C and considered great for the skin, bay leaves known for their digestive properties, green cardamom, coriander seeds and cumin. The elegant perfume of sandalwood powder lends a deep woody scent to this medley, while also being considered an important part of nerve (*muqawwi-i dimagh*) and cardio (*muqawwi-i qalb*) tonics that are crucial for nourishing the body.

After indulging oneself in the fragrance of one of the costliest woods in the world, *Amar Ayyar ki Zambeel*, i.e. our magical potli, unravels plantations of the tropical climates of Southeast Asia and India's northeast, especially Meghalaya, looking for dried galangal (paan ki jad or kulanjan). This is a fragrant rhizome that acts as a gastric tonic and is considered great for the liver. Today, with rising pollution, kulanjan has regained its reputation in helping remove phlegm and clearing our throat and the voice.

On further scrutiny of the ingredients in the potli, we are filled with the warm musky fragrance of dried spiked ginger lily (kapoor kachri), a rhizome that is considered excellent for hair growth. Kapoor kachri forms the understory of the subtropical Himalayan forests of Assam and Arunachal Pradesh, as it prefers to grow in the shade. Even in the nahari, it thrives under the shadows of other giants of the spice kingdom retaining its flavour.

The fragrant potli also includes star anise, black cardamom, mace and caraway seeds. In addition to be being sourced locally, these spices are imported from different places along the Indian Ocean trade routes.

Locating all the ingredients also means a quick stop in Kerala and Sri Lanka for their black pepper and cinnamon (dalchini). Then to Madagascar and Indonesia for cloves and cubeb or tailed pepper (kabab chini), not to be mistaken with all-spice. Kabab chini is a key ingredient in some family recipes of shami kabab, shikampur and haleem, and it is certainly a vital element in mine. It is considered a healthy digestive that helps to break down high fat content. Every tailed peppercorn is packed with strong flavours. One or two of its corns are enough to infuse a kilogram of meat with its warm peppery fragrance.

In order to source stone flower or lichen (patthar/dagad phul), we must come back to peninsular India through the rich plantations of the Western Ghats and the Nilgiris. This edible fungus grows on trees and rocks and has a pronounced sweet-smelling, earthy and aged scent. It ties Hyderabad to the local food practices of Maharashtra, an important part of the Deccan plateau. Hyderabad's bhojwar ka masala, Maharashtra's goda masala and Chettinad cuisine would be incomplete without it.

Towards the end of the cooking time, nahari is thickened with roasted chana dal powder (phule chane ka atta), beaten yoghurt and crushed fried onions, even as the texture remains soupy. The freshness of green chillies and generous bunches of coriander and mint leaves complements the complex flavours that come together in the cooking pot.

Some preparations are made richer by adding creamy and nutty flavours of chironji, poppy seeds and roasted khopra or dried coconut that has been ground to a fine paste. In short, it is wrapped in vivid flavours that hold a place of prestige in Unani and Ayurvedic medicines, while reflecting the global flows of commodities from across continents.

## Putting the dish together

In many ways, Hyderabadi nahari – with its sources from the local dawasaz – is at the confluence of many cultural histories that in the present day become a site for its living culinary practices. This dish can be located in the vastly globalising landscape of the Deccan which, in the past, has seen a constant movement of people, commodities and ideas, just as it does today.

In the present, muslin cloth can be substituted with stainless steel infusers, cooking over wood with pressure cookers and crockpots and DIY cleaning with the unmatched convenience of pre-cleaned trotters from the butcher shops or online stores. It is in these transformations that we can see Hyderabad's ever-mutating cuisine, animated by new cooking techniques, culinary exchange, trade and migration. The potli ka masala continues to initiate us into new vernaculars of a uniquely Deccani experience in our hybrid geographies. Whether in Hyderabad or the diaspora, the Deccan flavours come alive through this therapeutic potli.

As hakims and family elders humbly remind us, all healing is in the hands of the Almighty and thus the food we ingest, aromas we inhale and the many sensory gifts (*ne'mat*), are just a way (*zariya*) to nourish our soul (*nafs*) and body. Nahari is not your usual cliche of luxuries, nor will it leave you with clogged arteries: it is a celebration of bounties. It is a gift that ushers in the blessing of daylight (*barkat-i nahar*), making it synonymous with a promise of life emerging in the everyday.

## Everyday Meat Shorba

**Ingredients**

250g mutton or other meat with bones (shoulder or raan)
4–5 strands of vetiver roots (khus ki jad)
1 small piece of lichen/stone flower (dagad phul)
1 onion, finely chopped
1 tsp ginger–garlic paste
½ tsp turmeric
1 tsp red chilli powder
½ tsp black peppercorns
1 bunch of coriander leaves
2 green chillies
1 tbsp curd, beaten (optional)
saffron (optional)
water
salt to taste
oil/ghee

**Method**

1. Fry the onions to golden brown, then add the turmeric and ginger–garlic paste. Mix and continue frying.
2. Add the red chilli powder, followed by the meat and fry it all together until the meat changes colour and is ready to leave its moisture.
3. Add the peppercorns, 2 cups of water and salt to taste. Roll the vetiver roots and lichen in a muslin cloth or place them

in a tea infuser and drop them in the cooking pot. Cook in a 3-litre pressure cooker for 8–9 whistles on medium flame or slow cook till the meat is soft. You can add more water and salt as required.

4. Garnish the shorba with finely chopped coriander leaves and fresh green chillies. Savour with warm crispy parathas. An everyday shorba to rehydrate the body during summers and for the much-needed warmth in winters can be enjoyed at all times of the day.

## Nahari

### Ingredients

6 trotters, cleaned
3 tongues, cleaned and cut in two
1 bunch fresh mint leaves
1 bunch fresh coriander leaves
1 tsp turmeric powder
1 tsp red chilli powder
2 tsp ginger–garlic paste
1 packet potli ka masala (wrapped in a muslin cloth or a large tea infuser, tightly sealed)
2 medium-size onion (finely sliced, fried to golden brown and crushed)
4–5 tbsp beaten yoghurt
1 tbsp roasted chana dal powder (phule chane ka atta); add more, depending on the thickness you desire
3–4 green chillies (whole)

2 litres of water
salt to taste

**Method**

1. In a 10-litre pressure cooker, add the cleaned trotters and tongue with 2 litres of water, turmeric, red chilli powder, ginger–garlic paste and salt. At this step, you can also add half of the mint and coriander leaves for fragrance. Let it cook on low/medium flame for an hour. Once the aroma of the trotters thickens and the air gets heavier, you will know it is time. Let it cool. (You can do this step the night before and store the broth in the fridge.)
2. The second part of the story begins now. Make sure you crush the fried onions (by hand) and add them to the broth. Drop in the potli ka masala neatly tied in a muslin cloth and tightly sealed, for if the potli unravels in the nahari, it will take away all its magical subtlety and make the shorba bitter. Let it cook covered on low a flame for 20 minutes. You can add more water and salt if required.
3. Add the green chillies, remaining coriander and mint leaves and beaten yoghurt. Add the phule chane ka atta to thicken the nahari. If you prefer it thick, add more. Let it cook for 10–15 minutes and leave it covered for some time before serving. Enjoy your meal with crispy parathas or soft sheermals.

# Kashmiri Saag

*Iqbal Ahmed*

Although saag is referred to colloquially in Kashmir as a poor man's dish, it is eaten by rich and poor alike in the Valley. Furthermore, the Kashmiri diaspora is fond of growing this vegetable in their kitchen gardens in both Europe and America. In fact, saag is a broad term that refers to a variety of leafy vegetables grown in Kashmir, Punjab and other regions of the Indian subcontinent. However, it is the collard greens known as 'saag' that are most widely grown in Kashmir.

People living in Srinagar distinguish the saag grown on city land from its cousin, grown on the marshy land in Dal Lake and deemed to be less tasty. Red spinach is also known as the king of saag and is cooked as a delicacy. When the famous English actress Joanna Lumley travelled to Bradford for a TV documentary, she met a group of Asian women who informed her that they had grown Kashmiri spinach on a community allotment. She proudly told them that she too is a Kashmiri, having been born in Srinagar in 1946 – a year before the Raj ended.

Whenever I visited my grandma's home during my childhood in Srinagar, I was captivated by a large swath of land, not far from her home, on which only saag was grown. I would sit on a parapet wall and watch the city farmers tending a big crop while their womenfolk would click the saag leaves one by one before tying them in small bunches and throwing them in a basket. The men would draw water from the wells in a bucket by pulling a rope attached to a wooden pole that went up and down like a seesaw.

One of the women from this farm would come to our neighbourhood every morning. She brought a big basket of saag, balanced on her head over protective padded headgear, which she sold from door to door. She was quite tall and wore a long traditional garment known as a pheran. She counted the bunches of saag in fours and you could buy a score for a rupee. She would throw in an extra four bunches (like the sixteenth-century English bakers who added a complimentary thirteenth loaf to every dozen bought by their customers). Even then, some of her regular customers would bargain with her for four more free bunches.

In 1979 she went on a pilgrimage to Mecca which, in those days, took many months to accomplish as most of the pilgrims from Kashmir made the journey over land and sea, not by air. That year, there was a deadly incident at Mecca and some of the pilgrims died. We didn't see our saag-walli for several weeks after other pilgrims had returned to Kashmir and so we assumed that she must have gone to her heavenly abode.

Then one day she returned, with her basket of saag balanced hands-free on her head. Everyone in the neighbourhood was thrilled to see her and the older women gave her a warm, welcoming hug.

When I was about ten years old, I grew saag in our walled kitchen garden in the old town of Srinagar. One day a cockerel belonging to our neighbours jumped over the wall and devoured my crop. I was distraught when I saw all my efforts laid to waste. My cousin, who reared a few chickens at his home, was even more upset when his mother decided to cook one of them, and he refused to eat dinner because he couldn't bear to see one of his beloved chickens lying on his plate.

## A soothing broth

In Kashmir, saag is either cooked on its own or with lamb, but it is always served on its own at weddings. An expert cook adds a few big spoonfuls of lamb broth to give the dish a rich flavour. A school friend's mother once unwittingly added some lamb broth when she cooked saag for some guests who were vegetarians – fortunately they never found out. Some Kashmiri Pandits are not strictly vegetarian and eat lamb. I invited a Pandit friend to my home for dinner a couple of years ago and when I asked him if he preferred a vegetarian or non-vegetarian meal, he jokingly replied that he would gladly eat the food of the Rakshasa (demon) that day, thus revealing his predilection for a non-vegetarian meal.

Lamb broth is usually served in Kashmir when someone isn't feeling well, much as chicken soup is referred to as 'Jewish paracetamol' in northwest London. Incidentally, our family doctor in Kashmir would always advise a patient who was unwell to eat yoghurt with a hard-baked Kashmiri bread roll, as it was good for your gut.

For a long time, I didn't think you could cook kale as saag, though now it tastes just like it. I found Indian restaurants in London serving saag paneer, which in fact consists of spinach and cottage cheese. After I got married, my wife found curly kale on sale in a supermarket and started to cook it like Kashmiri saag. Since then she has been cooking it almost every day. Kale has become fashionable in London lately and is served as a salad with a lemon dressing.

Saag chawal is the staple food in Kashmir. In Punjab, saag is served with a roti, but in Kashmir it is always accompanied by chawal. Many years ago, a politician who suggested that Kashmiris should eat home-grown potatoes instead of rice in order to be more self-sufficient was mocked for such an outlandish idea. My Punjabi friends in London eat Kashmiri saag with relish when they come over for dinner. It doesn't matter to them whether it's served with roti or not.

One day I found out that the city farm near my grandma's home in Srinagar had been converted into a cricket stadium. I also discovered during my childhood that tobacco plants were being grown in another city farm in Srinagar. The green leaves of these plants looked like saag from a distance. The leaves were dried in the sun and turned into tobacco, to be smoked in hookahs. The dried tobacco was later mixed with a thick syrup.

In Srinagar, rumour has it that some *nouveau riche* artisans in the town filled their hookahs with milk instead of water, which has become a metaphor in Kashmir for outrageous spending. You can find glass hookahs filled with absinthe in a shisha lounge in Mayfair where they charge their Middle Eastern patrons more than £100 for a smoke.

It is customary in Srinagar to offer a hookah to a guest if he is a habitual smoker of the locally produced tobacco. I used to run errands for guests at my family home to buy tobacco from a shop in our neighbourhood. The only question the tobacconist would ask me, before wrapping it in an old newspaper, was whether I wanted the light or heavy kind of tobacco. I had to memorise each guest's preference.

The tobacconist would also buy old notebooks from schoolchildren to be used as wrapping paper, whereas printed textbooks were usually sold to other children at the end of the academic year. It was a most effective circular economy.

Some of the older women in Kashmir smoke hookahs. One of my great-aunts was among them and I found it fascinating to watch her tilt its copper pot with one hand for the pipe to reach her mouth. The pipes of the hookahs in Kashmir are rigid as they are made of bamboo and therefore you have to sit straight to smoke rather than leaning on a bolster when the pipe is of a flexible variety.

## A neighbour's dish

The other green vegetable grown abundantly in Kashmir is kohlrabi. Its leaves aren't as tender as those of collard greens and you have to cook them for a bit longer. The name of this vegetable is proverbial in Kashmiri for the daily grind. These days you can find all kinds of exotic vegetables, from kohlrabi to dudhi, on display at greengrocers in London. I sometimes buy kohlrabi at an international grocer's in Golders Green, more for its saag-like leaves than its bulbs.

It is a challenge for most parents to get their children to eat green peas, let alone a leafy vegetable like saag. Knowing my aversion to turnips, my mother would change its name from Kashmiri to Urdu whenever I asked her what she had cooked for dinner. At other times she would borrow a dish from our next-door neighbour when I refused to eat what she had cooked that day, since in one's childhood a neighbour's cooking almost always tastes better than your own mother's.

Nowadays, when I visit my parents in Srinagar, I ask my mother to cook saag. My father still grows it in his kitchen garden and shares it with his neighbours.

Grown on the marshy land in Dal Lake, saag is sold by weight, whereas the kind grown in the city is sold by the bunch. While preparing it for cooking, the leaves are checked one by one and the stem is removed if it is a bit tough. It is painstaking work and you usually end up getting rid of a bigger portion than the one you cook.

Kashmiris cook saag in many different ways. In its simplest form, saag is steamed and served as a dish in itself. Occasionally you would add a whole aubergine to a pot of saag to make it more palatable. In Kashmiri villages, many people pickle saag. Fish and saag are usually cooked together on special occasions. To mark the arrival of spring, my friend's mother always cooked fish and saag on Nowruz. The fish used is mostly the carp found in Dal Lake that is sold by fisherwomen in Srinagar.

In the summer of 2016, I ventured from my parents' home on my bike during curfew to stretch my legs and visit a friend I'd not seen for a long time who lived at the foot of the Zabarwan Mountains. On my way back, I saw a woman in colourful gear selling fish on Foreshore Road. I got off my bike to have a look at the fish in her tub. The fisherwomen in Srinagar usually hide their catch from the searching gaze of a prospective customer by covering their tubs with a moist cloth that also keeps the fish cool. They often take a big fish out to persuade a bargain-hunter to buy from her.

It is never easy for a man to bargain with these ladies because their smooth talk is so disarming and commanding of deference that they can out-bargain most of their potential customers. An exception was an uncle of mine who on one occasion encountered a fisherwoman in a market who addressed him as 'brother-in-law'. Being streetwise, he told her that he was no one's brother-in-law and she should quote a more realistic price for her fish.

## A hard bargain

One fisherwoman, whom I saw sitting on the bank of Dal Lake in Foreshore Road, poured all her fish into a plastic carrier bag and handed it to me before I'd even agreed to buy them. The fish were very small and I knew that my mother would be none too pleased with my purchase. I told the fish-seller that I didn't want to be thrown out of my parents' home. She took the bag back and offered to cut and clean the fish herself to save my mother the trouble of taking their guts out, a time-consuming business that requires expertise.

She cleaned the fish effortlessly in no time at all before handing them back to me in the carrier bag. When I asked her the price she said that I could pay her the next time I was around. I told her that I didn't live in the town and was only visiting my parents for a few days. She retorted that in that case I didn't need to pay her anything at all, thus putting me in the position of being indebted to her, which would be very much to her advantage in any future transactions with me. I had to insist that she accept my payment.

When I got home with the fish, I related the incident to my mother. She said that the fisherwoman was well known for her bargaining skills and had once sold fish to my cousin, together with the tub, even though he is known to be a cautious businessman. It made me smile, knowing that I didn't stand a chance of refusing the fisherwoman's offer. My mother observed that the fish I'd brought her were such small fry that she couldn't cook them with the saag, and so decided to serve the fish as an appetiser instead.

These days, whenever small fish are served as an appetiser, I'm reminded of the dried fish my grandmother liked to cook during my childhood.

## Saada Saag

I have a predilection for plain kale, or saada saag. I thus offer this recipe borrowed from my other half. Saada saag is better relished with chawal than roti.

### Ingredients

180g Kashmiri saag or kale
3 cloves garlic, chopped
½ tsp salt
2 tbsp vegetable oil
½ tsp cumin seeds
3 green chillies, chopped

**Method**

1. Chop saag into small pieces and wash it thoroughly with cold water.
2. Pour ⅔ litre of water into a large saucepan. Bring it to boiling point and then add chopped garlic and salt. Add saag and let it boil for 15 minutes.
3. Next, add vegetable oil, cumin seeds and green chillies. Let it simmer until the saag is tender.

# There's More to Dal Than You Might Think

*Rana Safvi*

After a grand wedding, with quite a few lavish meals consisting of every possible Awadhi meat and vegetarian dish, sweetmeats and flatbreads, the bridegroom's party returned to Sultan Manzil with the bride. In keeping with tradition, at the threshold the bridegroom washed the bride's feet in milk mixed with saffron strands. Next, the bride entered her new house to the strains of the melodious shehnai playing at the deorhi, or entrance. By this time all the ceremonies were over. These included the *munh dikhai*, a custom where the heavily veiled bride's face is shown to the bridegroom's relatives who then give gifts. After days of rituals, the bride and bridegroom were exhausted. However, there was still dinner to come, lavishly prepared for the many guests who had gathered to meet and greet the new bride.

Dinner brought one more custom. The bridegroom was requested, *Miyan, dulhan ko apni pasand ka ek luqma khilao*. 'Son, feed your bride a morsel of your favourite dish.' The bridegroom immediately reached for a bowl of arhar ki dal, prepared for an old and infirm relative. He took a spoonful onto his plate and, making a morsel of it with a chapati, lovingly fed it to his bride. Little was he to know the uproar that would follow.

'Arre! What will the dulhan think? There was so much to choose from and you fed her dal?' asked his mother.

'You said my favourite dish, Ammi. Dal is my favourite,' replied the groom.

Under my ghunghat – the dupatta pulled over my face to act as a veil – I smiled. After so many days of feasting, it was a relief to eat something simple and tasty. And now I also understood the way to my husband's heart.

Arhar ki dal continues to be my husband's favourite, and dal continues to be a regular fixture on our table. In that, we are not alone. It is a staple food of most Indians and, in a way, a unifying force as, throughout the subcontinent, we can see many forms of it.

## Humayun and the Safavids

My in-laws claim descent from the Safavids of Iran. Yet they were unaware that centuries ago their famous ancestor Shah Tahmasp (1514–1576) had also shown a preference for dal.

The Mughal emperor Humayun ruled for only a short time before he was ousted to spend many years of exile in Persia. There he picked up the finer tastes of life, which his warrior father Babur, the founder of the dynasty, had not possessed the luxury of leisure to enjoy. In an account of Humayun's reign by chronicler Bayazid Bayat, the head taster (*bakawal begi*) describes some of the feasts enjoyed by Humayun in Persia as well as the meals cooked in his camp.

When Shah Tahmasp heard of Humayun's imminent arrival in Herat, he instructed the governor to make special preparations for the royal guest, and invited Humayun to the holy city of Mashhad for a meeting. Twelve hundred dishes were to be cooked for the guest in every province until he reached his destination.

When Humayun was ready to return with the aim of retaking Hindustan, Shah Tahmasp first requested a Hindustani feast with appropriate food and music. Humayun was glad to oblige, and the event was held near Persepolis. A later account by Humayun's ewer-bearer Jauhar Aftabchi records that, apart from the music, the Shah was especially pleased with a dish referred to as khuske pulao with dal. He chose this dish over any of the others because it was a mode of cookery unknown in Persia. Though the Persians too ate khuske pulao, or buttered rice, they mixed it with egg instead.

## Dal through the ages

Dals find mention in Sanskrit, Hindi, Persian and Urdu literature, making this pulse the subject of stories and idioms since ancient times. Excavations at archaeological sites associated with the Indus Valley Civilisation have even revealed the presence of different dals. One has to only to look around the table to see how omnipresent dal is.

Dal is not only found on our dastarkhwans but its consistency makes it ideal for use in our buildings too. Skinned mash or urad ki dal was a stable component of the lime mortar prepared for construction before the use of cement, and it is still used for conservation. Its white colour and binding qualities ensured that it was used in all monuments requiring a marble finish.

Delhi's Moth ki Masjid inspires one of my favourite architectural stories. Moth or matki (dew bean) finds mention in Sanskrit literature, indicating that it has been cultivated in India since around 1000 BCE. There is a famous legend found in a Persian-language chronicle, *Khulasat-ut-tawarikh*, completed by Sujan Rai in 1695 during the reign of the Mughal emperor Aurangzeb. It shows that one day the Lodi sultan, Sikander Shah (1458–1517), found a grain of moth in the Jami Masjid. He picked it up and handed it over to his wise and sagacious minister Miyan Bhoiya, who paid obeisance and took it.

The minister thought that, since the grain had the honour of being touched by the Sultan, he should ensure that it received everlasting fame. Accordingly, he sowed it in an orchard attached to his house; the plant that grew from it yielded two hundred grains. He kept repeating this process until he had a full harvest a few years later.

Subsequently, he built a mosque from the proceeds of selling that harvest. He informed the Sultan about his labours and invited him to recite his prayers in the mosque, which was hereafter called Moth ki Masjid. Today, it is no longer a functioning mosque but it still continues to stand as a grand testimony to the power of that grain of moth.

Mash ki dal had clearly come out of construction material into its own. The skinned mash ki dal is a common sight on festive dastarkhwans. It is an excellent accompaniment for qorma as its dryness complements the curry.

In our house, arhar and masoor ki dals are staple, everyday food, while mash ki dal is cooked for festive occasions. A factor is that plain rice cooked for daily meals needs a dal with gravy, while, on festive occasions, the rice preparation is normally a biryani or pulao, making a dry dal more suitable.

Nowadays, dal is to be found in so many Indian dishes, be it shami kabab, dahi–vada, idli–dosa and sambhar and – as besan, or gram flour – in qormas and niharis, pakoris and parathas. Outside India, it finds its way into that Anglo-Indian invention of mulligatawny soup and into a range of vegetarian or vegan ready meals.

## Travel and celebrations

Dal is also traditionally used for celebrations and mourning. A story showcasing how food travels, as well as the syncretism of the Mughal court, is the following anecdote related by Munshi Faizuddin Dehlvi in his *Bazm-i akhir* (1885). The author was a courtier during the time of the last Mughal Emperor Bahadur Shah Zafar (1775–1862), serving as an attendant to the Emperor's father-in-law, Mirza Ilahi Baksh. He describes an important celebration called Jashn-i Tajposhi to commemorate the day of coronation.

The night before the jashn, or celebration, was called ratjaga, indicating the necessity to stay awake the whole night. Munshi

Faizuddin notes that the start of the function in the evening would be marked by the soaking of seven handfuls of yellow mung dal, or skinless split green gram, by the Emperor's chief consort. After this was ground, the Emperor would come into the ladies' section with much fanfare and put the first few vadas in the kadhai cooking pot to fry. In this way, the Jashn-i Tajposhi was officially inaugurated.

This practice was likely an influence of the Rajput women married into the Mughal family as, even today, any celebration in Rajasthan and parts of Uttarakhand begins with the frying of vadas made from dal. A similar practice is found in western Uttar Pradesh. In my family's qasba of Jalali in western Uttar Pradesh, no fried food is eaten during the month of Muharram. At this time, we observe mourning to commemorate the martyrdom of Husain, the grandson of the Holy Prophet, in the plains of Karbala in 61 AH or 680 CE. The end of the mourning is signalled by heating oil in the kadhais for the frying of vadas.

## Food for the prince and the pauper

Dal–roti or dal–chawal has become a shorthand for simple eating, often being described as the poor man's meal. But isn't what is nutritious for the common man also good enough for a king? A cook in Lucknow was to prove this.

In his famous account *Guzishta Lucknow*, Abdul Halim Sharar (1860–1926) describes an incident often associated with this saying, but attributed to different Nawabs. Sharar himself names the Nawab in question as Nawab Asaf-ud-Daula of Awadh (ruled 1775–1797).

According to him, a bawarchi, or chef, sought employment with the Nawab. He was asked, 'What do you cook?'

He replied, 'I only cook mash ki dal.'

He was asked, 'What salary will you take?'

He replied, 'Five hundred rupees.'

The Nawab sahib employed him. However, the cook put forward his conditions, saying he would only take up the job if certain conditions were met.

When asked, he said, 'When huzoor wishes to relish the dal cooked by me, it must be ordered a day before. And when I inform that it is ready, huzoor should partake of it immediately.' The Nawab agreed to these conditions.

After a few months, the bawarchi was ordered to cook the dal. He prepared it and informed the Nawab. The Nawab replied that he was coming and that everything should be laid out. The dastarkhwan was accordingly set, but the Nawab sahib remained engrossed in conversation. The bawarchi went up to the Nawab sahib and gently reminded him, 'The *khasa* (royal meal) is ready.' The Nawab still tarried, so he reminded him a third time.

When the Nawab sahib still did not come, the bawarchi picked up the pot of dal and emptied it onto the roots of a withered tree. Handing in his resignation, he left the palace. In oral history, the punchline of this story references a different dal, but still encapsulates the attitude of the belligerent bawarchi: '*Ye muh aur masoor ki dal!*' (You don't deserve masoor dal!).

The Nawab regretted the bawarchi's departure later and instituted a search for him, but found no trace. A few days later, it was discovered that the dead tree into which the dal had been poured had grown shoots and become green!

This story is, of course, exaggerated and far-fetched. However, it does showcase the high esteem in which a cook was held: that he could demand a king's ransom for a wage and put forward demands and conditions from a Nawab. We see the importance that dal, though these days considered a poor man's dish, could at one time command in India.

From these historical stories, we see that there's much more to dal than we think! The love affair with dal continues on my family's dining table and in millions of Indian homes across the world. Do explore your family stories and history, as you never know what treasures you will find.

## MASH KI DAL – A FAMILY RECIPE

### Ingredients

2 cups mash dal (white urad dal)
4 cups water
¼ tsp garam masala
green chilli to taste
2 tbsp desi ghee
1 large onion, sliced finely
2 whole dried red chilli
ginger, cut into juliennes and a slice
a few sprigs of mint leaves
salt to taste

### Method

1. Soak the dal in the water for one hour.
2. Boil the soaked dal with salt and a slice of ginger. Skim the top regularly to remove the foam with a large metal spoon.
3. Cook the dal for approximately 15 minutes, until it is done and the water absorbed. Strain if there is additional water.
4. Add garam masala, plus green chillies and a sprig of mint leaves to the dal. Cover the pot with a tight lid and leave to cook on simmer for 10–15 minutes. When the urad dal has cooked to perfection, it should be dry with each grain fluffy and separated, like rice in a pulao.
5. Remove the ginger, mint leaves and green chilli before serving. It should be plain white.

*For the tempering:*

1. Fry the finely sliced onions and whole red chillies in a generous amount of desi ghee.
2. Pour half of the fried onions and red chilli onto the dal when it is ready for serving. The extra ghee and fried onions can be served separately to be taken as per individual taste.
3. Garnish with ginger juliennes and a few mint leaves.

# Kanhi Served with a Side of Nostalgia

*Fehmida Zakeer*

Congee, kanji or kanhi is a simple unspiced dish which most people associate with illness. The food historian K. T. Achaya calls the rice congee an invalid repast, while Indian cuisine expert Colleen Taylor Sen notes that one of the most common ways to prepare rice under Ayurvedic guidance is to boil it into a gruel or porridge. She says, 'Rice gruel is prescribed for invalids or people who have gone through a regimen of purging and emetics.' In its most simple form, kanji, made by boiling rice in water, is a filling dish that is easily absorbed by the body, hence its widespread renown as a 'sickness food'.

Kanji has a presence in many cuisines the world over, but particularly those in Asian countries, including Japan, the Philippines, Indonesia, Thailand, Korea and China. In India, kanji and its variants exist in many regional cuisines, where it carries various names: jaou or phena bhaat (in Bengali), ganji (in Kannada and Hindi), sanpiau (in Mizoram), as well as kanhi (in Malayalam), a word deriving from the Tamil kanji which means 'boilings'. The base grain used in preparing this food may be rice, wheat or millet. The chosen grain is boiled in water, milk or coconut milk, either singly or in combination with various pulses, medicinal herbs and spices. Ultimately, the makeup and composition of congee varies according to the food practices of the region.

According to Eileen Yin-Fei Lo, an author of Chinese cookbooks, the oldest reference to this food is in writings from

China tracing back to 1000 BC during the Zhou Dynasty. Nearer to home, the first verifiable description of the gruel is in the sixteenth-century *Supa Shastra*, written by Mangarasa III, the Jain ruler of Kallahalli in Mysore. King Mangarasa III loved to cook and was deeply interested in tracing the origin of food recipes. He explored Sanskrit literature to learn about the art and science of cooking, and liked to put his knowledge into practice. Through the *Supa Shastra*, written in Sanskrit in verse form, he tried to impart his understanding of cooking techniques to help his readers cook food cleanly and tastefully.

Somewhat later, in 1900, another recipe for a version of congee, called pish-pash, appeared in *The Indian Cookery Book*, published by a well-known Calcutta-based company, Thacker, Spink & Co. The recipe calls for cooking long-grain rice, like basmati, with chicken, meat and spices, until the ingredients are mushy and tender, adding that it is a nutritious meal for invalids. This dish was also mentioned in *The Cookery Book of Lady Clark of Tillypronie*, published in 1909. According to the Hobson-Jobson dictionary of colloquial Anglo-Indian words and phrases, pish-pash is 'a slop of rice-soup with small pieces of meat in it, much used in the Anglo-Indian nursery'.

Perhaps the blandness of plain congee accounts for its survival through the ages. Its neutral profile provides an uncomplicated base for the hosting of multiple flavours, allowing itself to fit into the palate preferences of people across diverse cultures. When we look at how congee is consumed around the world, we see recipes that enhance the taste of the dish with delectable side dishes or by incorporating other ingredients into the original recipe.

When my family moved from Delhi to Chennai (then Madras) in the mid-1980s, our neighbours introduced us to nombu kanji during the fasting month of Ramzan. It was unlike any kanji we had ever seen or eaten. Flecked with chopped coriander and mint leaves, the kanji was light orange and had the faint aroma of biryani. Muslims in Tamil Nadu and many parts of Karnataka and Andhra Pradesh open their fasts during Ramzan with nombu kanji. The dish in fact derives its name from the word 'nombu', which means 'fast' in Tamil and Malayalam. The nombu kanji is not only made in homes but also in mosques in many regions of southern India. In mosques where worshippers are served food to open their fasts, nombu kanji is offered along with dates, juice, samosa or any fried snack. It is also distributed from mosques in the evening before sunset to anyone who comes to collect it, without any religious or status restrictions. During Ramzan, it is common to see people queueing up in front of mosque gates with steel containers to take some nombu kanji home.

Raw or broken rice and yellow mung dal form the base of this kanji. The rice and lentils are cooked in plenty of water with fenugreek, onions, tomato, green chillies, turmeric powder and a pinch of garam masala powder. Once the ingredients are well cooked, the mixture is tempered with onions fried in ghee along with cinnamon, cloves and ginger–garlic paste. Some people may add coconut milk or tiny mincemeat balls according to taste. Mint and coriander leaves, and sometimes grated coconut, are added to the mixture to add a note of freshness to the kanji.

Sometimes nombu kanji may also be made with the aromatic short-grained rice called jeeraga chamba, which increases the flavour profile of the rice gruel. The jeeraga chamba rice (also called seeraga samba and khaima rice) derives its name from cumin seeds because of its resemblance in size to the spice called jeeragam or jeera/zeera in many Indian languages. Chamba refers to the cropping season in Tamil Nadu known as the samba season during which this variety of rice is grown – the period from August to January. This cumin-sized rice easily absorbs flavours and is about one-third the size of the basmati rice. In the north Keralan Mappila cuisine as well as in the cuisines of some communities in the neighbouring state of Tamil Nadu, biryani is cooked with jeeraga chamba rice too.

In my native north Kerala Malabar Muslim region, although there is a practice of making kanji, or kanhi as it is called in

Malayalam, during Ramzan, the custom of opening fasts with kanhi is not very prevalent. In the Malabar region, kanhi is just one of the beverages made in rotation with other nutritious drinks during the fasting month.

In Malabar cuisine, the closest to a nombu kanji in popularity would be the light yellow-coloured jeeraga kanhi or jeerakanji made in many Mappila households during the fasting month. On her food blog, *A Big Sweet Tooth*, Rafeeda Abdul Raheem shares the following reflections on this dish: 'Jeerakanji or Cumin Rice Porridge is something that we make almost every night during the month of Ramzan. Cumin is a very good digestive, and [the kanhi] is a good source of energy. It is a filler and is normally something the men drink just before they go for the Taraweeh prayers [night prayers that could go on for an hour at least] or as the last meal before going to sleep.'

To learn more about the time-honoured congees of Mappila gastronomy, I reached out to Mrs Ummi Abdullla, who is considered to be the matriarch of that cuisine. In her eighties now, Ummi Abdulla brought out her first cookbook in 1981, featuring recipes for foods in Malabar Muslim cuisine. There had not been much awareness of this cuisine outside the community until that time. Since then, she has brought out nine cookbooks, three in English and the rest in her native tongue, Malayalam. In my conversation with her, she mentioned that during the fasting month of Ramzan, many people in the community make kanhi in some form or another. Even within the Malabar region, each area has its own special kanhi. For example, she said that in her hometown of Tikkodi and nearby regions, jeeraga kanhi made with cumin seeds is the popular choice, while in Kozhikode (formerly Calicut) and Thalasherry (formerly Telicherry), unique recipes for different flavourful kanhi exist in which the base grain may be rice or wheat.

I also approached the novelist and writer B. M. Zuhara, who is also sister to Ummi Abdulla, about the practice of making jeeraga kanhi during the fasting month. She mentioned that while growing up in Tikkodi, they had a tradition in their household of sending kanhi to the mosque so that it could be distributed among the worshippers. They sent the yellow-coloured jeeraga kanhi since it is filling and flavourful and also good for the stomach after fasting. Apart from the fasting month, Zuhara sometimes also makes jeeraga kanhi for dinner, especially after having a heavy lunch or attending a wedding or a party.

The preparation for the jeeraga kanhi involves cooking the rice in water and then mixing into it a smooth paste of coconut, turmeric powder, cumin and shallots. The base for this kanhi may be an aromatic rice such as jeeraga chamba or plain raw rice.

Ummi Abdulla's latest book of recipes is a coffee table book entitled *A Kitchen Full of Stories*, co-written with her granddaughter, Nazaneen Jalaludheen. Published in 2018, the book is both a memoir and a cookbook. It is packed with recipes that are accompanied by stories about Ummi Abdulla's childhood as well as the traditions and customs of the community. In this book, Ummi Abdulla lists kanhi as a light midday meal, taken around 11 a.m., between breakfast and lunch. At this brunch time, it could just be a glass of unpolished rice boiled to a mush and served with thick coconut milk, or it could be a special kanhi, depending on the mood of the day. Calling the kanhi a meal in itself, Ummi Abdulla writes, 'A simple and easy to make meal, the rice gruel soothes the body and soul. Whether it is a fever or a bad stomach, the kanji (minus the coconut milk) cures it all. It can even become a substitute for dinner in a pinch. In Mappila-speak, a kinnam (bowl) of kanhi keeps the doctor away. Kanhi is generally taken to be a food that digests easily since rice is well cooked in plenty of water until it is mushy and soft. Additionally, it has a hydrating effect on the body and the carbohydrate content makes it a good source of instant energy.'

Wheat grains replace rice in a special kanhi preparation that is considered a delicacy in Thalasherry and Kozhikode. Since the process for making it is quite laborious, the gothamba or wheat kanhi is made only for special occasions. After weddings, elaborate feasts are prepared for the bridegroom, and gothamba kanhi would be one of the items served at breakfast along with other special dishes. Wheat is soaked in water for an hour and then cooked along with chicken and chopped onions. After cooking, the chicken is removed from the mixture, shredded and placed aside. The boiled wheat is mixed with thin coconut milk and strained through a sieve – a time-consuming process requiring an abundance of patience. Thick coconut milk and shredded chicken are added to the strained wheat mixture along with diced shallots fried in ghee.

A shortcut method to make the wheat kanhi is to use a blender to mash the boiled wheat, forgoing the painstaking step of sieving the mixture. 'Though the taste is not the same as the kanhi prepared in the traditional way, it is nevertheless an easy way to prepare the wheat kanhi,' says Ummi Abdulla with a chuckle.

I found out from my maternal aunt, Zafeera Amin, that a sweet version of the gothamba kanhi also exists in the kanhi repertoire of Thalasherry. In this version, polished wheat is cooked along with chana dal and mixed well. Sugar, cardamom powder and thick coconut milk are added to the mixture. The sweet version of the wheat kanhi is considered a dessert and served with other desserts to the bridegroom after an elaborate dinner.

My mother makes an exceptionally flavourful parippu (lentil) kanhi during Ramzan by cooking equal amounts of jeeraga chamba rice and yellow mung dal along with diced onions. The boiled mixture is mashed well, and coconut milk is added to it along with a sprinkle of cardamom powder and diced shallots fried in ghee. The golden kanji with translucent onion bits floating in the creamy mixture feels like liquid silk as it slides down the throat. Sometimes she substitutes the yellow dal with green mung dal and boils it with rice and water. Grated coconut, soaked and rubbed in water, is added to the cooked mixture along with dried ginger, crushed and lightly fried in ghee. The light crunch of the grated coconut and gentle spiciness of the ginger elevates the flavour profile of this kanhi.

While kanhi still finds a place on the dinner table, what is slowly disappearing is the traditional ways of preparing the dish, says Ummi Abdulla. 'I try to follow the traditional methods as much as I can, but the ingredients we used to get previously are just not easily available today'. She cites the example of nurukku, or broken rice grains, left over after winnowing rice. 'In my ancestral home, during wedding celebrations, women sat around in the kitchen, cleaning and sieving bags of rice. After removing the clean grains, the remaining broken rice would be used to make plain kanji or jeeraga kanhi. The taste of the kanhi we make today is quite different from what we used to have.'

Perhaps one type of kanhi that has truly gone away from the Mappila kitchen is the kaadi. This kanhi, made out of discarded food from the kitchen, did not appear on mainstream dining tables even when it used to be made up to about three decades ago. Made out of thavidu, or rice husk, and fish heads, it was a wholesome one-pot dish that was often made and eaten in the kitchen. Sardines, ponyfish and catfish heads were especially prized when making this dish, according to my sixty-four-year-old aunt. It was a rustic and informal dish, made with whatever was available each day and mostly eaten as lunch by the maids, and also the women of the house, if they had a taste for it. My mother remembers making it with nurukku in our own house many years ago. She says relatives who had settled outside Kerala nicknamed it 'Malabar Biryani' and requested it on their yearly visits. However, the nickname was a misnomer considering that the dish did not rely on masalas or spices for its taste; its flavour came from the base ingredients used in making it.

Ummi Abdulla remembers her childhood days during the time of India's early Independence when her family had rice husk at home from the paddy fields they owned. 'Thavidu is very tasty to eat by itself. We used to collect the thavidu and mix it with jaggery before eating. The maids who helped in the kitchen would make kaadi for themselves, and sometimes we would also help ourselves to it.' She says that she has not made the dish for a long time now, simply because there is no thavidu to be found easily.

In the days when rice was cultivated in household farms, husking and pounding of paddy to extract grains were done by farm hands on the premises of the owners. Since the processes used to be done manually, the nutrient-rich skin and broken pieces could easily be gathered and distributed. It eliminated the wastage of precious grains even if they were broken, and was a healthy source of food, especially for the workers who had limited resources. However, due to the mechanisation of agricultural processes, the by-products of rice production are now lost in the whirl and speed of machines, ironically making them a scarce commodity today when people are in search of healthy food products.

The various kanhi recipes of the Malabar cuisine play with interesting combinations of ingredients to present the dish with different flavour profiles. However, it is more of a comfort food that is prepared and eaten when one wants to have a light meal or does not want to spend too much time in the kitchen. While it may never to get to be the centrepiece at an extravagant meal, this simple flavourful food will always be the one that evokes memories of home and family.

## Jeeraga Kanji – From Ummi Abdulla's *A Kitchen Full of Stories*

The gentle combination of cumin and turmeric is immensely soothing and is the perfect comfort food. The coconut in the recipe can be skipped if you don't want its flavour in the soup. The shallots add texture to this delightful soup.

This kanji tastes best when cooked with jeeraga chamba (also known as jeeraga samba/khaima) rice or any other type of small aromatic rice.

## Ingredients

½ cup pulao rice or ordinary rice
1 cup coconut, grated
1 tbsp shallots, chopped
¼ tsp turmeric
2 tsp cumin seeds
salt to taste

## Method

1. Grind coconut with cumin seeds, turmeric and shallots to a smooth paste.
2. Cook the rice in sufficient water until it is soft and mashes well.
3. Add the ground coconut mixture, 1 cup of water and salt.
4. Boil again for a few more minutes.
5. Serve hot with roasted pappadum.

Recipe reproduced from *A Kitchen Full of Stories: Mappila Kitchen Treasures by Ummi Abdulla* (2018) with the kind permission of Nazaneen Jalaludheen.

# Eggs in Mappila Cuisine

*Aysha Tanya*

In *How to Cook a Wolf* – a food guide first published amid wartime shortages in 1942 – the American food writer M. F. K. Fischer writes, 'Probably one of the most private things in the world is an egg until it is broken.' The egg, an anticipation of deliciousness to come, may be one of the most private things in the world, but its role in bringing together the Mappilas around a table cannot be overstated. Wedding festivities, naming ceremonies, Eid celebrations – you can be sure there is an egg or ten propping up various dishes on the table.

I understand the obsession with eggs. Could there be another ingredient as versatile as an egg? It can bind, glaze, thicken, aerate. It can be whipped, spun, set like custard, and scrambled into soft, creamy curds.

With an unmatched textural dexterity, the chicken egg is a true shape-shifter in the kitchen. It has been the personal mission of my community, the Mappila Muslims, to investigate every possible use for an egg – and I have to say, we haven't done too badly.

The Mappila community refers to the Muslims of the Malabar coast: the southern part of India's western coast, flanked by the Western Ghats on the east and the Arabian Sea on the west. This community emerged when West Asian traders came into contact with the local Malayalis. Although the Mappila community came into existence centuries ago, the ties that bind us to West Asia run deep to this day. Occasionally in my own family, after one too many cups of sulaimani tea, the elders might talk about the Arab woman my great-grandfather wed as his second wife. Sadly, she died fairly young from tuberculosis – thanks to the incessant prayers of my great-grandmother, my family maintains.

In the relatively small, close-knit Mappila community, holding on to a sense of identity has been important. We pass down our traditions and tales through a form of folk song called 'mappila paattu'. Songs of devotion, stories about the Prophet and prominent Sufi saints, parables about love and marriage and, in one case, a detailed description of the delicacies one mother-in-law is whipping up for her son-in-law are all themes explored in mappila paattu. My grandmother made sure that every one of her grandchildren had a mappila paattu recorded in their name. As a child listening to this cassette of songs that mention me and my parents, placing us within a larger family context, gave me a strong sense of belonging – and helped provide much needed distraction at mealtimes!

However, I would argue that it is our food that offers the strongest sense of identity. My own family story begins with my great-great-grandfather, Uppi Haji, falling in love with and marrying his wife Kadeeja after eating a lunch she had cooked for him. Mappila culinary traditions are heavily influenced by the Arabs, English, Dutch, Portuguese and French, all of whom came to the Malabar coast for trade. Our food is a loud and raucous expression of our fascinating history.

The Mappila cook has an appetite for the absurd and the dramatic. As conservative people, food is a matter of great pride, and an integral form of self-expression. The egg, with its Swiss army-like versatility has been an aide to this end.

The 'aha' moment in many of our elaborate dishes is a boiled egg, adding an element of drama, laced with irony. Hidden painstakingly in an elaborate dish, revealing itself proudly, as though it were a Fabergé, is the humble hard-boiled egg. Take kozhi thalayana (chicken pillow), for instance. A billowy pastry encases a whole chicken that is stuffed with a boiled egg. Or the turki-pathiri, or bomb as we lovingly call it, a deep-fried meat parcel that when cut into reveals a smaller meat packet stuffed inside, with a perfect boiled egg enclosed within it, like a precious jewel. For those who would like to up the ante, there is adu porichathu (fried goat – the name hugely underselling the dish) for which a whole goat is roasted, stuffed with a whole chicken, and lastly – you guessed it – stuffed with a boiled egg.

It is hard to point to one single reason for the Mappila proclivity for eggs. It could be that many households raised hens in their backyards, and the eggs needed creative ways of being used. Perhaps the ingredient's popularity lies in it being a relatively cheap source of protein. But my suspicion is that it is indispensable in the Mappila kitchen because there is no ingredient that offers a cook as much power as an egg does.

From a long list of egg-centric dishes from the Mappila repertoire, here are three where the egg plays a substantial, albeit completely unique, role.

## Panjara pata

Slowly falling out of favour in the community, panjara pata is technique-driven and infamously finicky. I first heard about it a few years ago when I was interviewing Ummi Abdulla, the woman who has single-handedly taken Mappila food around the world through her seminal cookbook, *Malabar Muslim Cookery*. Ummi Abdulla recalls that her grandmother would make these in secret, far from the prying eyes of the rest of the household. This was because if anyone were to put an evil eye on it, the panjara pata simply would not froth up to its full extent, making for a flat, greasy version.

The name panjara pata translates to 'sugar insect', and in this case, one can assume the insect referred to is the bee: the perfectly made panjara pata, made far from the evil eye of onlookers, has a hollow, hexagonal structure, much like that of a honeycomb.

Like many foods in the Mappila culinary canon, it starts with eggs and ground rice, which are placed in a large bowl and whipped into a frothy frenzy. The two ingredients completely transform into a light, airy cloud-like mass at the hands of the expert cook. The froth is then gently scooped up and lowered into a pot of oil, where it spreads out to take the shape of the pot. As this sets and turns colour from a pearly white to a light golden, another round of froth is whipped up and ladled into the same pot. This process continues until you have a thick yet light and crisp disc. It is served with a sprinkling of sugar and a ripe banana, and then, in what can only be described as an unexpected move, this carefully created honeycomb is ruthlessly crushed in a matter of seconds until it is a glorious mess of smooshed banana and crumbles of golden shards. Crunchy, with pockets of soft, honey-sweet banana, a smattering of sugar, it is a textural delight.

## Mutta mala

These days, as Mappila cuisine gains popularity across India, mutta mala has become its most well-known ambassador. In many ways, it is a fitting advocate – with roots elsewhere, using just a few ingredients to create a dish whose sum is so much greater than its parts.

Mutta mala is the Mappila version of the Portuguese *fios de ovos*, made in former Portuguese colonies around the world, including Hong Kong and Brazil. Here, in the Malabar region, it is synonymous with celebrations.

Ramsheed K. T., who runs the catering company Malabar Kitchens, says that for a party, he will use no less than a hundred eggs, sometimes going up to two hundred, to make mutta mala. Breaking these eggs carefully, making sure the yolk remains whole, is a task that requires a fair bit of patience and a delicate hand. Often, duck yolks are added to the chicken egg yolks, to impart a deeper yellow colour.

To make the mutta mala, first the yolks are separated and strained through a muslin cloth. Next, the strained yolks are poured into a ladle with a quarter-inch incision on the bottom that acts as a nozzle. A thin stream of this yolk drizzles down through the ladle into a vat of bubbling sugar syrup. As soon as this stream of pale-yellow liquid hits the hot sugar, it turns into a sunshine-coloured noodly strand. The name mutta mala, meaning 'egg necklace' or 'egg garland', then begins to make sense. The texture of mutta mala is easy to fall in love with – it's springy yet soft and buttery. It tastes of the richness of egg yolks, with an almost candied sweetness from the sugar syrup. Yet, even among those who have grown up eating it, mutta mala is a divisive subject. There are those who simply can't stand the strong flavours and there are others who are zealous in their devotion.

The egg whites that remain after making mutta mala are turned into another dish called pinjanathapam. The whites are whisked with a few spoons of the leftover sugar syrup and steamed to form a cloudy white, soft-set slab that is carefully cut into diamond-shaped pieces. Scented with the sweet warm thrum of cardamom, its subtle flavours are the perfect contrast to the richness of mutta mala. The two are always displayed together – mutta mala usually in the centre and the pinjanathapam placed carefully around it – a soft tangle of gold necklaces, surrounded by diamonds.

## Chattipathiri

A chattipathiri is far less of a party dish than either the panjara pata or the mutta mala. It is typically served as a teatime snack or as part of the iftar spread during the month of Ramzan. The casual setting that chattipathiri is usually served in belies its tedious preparation process. First, translucent sheets of pastry are made from flour and water. Next, the fillings. Traditionally, these chattipathiri fillings – and, yes, there is more than one filling – would be made with meat, incorporating both savoury and sweet flavours. However, these days chattipathiri is either sweet or meat-based. As something of a compromise, the sweet variation in some households, including mine, includes savoury elements. In my family's rendition, onions, coriander powder and chilli powder feature in the sweet version. Three fillings, one made of almonds and raisins, another with split Bengal gram and another with – surprise! – eggs, are layered between ten layers of pastry. This dish is nothing if not proof that there are very few lengths that the Mappila cook will not go to for a good snack. After the careful layering, as a final anointment a rosewater-scented custard is poured over the dish.

Like many Mappila dishes, the exact roots of the chattipathiri are unclear, but it bears resemblance to the North African *bastilla*. Like chattipathiri, a traditional bastilla is sweet and savoury, made from stacking thin layers of pastry. The meat of choice in the Moroccan version, however, is pigeon – and, rather than a custard bath, crushed almonds and powdered sugar add that final flourish on the bastilla.

## Mapping Malabar's food history

Mapping the food history of the Malabar region has proven to be quite difficult, with simply not enough primary sources from which to draw. Often, it is through pure coincidence that we are able to draw parallels and make connections as to where a certain dish, previously thought to be unique to the community, comes from. For instance, we learned about the similarities between chattipathiri and bastilla thanks to my mother's great enthusiasm for watching cooking shows from around the world. In an episode on Moroccan cooking, she came across a cook making bastilla.

Her excitement at finding what is likely to be a relative of the chattipathiri feels poignant to me as a food writer trying to map her community's culinary history. Finding pieces of who we are, where we come from and what we ate, often scattered in faraway places, is both a joy and a relief. As the French author and researcher Luce Giard writes, 'Every dietary habit is a tiny historical cross-roads.' In Malabar, which has served as an international trading hub for millennia, this is especially true. As interest in the culinary history of the Mappilas deepens, I'm certain we will uncover more about the roots of our eating habits, including our penchant for eggs. In the meanwhile, I'll be here cooking and keeping my culinary traditions alive, one egg at a time.

## Mutta Mala and Pinjanathapam

**Ingredients**

15 eggs
300g sugar
500 ml and 250 ml water
¼ tsp cardamom, finely powdered
vanilla essence (optional)

*Note:*

We use a coconut spoon, or charatta kayil, that has a small hole at the bottom to make the mutta mala. Alternatively, you could also use a disposable drinking cup with a tiny hole poked into the bottom.

## Method

*To make the mutta mala:*

1. Separate the yolk and white of the eggs carefully. While separating, be sure not to get any white into the yolk and vice versa. Pass the yolk through a muslin cloth into a clean, dry bowl.
2. Boil 500 ml water in a wide, heavy-bottomed vessel (uruli) and then add the sugar. Reduce the heat to low and continue to boil the sugar syrup until you get a 'one-string' consistency.
3. Plug the hole in the spoon or disposable cup with your finger while filling it with egg yolk. Increase the heat and, when the sugar syrup starts to boil, release the yolk over the boiling sugar. You should move your hand in concentric circles to form thin, delicate strands of yolk. To get strands of the right thickness, the speed with which you move your hand is crucial: too fast means the strands will break and too slow will result in thick ribbons. Continue the process until you have released all the yolk in the spoon or cup.
4. Once the yolk has been cooked, reduce the heat. Remove the cooked strands from the syrup using a flat spoon, being careful not to break them. Transfer the mutta mala to a platter.
5. Rub a drop of vanilla essence into your palm and gently press it into the mutta mala.
6. Add 2 tsp water to the syrup and let the syrup boil again to come back to a one-string consistency.
7. Repeat the process with the remaining yolk.

*To make the pinjanathapam:*

1. Cool the remaining syrup and then mix it into a large bowl containing the egg whites.
2. Add cardamom powder and mix well, being careful not to incorporate air into the egg mixture.
3. Pour the mixture into a greased 9-inch round cake pan.
4. Place the cake pan over a pot of boiling water and cover. Steam for 15 minutes. The top should be set, but still soft to the touch.

5. Once the whites have cooled, cut them into triangles and remove from the pan.
6. Serve the triangles on top or around the mutta mala on a platter.

# Tracking the Culinary Journey of Rampuri Adrak Halwa

*Tarana Husain Khan*

Adrak halwa, according to author Muneeza Shamsie, was a specialty of my hometown, Rampur. Yet, I don't remember ever eating this halwa or it being cooked in our home while I was growing up. Muneeza's mother, Jahanara Habibullah, was sister-in-law to the last Nawab of Rampur, Raza Ali Khan (ruled 1930–1949), and had experienced the finest culinary traditions of the famed royal dastarkhwan. An adrak halwa recipe was adapted by Muneeza's gourmand father, Isha'at Habibullah, from the cooking techniques of their two Rampuri khansamas. She inherited the sweetmeat recipe from her parents' cooking diary and had then added it to her article about her family's gastronomic journey from Rampur to Karachi, republished in this collection. The recipe required three straight hours of cooking and at the time there was a shortage of gas supply in her country of Pakistan.

At this point, I gallantly stepped in. I was curious about the adrak halwa. My plan was for my old cook Akhtar bhai and me to take turns in stirring and sautéing the halwa.

Adrak halwa had disappeared from our own family winter dining table, along with several other dishes which were expensive or tedious to cook. The memory of adrak halwa being cooked for my grandfather and set in a silver bowl from which Nana Abba took a spoonful in the cold winter mornings is probably a collective family memory which has morphed into a lucid mental picture.

Culinary wisdom, which I must have somehow stored in my embryonic cooking brain, dictated that October was the perfect time to cook adrak halwa. The young ginger shoots become available that month. Muneeza's recipe called for an elaborate list of ingredients and a painstaking procedure which began by soaking the ginger shoots overnight before grinding them three times with some milk on a sil-batta. I conserved the manpower, also known as Akhtar bhai, for sautéing, and instead used a mixer-grinder. The ginger paste then needed to be put through a sieve to remove its fibres. After this, the smooth ginger paste was cooked in milk, ghee and cream until it became thick enough to drop from a spoon. The actual work began when we added sugar and began to sauté it to a deep golden hue. It took an hour of rigorous stirring for the ghee to separate from the halwa.

Oral history suggests that the halwa was devised by the Rampur khansamas when one of the Nawabs was advised by his hakim to eat ginger for knee pain. The Nawab, who hated ginger, was surreptitiously fed the halwa and became fond it. Looking at the glistening layer of ghee which had settled on top of the halwa, and thinking of the amount of sugar that went into it, it didn't seem a very healthy preparation. Indeed, I drained off half the ghee!

I tested the halwa on my unsuspecting cousin and his non-Rampuri wife. His wife curled her lip and said she had never tasted a more obnoxious sweet dish. My cousin asked for a second helping. I loved the halwa, but it had a sharp spicy, gingery aftertaste that clung to the back of my throat. My husband said it tasted like a hakim's majoun, or medical concoction, and that I should have sautéed it more; he remembered a darker adrak halwa being cooked in his ancestral home. I gritted my teeth, smiled and told him that he could join us in sautéing the next time we prepared adrak halwa.

Muneeza's article was published in *Scroll* and became terrifically popular – with my contribution in cooking up the halwa much appreciated too. As a food researcher, I was intrigued by the so-called Rampuri adrak halwa and decided to dig deeper. Working on the research project 'Forgotten Food', I was engaged in translating nineteenth-century cookbook manuscripts preserved in the Rampur Raza Library. I turned to these manuscripts to discover this halwa's origins. Was it actually created for an ailing Nawab in the huge Rampur kitchens or amalgamated from other cuisines of the time? As I knew from my own research, culinary exchange was the norm of the time. Rampur cuisine had acquired several dishes and modified Pathan cuisine under the influence of Mughal and Awadhi cooking.

Rampur Nawabs were known to be culinary connoisseurs and used their elaborate dining tables as a facet of diplomacy. Persian cookbook manuscripts were collected and commissioned by the Nawabs, just as we collect recipe books today. These manuscripts functioned as a frame of reference and a guide for culinary transformation. Some of the Persian cookbook manuscripts at the Raza Library are copies of original Mughal or Awadhi cookbooks; a few were commissioned by the Nawabs as a type of reference book.

One slim volume, *Nuskha hai ta'am*, identifies Nawab Kalbe Ali Khan (ruled 1865–1887) as its author. It begins rather unconventionally with recipes for eleven styles of halwas, most of them variations of the iconic halwa sohan. Adrak halwa doesn't merit a single mention in this manual of Rampur cuisine.

Another cookbook, *Risala dar tarkib ta'am*, written under the patronage of Khansahib Muhammad Shah Khan of Nankar – possibly a nobleman from the Rampur tehsil of Nankar – was collected in 1816. This too neglects the adrak halwa in its vast repertoire of Mughal and Awadh-inspired dishes.

These two volumes are the only ones which can be conclusively said to have been written under the patronage of the Rampur aristocracy. However two other volumes in the Rampur Raza collection, *Risala dar tarkib ta'am* and *Khwan-i ne'mat*, have exactly the same recipe for adrak halwa. It calls for just three ingredients: ginger, sugar and ghee. No milk, cream, spices or aromatics are prescribed.

*Alwan-i ne'mat*, another Urdu cookbook, edited by Munshi Bulaqi Das Dehlavi for publication in 1876, has a similar recipe. Interestingly, all three recipes call for blanching the adrak in water before grinding, supposedly to reduce the spicy aftertaste. Blanching was not a requirement in Muneeza's recipe. Adrak halwa therefore appears to have been a dish cooked in the nineteenth century within the broad remit of Mughal cuisine. *Haft Khwan Shaukat*, the oldest surviving cookbook printed in Rampur, which ran to three editions – in 1873, 1881 and 1883 – after it was compiled by a gentleman from Bhopal, also doesn't contain an adrak halwa.

By this point, I had become convinced that adrak halwa was originally a Mughal dish possibly not even cooked in Rampur in the nineteenth century. To confirm my hunch, I next looked through *Shahi Dastarkhwan* – the last cookbook from princely Rampur written in 1945 and published in 1957, and the only one ever written by a Rampuri khansama – on the basis that it included several dishes from Rampur cuisine of that time. Many of these dishes have since vanished from Rampuri dining tables, meaning that they only exist in food memories. Latafat Ali Khan Rampuri, the author of *Shahi Dastarkhwan*, describes an elaborate adrak halwa recipe with the list of ingredients corresponding to Muneeza's heirloom recipe: milk, cream, spices and aromatics along with the three main ingredients. As in Muneeza's recipe, there was no blanching of ginger before grinding. Instead, the ground ginger was boiled in milk. Latafat Ali Khan ends with the important line: '*Ye halwa Rampur ki tarz par banane ki tarkib hai, ummid hai ki pasand farmaya jayega*.' ('This halwa is prepared by the special Rampur recipe, I hope you will like it.') Sometime in Rampur's culinary history, the adrak halwa had evolved under the hands of the local khansamas into an exquisite sweetmeat with a differentiated procedure and sumptuous ingredients.

Today adrak halwa is rarely cooked in Rampur houses, probably because of the tedious method. Most Rampuris buy adrak halwa from Amanat bhai's shop which is renowned for its halwa sohan. My quest for Rampuri adrak halwa thus took me next to Amanat bhai's kitchen workshop above his famous lal dukan. The founder, Amanat bhai, had set up shop in the 1930s outside the Rampur fort, becoming famous because he supplied halwa sohan, boondi ladoos and other sweets to Nawab Raza Ali Khan, his son Nawab Murataza Ali Khan and other members of the royal family. The shop is now looked after by Amanat bhai's grandson, Haris Raza, who inherited the business and the recipes from his father. When he prepared adrak halwa, Haris measured out wheatgerm flour and semolina, mixed it in milk and cooked it in a large kadhai, only adding ginger paste when the mixture became brownish. This concoction required a completely different recipe and method. Samnak (wheatgerm flour) is the base for Rampuri halwa sohan, but it never appeared in the heritage recipes for adrak halwa. Amanat bhai's adrak halwa – which had a fabulous taste with only a slight gingery tang – is actually a variation of halwa sohan adapted to suit popular taste buds.

As the stars of my halwa journey aligned in perfect symmetry, the district administration of Rampur in collaboration with the Women's Welfare Department decided to organise a halwa festival in October 2021. All the khansamas and lady chefs of Rampur – the latter of whom had started home catering during the pandemic with help from the district authorities – were invited to present their halwas at a tasting festival, *Zaika-i Rampur*. There was much excitement among the khansamas – a culinary manifestation of a prince's ball for the Cinderellas of Rampur's gourmet cooking scene. The prize was an allotment of shops at Rampur's annual *Hunar Haat* exhibition. For our 'Forgotten Food' project, I had been working with some khansamas to revive the heirloom dishes of Rampur cuisine and collect the recipes for a Rampur cookbook. As a corollary to our efforts, the project sponsored Chef Suroor and Bhura khansama to set up their stall for *Zaika-i Rampur.* Since we were also producing a documentary on Rampur cuisine for the project, I invited the film crew to capture Bhura bhai cooking his sweetmeats at my own home.

The halwa that I was most interested in was, of course, adrak halwa, and so I watched Bhura bhai closely as he prepared a wood chulha and made a ginger paste. I was in for a surprise when Bhura bhai fried the ginger paste for a few minutes in a lot of ghee and then cooked it in milk. His explanation was that the frying reduced the ginger tang. There was no blanching or boiling in milk. Even the dried fruits for the garnish were fried and added to the halwa. This was the fourth kind of halwa recipe I had seen – indicative of the circuitous transformations that adrak halwa had undertaken through the centuries.

The ingenuity of the Rampur khansamas was in full display at the halwa festival. Several weird and wonderful halwas were cooked and tasted that day – including neem halwa, meat halwa, turmeric halwa and date halwa. My brain was on a sugar high. Mehfooz khansama's adrak halwa had an earthy taste; he had used jaggery and honey to make the halwa for the more health conscious. However, he followed the same procedure as Bhura bhai.

Over the course of my culinary journey, I had tasted at least seven variations of adrak halwa. I could sit on an adrak halwa jury if one were ever called up! I can now say with some authority that the oral history referencing the Nawab with knee pain cannot be corroborated. At some point near the beginning of the twentieth century, adrak halwa had started being prepared in Rampur in an elaborate form quite different from the Mughal–Awadh style. As time went on, the people of Rampur made it a part of their winter halwas, adapting and evolving it. They had eaten it with gusto to combat the cold and heal stiff joints. But, eventually, it passed into memory as a lost but not forgotten sweet treat of Rampur cuisine.

## Rampuri Adrak Halwa – Adapted from Latafat Ali Khan Rampuri's *Shahi Dastarkhwan*

**Ingredients**

500g young ginger shoots
500g ghee (you can reduce this to 300g if you prefer)
5–6 green cardamoms
2 black cardamoms
½ litre milk
500g sugar, or to taste
500g khoya
100g almonds, blanched and made into paste
125g fresh cream, well beaten
a few strands of saffron, soaked in warm water
3–4 drops of kewra
50g almond juliennes for garnish

**Method**

1. Wash the ginger thoroughly and peel it. Soak in water to soften it. Once softened, grind it finely on a sil-batta. You can also use an electric mixer or grinder, but it is important that the paste should be smooth with no fibres.
2. Add kewra to the saffron.
3. Heat the ghee and add the green and black cardamom. Let them fry for a few seconds, then set aside.
4. Put the ginger paste in half a cup of milk in a pan, then boil it on low heat until the ginger becomes tender.

5. Add the sugar and continue to cook for 5 minutes, stirring constantly. The sugar should completely dissolve and the mixture should start bubbling.
6. Add the khoya and almond paste. Continue to cook on low heat, stirring until the halwa mixture starts changing colour.
7. Sauté the halwa mixture, adding splashes of milk and ghee mixture to ensure it doesn't burn. Add cream and continue to sauté. Keep the heat low. When ready, the halwa will have a perfect dark golden colour. The consistency should be thick, so that it can be dropped from a spoon. The total cooking time should be around two hours.
8. Add the saffron water and kewra, then remove from heat.
9. Garnish with almond juliennes before serving. This halwa can be kept for at least ten days in the refrigerator.

# Biographical Notes

**Aliya Nazki** is journalist and food blogger. She was born in Kashmir and lives in London.

**Ashok Malhotra** is Senior Lecturer in History at Queen's University Belfast and the author of *Making British Indian Fictions, 1772–1823* (2012). His current project examines the ways in which early twentieth-century medical research of the British Raj influenced discourses pertaining to nutrition and race in Britain, colonial India and North America.

**Ayesha Mualla** is a research scholar at the Department of Sociology, Shiv Nadar University, with an interest in the olfactory and gustatory landscape of Hyderabad, Deccan.

**Aysha Tanya** is a food writer who co-founded the *Goya Journal*. She is the author of the cookbook *The Family Table* (2019), documenting the recipes of the Arinhal Karuvantevalappil family from northern Kerala.

**Bina Shah** is a Karachi-based writer and the author of five novels and two collections of short stories. Her latest works are the feminist dystopian novels *Before She Sleeps* (2018) and *The Monsoon War* (2023). She has been a regular contributor to the *New York Times*, *Al Jazeera* and the *Huffington Post*, and is a frequent guest on the BBC. In 2022 she was awarded the rank of Chevalier in the Order of Arts and Letters by the French Ministry of Culture.

**Claire Chambers** is Professor of Global Literature at the University of York, where she researches and teaches writing from South Asia and the Perso-Arab world. She edited *Desi Delicacies: Food Writing from Muslim South Asia* (2021) and her most recent monograph was *Making Sense of Contemporary British Muslim Novels* (2019).

**Farah Yameen** does work in digital archiving and public history dealing with diverse subjects: cultural geographies and the individual person, democratic movements, personal histories of journalism and, lately, food.

**Fehmida Zakeer** is an independent writer from Kerala. She writes on food, culture, lifestyle, environment, gender and books. Her translation of Malayalam author B. M. Zuhara's memoir, entitled *The Dreams of a Mappila Girl*, was published recently (2022).

**Fida Husain** is a PhD scholar at Jawaharlal Nehru University, New Delhi, who works on early Western narratives of Ladakh.

**Iqbal Ahmed** was born in Kashmir and has lived in London since 1994. He has been writing and travelling, and is the author of five books.

**Jayanta Sengupta** is a historian of modern South Asia and the author of two books. He is currently Secretary and Curator of Victoria Memorial Hall, Kolkata, India's most-visited museum.

**Marjan Wardaki** is a postdoctoral research fellow at Yale University. She specialises in the intellectual histories of modern South Asia and Europe, with a particular emphasis on the interconnection between the history of science and the history of migration.

**Md Chingiz Khan** is visiting faculty at Jamia Hamdard University, New Delhi. Formerly, he was a PhD Research Scholar at the Centre for Historical Studies, School of Social Sciences, Jawaharlal Nehru University, New Delhi. He has achieved several national honours, including the Namaste Governor Acharya Award, the Institute of Scholars Young Researcher Award and the National Award for Social Excellence.

**Mobeen Hussain** is an early-career historian of the British Empire with expertise in race, caste, gender, medicine and consumption in South Asia. She is currently a junior research fellow at University College, Oxford and previously a postdoctoral research fellow for Trinity College Dublin's Colonial Legacies project. She is also working on her first monograph on race, colourism and skin-lightening in colonial India.

**Moneeza Hashmi** is a broadcaster, television producer, media consultant, and former general manager of Pakistan Television. She is the author of *Who Am I* (2014), a collection of interviews with iconic Pakistani women, and *Conversations with My Father* (2022), a memoir of her life with her father, the renowned poet Faiz Ahmed Faiz.

**Muneeza Shamsie** is a Karachi-based writer and critic. She is the author of *Hybrid Tapestries: The Development of Pakistani English Literature* (2017). She is also the bibliographic representative for Pakistan of the *Journal of Commonwealth Literature* and an area editor of the online *Literary Encyclopedia*.

**Noor Khan** retired as the Principal of Karamat College, Lucknow, where she also taught English. As a member of the core organising group of the Mahindra Sanatkada Lucknow Festival, she has worked tirelessly to generate awareness about Lucknow's cultural heritage. She is also a trustee of Lucknow Bioscope, an online city museum for conserving the social and cultural heritage of Lucknow.

**Rana Safvi** is a historian, writer and chronicler of Delhi, with particular interests in medieval heritage, monuments, food and culture. She has written many books, including *Where Stones Speak* (2015), *The Forgotten Cities of Delhi* (2018) and *Shahjahanabad* (2019). Her latest translation is *Tears of the Begum: Stories of the Survivors of the Uprising of 1857* (2022).

**Razak Khan** is a research fellow at the Centre for Modern Indian Studies, Georg-August-Universität Göttingen. He is the author of *Minority Pasts: Locality, Emotions, and Belonging in Princely Rampur* (2022).

**Rizvina Morseth De Alwis** is a writer and activist from Sri Lanka. She is the author of the prize-winning novel *It's Not in the Stars* (2015). Her upcoming novels, *Memory of Loss* and *Talking to the Sky* were shortlisted for the Gratiaen Prize in 2016 and 2021 respectively. She also co-authored *Feminist Engagements with Violence*. She worked for the United Nations and lived in several countries in Southeast Asia, and currently resides in Colombo.

**Sadaf Hussain** is the author of *Daastan-e-Dastarkhan* (2019) and *The Carrot Soup* (2023), as well as many food articles. He is also a consultant chef based in Delhi. He was one of the top *MasterChef India* contestants in 2016 and, since then, he has featured in Indian food-based shows on TV and online.

**Samina Naqvi** is an educator and cultural enthusiast with a deep proclivity to keep the present generation connected with their heritage.

**Saumya Gupta** is Associate Professor in History at Janki Devi Memorial College, University of Delhi, and a Fellow at Nehru Memorial Museum and Library (2021–2023). Her research focuses on urban social history, Partition studies and north Indian foodways.

**Sheikh Intekhab Alam** is an architect and educator with an interest in urban regeneration. He is the founder of EMARA Architecture and Urbanism. His research and work interests revolve around traditional wisdom in built environment practices. He also teaches at the Jindal School of Art and Architecture, O. P. Jindal Global University.

**Sikander Malik** is a cultural curator, a storyteller and a heritage activist from Bhopal. He is also a professional copywriter who loves to write on Bhopal's history, culture and, more recently, food stories.

**Siobhan Lambert-Hurley** is Professor of Global History at the University of Sheffield. Her latest books are *Elusive Lives: Gender, Autobiography and the Self in Muslim South Asia* (2018) and *Three Centuries of Travel Writing by Muslim Women* (with Daniel Majchrowicz and Sunil Sharma, 2022).

**Taran N. Khan** is a journalist and author of *Shadow City: A Woman Walks Kabul* (2019), which won the Stanford Dolman Travel Book of the Year and Tata Literature Live! First Book Award in 2021.

**Tarana Husain Khan** is a writer and cultural historian based in Rampur. She is the author of the award-winning historical novel *The Begum and the Dastan* (2021). Her latest book *Degh to Dastarkhwan: Qissas and Recipes from Rampur* (2022) has been published by Penguin Random House India.

## Praise for *Desi Delicacies*

'Perfectly encapsulates food's vital role in Muslim culture, as sustenance as well as a social service. The anthology is a treasure trove, but be warned: making any of the recipes will have your entire family flocking to the dining table. This togetherness is what *Desi Delicacies*, its writers and Claire Chambers achieve' – ***Dawn***

'A delightful anthology. Full of mysteries from the kitchen of Muslim households of the Indian subcontinent, *Desi Delicacies* narrates the pathos and the glee food evokes in the minds of the people, numbering over a billion across the globe' – ***Daily Star***

'A mouth-watering collection of stories and essays … eminently readable. The problem with a book like this is that it sends you straight to the kitchen … Shows that food, really, has no religion' – ***Hindu***

'Curious, eclectic … I savoured Rana Safvi's impressively magisterial exegesis on the cultural, social and political history of the signature speciality of Mughlai cuisine. I also loved Nadeem Aslam's very brief but deeply affecting "The Homesick Restaurant"' – ***Hindustan Times***

'*Desi Delicacies* has a deeper purpose behind it to record culinary memories, local food heritage and forgotten grains. This is a unique anthology based on Muslim food culture – perhaps delectable would be the correct word' – ***Outlook Traveller***

'[*Desi Delicacies*] shows there's more to the cuisine of South Asian Muslims than rich, meaty food' – ***Scroll***

'A dazzling, dizzying array of fiction and non-fiction, which informs as much as it provides some much-needed escapism … This ambitious endeavour is a feel-good celebration of what food means to Muslim South Asian households, and the legacy Muslim cooking has had on South Asia. It captures the complexities, the feelings and associations people have with the dinner table. Perhaps most of all, it shows readers that our mutual love of food and our communities binds us together, even when we are geographically apart' – ***Youlin Magazine***